Perspectives
Psychology

INTRODUCTORY PSYCHOLOGY

This series of titles is aimed at A-level psychology students in sixth forms, further education colleges and on degree courses and those wishing to obtain an overview of psychology. The books are easy to use, with comprehensive notes written in coherent language; clear flagging of key concepts; relevant and interesting illustrations; well-defined objectives and further reading sections to each chapter; and self-assessment questions at regular intervals throughout the text.

Published

INDIVIDUAL DIFFERENCES
Ann Birch and Sheila Hayward

DEVELOPMENTAL PSYCHOLOGY (Second Edition)
Ann Birch

BIOPSYCHOLOGY
Sheila Hayward

COGNITIVE PROCESSES
Tony Malim

SOCIAL PSYCHOLOGY (Second Edition)
Tony Malim

RESEARCH METHODS AND STATISTICS
Tony Malim and Ann Birch

COMPARATIVE PSYCHOLOGY
Tony Malim, Ann Birch and Sheila Hayward

PERSPECTIVES IN PSYCHOLOGY (Second Edition)
Alison Wadeley, Ann Birch and Tony Malim

PERSPECTIVES IN PSYCHOLOGY

Second Edition

Alison Wadeley
Ann Birch
Tony Malim

palgrave
macmillan

First edition 1992
Second edition 1997

Published by
PALGRAVE MACMILLAN
Houndmills, Basingstoke, Hampshire RG21 6XS and
175 Fifth Avenue, New York, N. Y. 10010
Companies and representatives throughout the world

PALGRAVE MACMILLAN is the global academic imprint of the Palgrave Macmillan division of St. Martin's Press, LLC and of Palgrave Macmillan Ltd. Macmillan® is a registered trademark in the United States, United Kingdom and other countries. Palgrave is a registered trademark in the European Union and other countries.

ISBN 0–333–67507–X

This book is printed on paper suitable for recycling and made from fully managed and sustained forest sources.

A catalogue record for this book is available from the British Library.

Transferred to digital printing 2003

Copy-edited and typeset by Povey–Edmondson
Tavistock and Rochdale, England

Printed and bound in Great Britain by
Antony Rowe Ltd, Chippenham and Eastbourne

Cartoons by Sally Artz

To my mother and late father
with love and admiration

A.W.

Contents

List of Figures

Preface to the Second Edition

This book aims to provide those engaged in the study of psychology with an overview of psychological science. It begins with an account of the historical background of psychology, looking at different strands within its development from being a branch of philosophy to its emergence as a science. Chapter 2 examines different theoretical approaches which have developed and which currently influence psychological theory and practice.

Chapter 3 presents a discussion of major issues and debates in psychology, such as the heredity/environment debate, reductionism and free will and determinism. Chapter 4 examines controversies in psychological research, including the use of the scientific method and biases in psychological research. Ethical issues in psychology are explored in Chapter 5, and Chapter 6 examines some controversial applications of psychological research, for example advertising, propaganda and warfare. Finally, Chapter 7 looks at vocational fields open to psychologists.

The authors have attempted to present this overview simply and concisely in the form of comprehensive notes. There is, of course, a thin dividing line between clarity and succinctness on the one hand and oversimplification and distortion on the other. Every effort has been made to avoid the latter. Psychology is a rich and varied discipline containing many complex ideas. Some of these cannot be adequately expressed briefly; therefore at the end of each chapter there are suggestions for appropriate further reading.

For the independent student each chapter begins with objectives to be met during the study of the chapter and each section within chapters ends with self-assessment questions, so that the reader may test his/her understanding of the section. The reader is advised to work through the text a section at a time and to consider the self-assessment questions as they present themselves and again after further reading has been undertaken.

The authors believe that this book will meet a long-felt need and that readers will find it both enjoyable and useful in relation to their study of psychology. It is a book which students may look at when new to psychology and again when they are more familiar with the subject.

Alison Wadeley
Ann Birch
Tony Malim

DARWIN'S THEORY LIVES ! I SURVIVED
THE MONDAY MORNING RUSH-HOUR !

Psychology: Historical Sketch **1**

At the end of this chapter you should be able to:

1. propose a definition of psychology;
2. trace the historical development of psychology from its philosophical roots to its emergence as a separate, scientific discipline;
3. reach an understanding of the concept of schools of psychology;
4. describe and make some assessment of the schools of structuralism, functionalism, behaviourism, Gestalt psychology and psychoanalysis; and
5. identify some of the contributions made by these schools to contemporary psychology.

SECTION I   EARLY BEGINNINGS

What is Psychology?

Perhaps the most widely accepted definition of psychology is that it is the scientific study of behaviour and experience. That is to say that, through systematic research, psychologists aim to explore questions about the way human beings, and sometimes animals, behave and how they experience the world around them. This apparently simple and straightforward definition requires further explanation if the reader is to gain an adequate view of the nature of psychology and, indeed, the whole of this book is concerned with that explanation. The aim of this chapter is to give a brief account of the early development of psychology and to examine significant events in the history of the subject up to about the middle of the twentieth century.

Psychology as a scientific discipline has a short history – only just over a hundred years. As a branch of philosophy it dates back to the time of Plato and Aristotle. The word 'psychology' is of Greek origin: 'psyche' can be freely translated as 'mind' or 'soul', and 'logos' indicates 'study' or 'line of teaching'; thus we have 'study of the mind'. This definition exemplifies what psychology was essentially about up to the end of the nineteenth century.

It was in 1879 that Wilhelm Wundt opened the first psychological laboratory in Leipzig, Germany. It is generally agreed that this event heralded the beginning of psychology as a scientific discipline in its own right. Prior to this, psychology had generally been regarded as a branch of philosophy. Before we consider the development of psychology as a scientific discipline, it will be of benefit to examine briefly the influence of some philosophical ideas.

Pre-scientific Psychology

René Descartes (1596–1650), the French philosopher, had an important influence on the development of psychology as a discipline distinct from philosophy. Before Descartes, human beings tended to be viewed by philosophers as unique, mysterious products of God's will, whose mental life was beyond rational explanation. Influenced by scientific discoveries of the time in the field of medicine, most notably Harvey's discovery of the blood circulatory system, Descartes adopted a more analytical stance. He attempted to view the human being as a machine which could be studied and whose workings could be understood and explained. In his theory of **interactive dualism** he made a distinction between the mind (thinking, remembering, knowing) and the body (physiological processes). The interaction of mind and body, he believed, took place in the brain and the seat of the mind was narrowed down to the pineal gland, a structure in the brain which serves to initiate hormonal activity.

The seventeenth century also saw the birth of the British Empiricist Movement, led by a group of philosophers, the most notable of whom were John Locke and Thomas Hobbes. The empiricists attempted to make sense of the human mind through the use of systematic and objective methods of study, rather than through reasoning or intuition. Mental life, they contended, was composed of 'ideas' which arose from sensory experience and entered the mind by means of perception. In contrast to Descartes, who believed that some ideas are present at birth, the empiricists saw the development of the mind as arising from experiences of and interaction with the environment. Thus the early seeds of the heredity–environment (nature–nurture) debate were sown (see Chapter 3, Section III).

In the early part of the nineteenth century there was a strong upsurge of philosophical opinion which contended that the study of human mental activity was worthy of attention in its own right outside of the discipline of philosophy. This move was greatly advanced by the work of a group of German physiologists – Weber, who used weights to study muscle sense, Helmholtz, who made an outstanding contribution to the study of vision and hearing, and Fechner, who investigated visual discrimination and perception. The findings of these early physiologists greatly influenced psychology as we know it today.

Scientific Psychology

As previously indicated, the establishment of psychology as a scientific discipline in its own right is generally linked to the setting up in 1879 of the first psychological laboratory by Wilhelm Wundt. Before looking further at the work of Wundt and his contemporaries, it might be useful to examine the concept of schools of psychology.

Schools of Psychology

As psychology developed as a discipline which was founded on the use of empirical methods (based on observation and the collection of data) there emerged a number of different schools of thought. Schools, in this context, can best be thought of as groups of psychologists who held common beliefs about both the subject matter of psychology, that is what facets of mental functioning should be studied, and what methods of study should be used. Most schools developed as a revolt against traditional methods and beliefs at the time. However they did not always replace earlier schools, but sometimes existed alongside them. Schools, as such, do not now exist, but each has provided ideas (some more influential than others) which have influenced contemporary approaches to psychology (see Chapter 2). Therefore a knowledge of them can help us to make sense of the multitude of ideas and methods which currently characterise psychology.

Sections II to V contain a brief description of six major schools of psychology: structuralism, functionalism, associationism, behaviourism, Gestalt psychology and psychoanalysis.

Self-assessment Questions

1. How would you define psychology?
2. What event is generally regarded as the beginning of psychology as a scientific discipline distinct from philosophy?
3. In what way did the philosopher, Descartes, influence philosophical thinking about the nature of the human mind?
4. Outline the main contributions to psychology of (a)
   the British Empiricists;(b)
   the nineteenth-century physiologists, Weber, Helmholz and Fechner.
5. What do you understand by 'schools of psychology'?

SECTION II STRUCTURALISM AND FUNCTIONALISM

Structuralism

Inspired by the pioneering work of Fechner and other scientists, **Wilhelm Wundt** and his many collaborators founded the school of structuralism. Wundt believed that psychology should concern itself with the elementary processes of **conscious experience**. The structure of consciousness and immediate mental experience, he contended, could be broken down into basic elements and compounds in the same way that, in chemistry, one can describe the structure of water or air.

The elements of conscious experience were considered to be of two kinds:

- **sensations** – sights, sounds, tastes, smells and touch, which arise from stimulation of the sense organs; and
- **feelings** – love, fear, joy, and so on.

The term **image** was also used to describe experiences not actually present.

Three primary questions were addressed:

1. What are the elements of experience?
2. How are they combined?
3. What causes the elements to combine?

An experience such as meeting and recognising an old friend in the street was thought to be composed of many independent sensations, feelings and images, which were drawn together and synthesised by the mind.

Introspection

In an effort to study the elements of consciousness in what they believed was an analytical and objective way, structuralists devised a technique known as **introspection**. This simply means that people were asked to consider and report on their own mental processes as they experienced a particular object or event. This was to be done in a pre-specified and systematic way and required much training. For example, to be introspective about a flower, the reporter would be asked to describe the sensations of experiencing it in terms of its shape, size, colour, texture and so on.

The method of introspection proved difficult and inadequate, largely because of conflicting findings between introspectionists in different laboratories. Reaching agreement on the basic elements of a particular mental experience proved an impossible task and (predictably, perhaps) reporting on mental activity in humans was not quite so straightforward as observing what happens in a test-tube when two chemicals are combined.

Another prominent member of the structuralist school, Edward Titchener, developed and extended Wundt's ideas and later introduced them to the USA.

Structuralism declined in the early 1920s, partly through the failure of introspective methods to provide a coherent and generally accepted account of human mental activity and partly through the emergence of schools which offered alternative approaches to the study of psychology. These schools included functionalism, behaviourism and Gestalt psychology, each of which developed at least in part as a reaction against structuralism.

Functionalism

Whilst the structuralists emphasised the structure of mental activity, the functionalists were concerned with the purposes, or functions, of mental processes. Functionalism was strongly influenced by biology and many of the concepts 'borrowed' from that discipline continue to influence psychology today.

Darwin and Natural Selection

The work and ideas of **Charles Darwin** had a monumental impact on the emergence of functional psychology. Darwin's revolutionary theory of evolution provided an account of the way living organisms change and develop over time through a process of **natural selection**. Living organisms have characteristics such as extreme strength, speed of movement and temperament, which are variable even within the same species. Organisms whose characteristics were best suited to their environment survived and reproduced, while organisms whose characteristics were less adaptable died out. Survivors would transmit to the next generation those characteristics which enabled them to survive. In this way a particular species might change quite extensively over several generations and, in some cases, an entirely new species could evolve.

The notion that humans had descended from animals was revolutionary – and shocking to many people. Amongst psychologists it led to a belief, which for many still persists, that by studying animals a greater understanding might be reached about the nature of human beings. (See Chapter 5 for a discussion of the use of animals in psychological research.) Darwin's work also drew attention to the importance of studying individual differences between members of a species. This idea was taken up and continues to provide an importance focus in psychology today, particularly in the field of psychometrics , the study of mental testing.

William James (1842–1910) was a leading figure in functional psychology and his work has made a very significant impact on contemporary psychology. Influenced greatly by Darwin, James held that the function of consciousness was to enable humans to behave in ways which would aid survival through adaptation to the environment. Where these adaptive behaviours were repeated frequently they became **habits**. Habits, James believed, provided stability and predictability in society.

The range of topics studied by James was immense and few psychologists would disagree that he was responsible for opening up the scope of psychology. In addition to a study of the functions of consciousness and the role of habits, he turned his attention to emotions and to the concept of self. As with the structuralists, his main method of study was introspection, though he encouraged the use of experimentation. His emphasis on the importance of observing similarities and differences between varying species greatly influenced the development of comparative psychology. The work of John Dewey (1859–1952) at the University of Chicago further established the ideas of functionalism. This work led to a new trend, that of attempting to apply research findings to practical problems. For example, the first intelligence tests for use with children were developed by the functionalists.

Self-assessment Questions

1. What did the structuralists, led by Wundt, consider to be the appropriate subject matter of psychology?
2. Evaluate the use of introspection as an effective method of study.
3. How did the work of Charles Darwin influence or change the study of psychology?
4. What were the aims of the functionalists?
5. Outline some important contributions to contemporary psychology made by William James.

SECTION III   ASSOCIATIONISM AND BEHAVIOURISM

Associationism

This refers to the movement concerned with studying the the idea that learning amounted to the forming of associations. The work of three scientists is important in this context: Herman Ebbinghaus (1850–1909), Edward Thorndike (1874–1949) and Ivan Pavlov (1849–1936). There follows a brief account of some of their main contributions.

The work of **Ebbinghaus** is often regarded as the basis of modern research into memory. Using himself as a subject and 'nonsense syllables' such as TAF, ZUC, POV as his experimental material, Ebbinghaus systematically studied factors which influence learning and forgetting. Nonsense syllables were used in preference to real words because Ebbinghaus believed they contained no meaning and thus offered a device which would enable him to study 'new' learning. New learning was regarded as the *forming of associations* within material which is not already associated with previous learning. His meticulous and painstaking methods of study, carried out over several years, produced much reliable quantified data. His work provided insights into remembering and forgetting which still hold good today. For example, he demonstrated that material is forgotten quite quickly in the first few hours after learning, but then the rate of forgetting becomes progressively slower.

Pavlov, a Russian physiologist, made a significant contribution to the study of learning through experiments with animals. During his investigations into the salivary reflex in dogs, Pavlov discovered that a stimulus, for example food (the unconditional stimulus), which is naturally linked with a particular reflex response, for example salivation (the unconditional response), can become associated with other stimuli which are present at the same time. In one series of experiments he showed that a dog, when offered food as a buzzer (the conditional stimulus) is sounded, will, after several presentations, begin to salivate when the buzzer alone is sounded. (Salivation now becomes the conditional response.) Thus an *association* is formed between the food and the buzzer and between the buzzer and the salivation response. This learning process became known as classical, or Pavlovian, conditioning. Its principles have since been applied to the study of human behaviour, for example as an explanation for the development of irrational fears or phobias.

Like Pavlov, **Thorndike** studied learning in animals. However, where Pavlov was interested in reflex, or *involuntary*, behaviour, Thorndike studied the *associations* formed between a stimulus and *voluntary* responses. His early experiments involved the use of a cat in a 'puzzle box' – a cage from which the animal could learn to escape by pulling a loop of string. Thorndike measured the time taken by the cat to escape as an indicator of learning. His data showed that learning the correct 'escape' behaviour happened gradually. The 'reward' (freedom), he contended, was responsible for 'stamping in' the appropriate response. This insight formed the basis of Thorndike's **Law of Effect**, which has been developed further by Skinner in his study of operant conditioning (see Chapter 2, Section III).

Behaviourism

While functionalism was at its height in the USA, a young student, **John Watson** (1878–1958) graduated in psychology at the University of Chicago. He went on to revolutionise psychology by changing it from the study of conscious experience to the study of behaviour. In an influential paper, 'Psychology as the behaviourist views it', in

1913, Watson attacked the structuralist emphasis on consciousness and mental experience and also condemned the use of introspection as a method which claimed to be reliable and objective. Psychology, he believed, should be about the study of observable behaviour that all could agree upon and the aim of psychology should be to describe, predict, understand and control behaviour. He contended that psychologists should '. . . never use the terms consciousness, mental states, introspectively verify, imagery and the like' (1913, p. 166).

Behaviourists did not reject the existence of mind and consciousness as critics have sometimes suggested. Rather they viewed these concepts as impossible to observe and contributing little to a scientific approach in psychology.

Watson and his colleagues believed that behaviour is moulded by experience. He therefore had a natural interest in learning and his view of learning relied to a great extent on Pavlov's account of classical conditioning described earlier. However complex a piece of behaviour might be, it was possible, behaviourists believed, to break it down and analyse it in basic **stimulus–response units.** Much of the behaviourists' research into learning was carried out on animals, rather than humans, partly because animals were easy to obtain and greater control could be exercised over their environments, and partly because they accepted the idea that humans and animals are related both physiologically and behaviourally.

Though Watson's view of the nature of human beings was considered by critics to be mechanistic and oversimplified, his focus on the study of observable behaviour allowed him to formulate clear hypotheses which could be tested by experimentation. This shift in emphasis towards the use of more objective and systematic methods was one of his greatest contributions to psychology.

Following the work of Watson and his followers, behaviourism gathered strength and its principles and methods of study became an integral part of psychology. By the middle of the twentieth century it was widely accepted that psychology was about the study of behaviour rather than conscious experience. This momentum has been sustained to a large extent in contemporary psychology by the efforts of the behaviourist, B. F. Skinner (see Chapter 2, Section III). Skinner extended principles derived from his work with animals to a consideration of human behaviour. However, as will become clear in Chapter 2, although behaviourism has left an indelible mark on contemporary psychology, alternative perspectives have been offered, largely through the emergence of cognitive psychology (Section IV) and humanistic psychology (Section V), which have modified its influence and endorsed the value of also studying mental processes and conscious experience.

Self-assessment Questions

1. Briefly outline the main contributions made by the associationists.
2. Outline Watson's objections to structuralist psychology.
3. What did the behaviourists consider should be the aims of psychology?
4. Briefly explain the process of learning known as classical conditioning.
5. Why was Watson particularly concerned with the study of learning?
6. In what way did the behaviourists influence methods of study in psychology?

SECTION IV   GESTALT PSYCHOLOGY

Functionalism and behaviourism came into being in the USA partly as a protest against structuralism. Around the same time, another movement against structuralism developed in Germany – the Gestalt School. The leading proponents of the Gestalt view were Max Wertheimer (1880–1943), Kurt Koffka (1876–1941) and Wolfgang Köhler (1887–1967).

Gestalt psychologists opposed the atomist approach of the structuralists and later the behaviourists. **Atomism** is a belief that, to understand a phenomenon, it is best to break it down and investigate its constituent parts. (See Chapter 3 for a discussion of the related concept of reductionism.) In contrast, Gestalt psychologists argued that people perceive the world in 'wholes'. 'The whole is greater than the sum of its parts' exemplifies this view. Gestalt, roughly translated, means 'whole', 'shape' or 'configuration'.

Wertheimer produced an early demonstration of this holistic approach through his experiments on apparent movement. He showed that, when two lights were presented a small distance apart and then switched on and off alternately, at certain time intervals a person reported seeing not two lights being lit, but one light which appeared to move from one location to the other. Wertheimer called this effect the **phi phenomenon**. He claimed that it contradicted the structuralist view that perception could be understood by analysing the basic elements of the perceiver's experience. The phi phenomenon is more familiar to us in the form of apparent movement in illuminated advertisements and the like. Further research by the Gestaltists led to the development of a set of principles of perceptual organisation. Such organisation, they believed, arose through the brain's innate ability to structure and organise the perceptual field into meaningful 'patterns' rather than perceiving the separate elements. Figure 1.1 illustrates some of the main Gestalt principles of organisation: figure/ground; proximity; similarity; closure.

The Gestalt principles of organisation can be subsumed under the overall guiding principle of **Prägnanz**. This refers to the principle governing the brain's attempt to perceive objects in the 'best' and most meaningful way. Critics have pointed out that these principles are purely descriptive and offer no explanations as to how or why the brain operates in this way.

Learning and problem-solving also received much attention from the Gestaltists. **Köhler** investigated problem-solving in apes. One study involved an animal in a cage with food out of reach beyond the cage. Inside the cage were a number of sticks which, if slotted together, were long enough to reach the food. After a period of inactivity, the animal quite suddenly solved the problem by slotting the sticks together and reaching for the food. Köhler claimed that, because all the elements for the solutions were available, the animal perceived the problem situation as a whole, formed a hypothesis about its solution and responded appropriately. He called this process 'insightful learning'.

The tendency of the Gestalt psychologists to rely for their data on subjective observations and reports of conscious experience, rather than carefully controlled behavioural methods, attracted criticism from the behaviourists. Gestaltists have also been accused of posing more problems than they actually solved. Nonetheless the influence of Gestalt psychology is great in some areas of contemporary psychology, for example in the study of perception and problem-solving. Also the concept of 'wholeness' has been adopted in Gestalt approaches to therapy. Gestalt views can also be detected in some contemporary approaches to learning in the field of education. For example, work on discovery learning is rooted in early Gestalt ideas.

FIGURE 1.1
Gestalt Principles of Perceptual Organisation

Figure/ground: focusing attention on an object causes it to 'stand out' sharply from its context, whilst the context or 'ground' is less clear. This ambiguous figure illustrates a situation where the figure and ground reverses as the brain switches attention from one to the other.

Proximity: the dots are perceived in groups of two rather than as eight separate items.

Similarity: these equally spaced dot are perceived in groups of two.

Closure: this figure is perceived as a circle rather than as four curved lines.

Self-assessment Questions

1. How might the term 'atomism' be applied to the work of the structuralists and the behaviourists?
2. Explain how the views of the Gestalt psychologists contrasted with the atomist approach of the structuralists and behaviourists.
3. How does the phi phenomenon illustrate the views held by the Gestaltists about perception?

4. What, according to the Gestaltists, is the purpose of perceptual organisation? Explain the principle of Prägnanz.
5. Briefly evaluate the contribution made to psychology by the Gestaltists.

SECTION V   PSYCHOANALYSIS

The school of psychoanalysis stands apart from the other schools in that the focus of attention is neither the nature or functions of consciousness, nor the stimulus–response links which influence behaviour. Psychoanalysis, which developed from the work and theories of Sigmund Freud (1856–1939), proposed an account of human mental activity which relied heavily on the notion of an **unconscious mind**.

Towards the end of the nineteenth century, science had been making huge advances and psychologists believed that the time was near when a full understanding of human mental life and behaviour would be reached. This view was shared by Freud, a young physician working as a neurologist in Vienna.

However, in the course of treating psychiatric patients over many years, Freud became convinced that many of the nervous symptoms displayed by patients could not be explained purely from a physiological point of view. Nor could the rational and systematic laws of science be applied to irrational and self-defeating behaviours such as phobias (excessive fears) and conversion hysterias (physical complaints that have no apparent physiological cause). It was against this background that Freud developed his now famous psychoanalytic treatment of neurotic disorders. His therapeutic work led to the development of a comprehensive theory of personality and child development which focused largely on the emotional aspects of human functioning. Thus the term **psychoanalysis** can relate both to the treatment and to the theory. Freud's starting-point was a thorough analysis of his own personal experiences and the development of case studies of his patients.

Psychoanalytic Theory

- The human personality contains and is greatly influenced by an unconscious mind harbouring repressed ('forgotten') memories which determine conscious thoughts and behaviour. A third level of consciousness, the preconscious, contains thoughts which may not be conscious at a given time, but which are accessible to us.

- Human beings are born with a number of **instinctual drives** which regulate and motivate behaviour even in childhood. The source of these drives is psychic energy and the most powerful, the **libido**, is sexual in nature.

- The personality consists of three major structures: the **id**, which is biologically determined and represents all the instinctual drives which are inherited; the **ego**, which develops in order to help satisfy the id's needs in a socially acceptable way; and the **superego**, representing the individual's internal framework (conscience and ego ideal) of the moral values which exist in the surrounding culture. Figure 1.2 illustrates the way in which these structures occupy different levels of consciousness in the mind: the conscious, the preconscious and the unconscious.

- Experiences gained in early childhood have a crucially important influence on emotional and personality development. Development of the personality is seen as proceeding through a number of **psychosexual stages**. During each stage, satisfaction is gained as the libido is directed towards a different part of the body. Failure to negotiate satisfactorily a particular stage results in **fixation**, or halting of development at that stage. Fixation causes the individual to retain some of the characteristics of that stage in later life and in severe cases may result in neuroses in adult life.

Freud's work attracted many followers, but his theory also generated much debate and controversy. His notion of 'infantile sexuality' outraged Victorian society. Many psychologists believed his methods of study to be unscientific and the concepts he employed vague and difficult to verify (See Chapter 2 for a more detailed critique of psychoanalytic theory.) Even among his original followers there were dissenters, such as **Carl Jung** and **Alfred Adler**, who eventually broke away from Freud to develop their own modified versions of his theory.

Jung's version of psychoanalytic theory differed from Freud's in two main respects:

1. Freud's conceptualisation of the unconscious mind was extended by Jung, who proposed that there existed also a **collective unconscious**. Jung reasoned that the human mind should contain

FIGURE 1.2
Structure of the Personality (Freud)

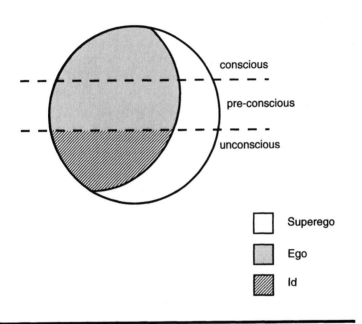

a record of human experience in the same way as the body reveals the past structures of our ancestors. The collective unconscious, Jung believed, is not directly available to us but is revealed in the myths and artistic symbols that different cultures create. The collective unconscious contains archetypes, universal symbols that occur again and again in art, literature and religion.

2. The libido was seen by Jung as primarily spiritual in nature rather than essentially sexual, as had been posited by Freud.

Jung was also concerned with personality 'types'. He was responsible for proposing that humans are born with a temperament which is either **introverted** (primarily concerned with oneself) or **extraverted** (primarily concerned with the outside world). Introversion and extraversion have subsequently become important concepts in contemporary theories of personality.

Adler regarded the need for power and superiority as the most important human drive. Whilst not denying the existence of unconscious motives, he saw human motivation as being largely conscious. He had considerable success in treating mental disorders, particularly with young people suffering from minor maladjustments. His methods were quicker and simpler than those of Freud and therefore were less likely to become a dominating force in the life of a patient. Birth order, the order in which children are born within a family, was viewed by Adler as an important influence on the development of personality.

Psychoanalysis as a Therapy

Psychoanalysis as a therapy is very widely used in the treatment of neuroses and sometimes in the treatment of non-neurotic disorders. There is an assumption by psychoanalysts that it is in the unconscious part of the personality that conflict occurs. Therefore the aim of psychoanalysis is to explore the individual's unconscious mind in order to understand the dynamics of abnormal behaviour.

During treatment the individual is encouraged to re-experience traumatic events and feelings encountered in childhood, express them in a safe context and then return them, devoid of anxiety, to the unconscious.

In classical psychoanalysis, therapy involves **transference** – the client's projection and displacement of thoughts and feelings onto the analyst; **free association**, where the client says whatever comes into his/her mind, no matter how trivial or irrelevant it may seem; and **dream analysis**, which involves the analyst interpreting the content of the client's dreams.

Though the psychoanalytic process may sound quite straightforward, it is usually difficult and time-consuming.

Psychoanalytic theory and methods of treating mental disorders are still a significant force in contemporary psychology. Many of Freud's original ideas have been adopted and in some cases modified by subsequent psychoanalytic theorists, known as post-Freudians (see Chapter 2, Section II).

Self-assessment Questions

1. Explain the two applications of the term 'psychoanalysis'.
2. What methods were used by Freud to arrive at his theory of personality and child development?
3. Briefly explain the Freudian concepts of unconscious mind and libido.
4. Outline the three structures of the personality proposed by Freud.
5. For what reasons did Freud's work attract criticism?
6. Briefly explain how the psychoanalytic theories of Jung and Adler differed from that of Freud.

FURTHER READING

R. E. Fancher (1979) *Pioneers of Psychology* (New York: W.W. Norton).
D. Schulz, *A History of Modern Psychology*, 4th edn (New York: Academic Press, 1987).

O.K. — SO WE'LL LEAVE THE FREE ASSOCIATION AND GO INTO DREAM ANALYSIS.

Theoretical Approaches to Psychology

2

At the end of this chapter you should be able to:

1. describe and evaluate five major theoretical approaches to psychology: physiological, psychoanalytic, behaviourist, cognitive and humanistic;
2. discuss different levels of explanation of psychological functioning; and
3. consider a number of issues and debates about the nature of the person in psychology, including heredity and environment, free will and determinism the mind/body problem and reductionism.

Introduction

As outlined in Chapter 1, for the first 50 years or so of its existence as a separate discipline, psychology was organised around separate schools, each with its own distinct ideas of what psychology should be about and how it should be studied. Psychologists tended to identify themselves as structuralists, functionalists, behaviourists, psychoanalysts or Gestaltists. Today, with the realisation that the problems psychologists have set themselves will not be solved by one particular set of ideas and methods, it is accepted that many different routes must be taken if a full understanding is to be reached about psychological functioning. Psychologists are now often classified according to their professional commitments – clinical psychologist or educational psychologist, for example – or to their specific fields of study, such as social, developmental or cognitive psychology (see Chapter 7).

However, though schools as such no longer exist, within each field of psychology can be seen many different **approaches** to the study of psychological phenomena, and some of the ideas of the early schools continue to influence many of the modern-day approaches. 'Approach', in this context is not easy to define exactly, but it is to do with basic assumptions that are made about what human beings are like, theories used in order to help explain human and animal behaviour and the kinds of research methods used to study them. For example, the learning theory approach, influenced heavily by the behaviourist school, still strongly emphasises the effects of the environment on psychological functioning and continues to use the concept of reinforcement in attempts to explain and change human behaviour. Also the experimental method is still the major technique used in research, in preference to more subjective methods.

Five major approaches in psychology are **physiological**, **psychodynamic**, **behaviourist** (or learning theory), **cognitive** and **humanistic**. Each will be discussed below. There is some overlap between these approaches and they should not be seen as separate, competing bodies of knowledge and theory. Rather they represent different but complementary views and methods of understanding psychological functioning.

SECTION I THE PHYSIOLOGICAL APPROACH

Psychologists who take a physiological approach, as the name implies, look to biology as a means of describing and explaining psychological functioning. Our behaviour, even what we think and feel, is assumed to be linked to our physiological make-up. For example, schizophrenia may be seen as arising almost entirely from malfunctions in biochemical processes in the brain. Some of the labels attached to researchers who take this approach, albeit in rather different ways, are biopsychologist, neuropsychologist, psychobiologist and physiological psychologist.

Physiological psychologists are interested in a wide range of phenomena and issues. Research has developed rapidly over recent years into the functions of the nervous system (particularly the brain) and the hormonal system, and into how these two systems interact and influence behaviour and mental activity. Some of the questions that have been asked by scientists in the course of this research are:

- What activities occur in the nerve cells (neurons) of the brain and senses when we perceive patterns or colour?
- To what extent does the brain function as a single unit and to what extent as a collection of 'parts', each with its own particular function (localisation of brain functions)?

- What activities occur in the brain during different states of consciousness, such as wakefulness, sleep and coma?
- What are the links between the hormonal system and emotion, aggression and sex differences in behaviour?
- What physiological mechanisms underlie needs and motivations?
- What changes take place in the nervous system when a memory has been established or something has been learned?
- How might a person's mental state affect his or her health?

Another aspect of the biological approach is interest in the role of heredity in behaviour. In the relatively short time since Darwin suggested that variations among individuals of a species could be passed on to future generations, much knowledge has accumulated regarding genetic transmission. For example, it is known that inheritance occurs through a chemical code carried in the genes. However, while the transmission of physical characteristics is well-understood, the role of heredity in behavioural characteristics such as intelligence and personality is less clear-cut. Linked to this has been interest in the relative importance of heredity and environment in the development of psychological characteristics (the nature–nurture debate), a long-standing controversy in psychology. It is now generally accepted that the key question that needs to be addressed is not which of the two, heredity or environment, is the more important, but how do the two *interact* to influence the development of behaviour? This question will be addressed later in the chapter.

Reductionism and the Mind/Body Problem

There are some scientists who believe that all psychological phenomena can be explained by reference to ('reduced to') physiological activity, particularly brain processes. This philosophical viewpoint has been termed **reductionism**. The term may be used also in relation to views held by behavioural and other psychologists.

Reductionism in relation to physiological psychology implies that, if we are to understand psychological functioning, we must analyse these functions in terms of ever smaller units of analysis, such as nerve activity, muscle movements or chemical processes. This view, taken to its logical conclusions, could lead to psychological explanations of behaviour becoming redundant. (A more detailed discussion of reductionism will appear later in the chapter.)

The reductionist issue is closely linked to a continuing and extremely controversial issue, that of the **mind/body problem**. This issue is concerned with the relationship between the mind (or awareness) and the neurophysiological processes within the body, how the two interact and the influence of one on the other. The debate began in the seventeenth century, with the work of the philosopher, René Descartes (see Chapter 1). Descartes' theory put forward the view that the human body, like that of animals, was basically a machine. However, what distinguished humans from animals was the existence in the former of a soul which was intangible but which interacted with the physical body through the pineal gland located in the brain.

In modern times most people would equate the term 'mind' with 'brain'. But the word 'mind' was originally created to identify a psychological rather than a physiological concept. The mind is usually regarded as the root of awareness, or consciousness, rather than as a physiological mechanism. Many examples exist of the effect of body on mind (a cup of coffee may act as a stimulant) and also of mind on body (for some the prospect of flying or even a visit to the dentist can produce trembling and sweating). Also research has confirmed that the brain is involved in the experience of consciousness, though it is not certain how and to what extent. Therefore the question remains: if it is impossible to link the intangible mind to a particular part of the body, how can we study the interaction between the two? There is currently no adequate answer. However, knowledge is constantly expanding and, as our understanding of physiological mechanisms increases, it becomes clear that mind and body are closely integrated.

Some Research Findings from Physiological Psychology

There follows a brief outline of some research which has focused on the physiological mechanisms underlying behaviour. The aim here is to provide the reader with a 'feel' for the kinds of investigations carried out and some of the techniques used.

- In 1861, **Paul Broca**, a doctor, demonstrated by post-mortem autopsy that a patient's inability to speak arose from a defect in a specific area of the brain. This evidence of **localisation of brain function** contributes to the gradually emerging view that behaviour had a physical base.

- In the 1920s, **Karl Lashley** carried out a series of classic experiments in which he demonstrated that learning and memory in rats is impaired if part of the cortex of the brain is removed. Lashley used a technique known as **ablation**, the removal of parts of the brain by surgery or by burning out with electrodes. Many of his experiments demonstrated that the amount of brain tissue destroyed appeared to be more important to the animal's behaviour than the specific part of the brain involved (Lashley, 1929). He believed that all parts of the brain were probably involved in every action (the Law of Mass Action).

- Much research has been carried out into **electrical stimulation of the brain** (ESB). ESB involves the stimulation of neurons by means of a mild electrical current passed through an implanted electrode. Typically the main aim of this research is to investigate the effects of such stimulation on behaviour, particularly emotions. In the 1950s, using ESB, **Olds and Milner** identified **pleasure centres** in the brains of rats – areas which, when stimulated, led the rat to return to the area of the cage where it had been stimulated.

- Much well-established research has highlighted the close inter-action between mental processes and physiological changes within the body. **Hans Selye** (1956, 1974) has pioneered research into the physiological changes associated with stress in both animals and humans. Selye's work led him to propose the **General Adaptation Syndrome** (GAS), which describes the hormonal, biochemical and other bodily changes which occur and which interact with psychological factors within the in-dividual during the experience of stress.

- The notion that people can influence their own health by their thoughts or feelings used to be treated with scepticism. However, the work of **Cousins** in the 1970s led to the development of research into **psychoimmunology** – the study of mental states and their effect on health (see Cousins, 1989, for a review) Cousins, a newspaper editor, was diagnosed with Hodgkin's Disease, a form of cancer which affects the immune system; doctors did not expect him to live long. However, he recovered, claiming that this was due at least in part to his determination to think positively and find ways of lifting his spirits.At first, Cousins' beliefs were dismissed as untenable, but as fresh information became available about the functioning of the immune system, his ideas were treated more seriously. Today, scientists, using advanced biochemical techniques, are attempting to identify some of the body's chemicals and hormones which are influenced by different mental states and which may affect the responses of the immune system (Maier and Laudenslager, 1985; Pert, 1990).

- A great deal of research has been carried out in an attempt to understand the nature and causes of schizophrenia. Some of this work has indicated the influence of social, cultural and family factors on the development of the condition. A major line of enquiry has focused on possible biological differences between schizophrenic individuals and other people. For example, evidence is accumulating that schizophrenia, or some variants of it, may have a genetic base. Using advanced techniques of molecular biology, Sherrington *et al.* (1988) have located a genetic abnormality in members of a family having an unusually high incidence of schizophrenia. Research such as this does not, however, rule out other possible causes of schizophrenia.

Evaluation of the Physiological Approach

The physiological approach endeavours to work towards an understanding and explanation of the biological basis of behaviour. It is unique as an approach within psychology in the range of factors it considers and in the level at which it seeks to explain them. The physiological approach is the only one which attempts to relate behaviour to the workings and genetic make-up of the body. Other approaches, for example psychoanalysis, may subscribe to the view that behaviour is biologically based, but the concepts used and the phenomena studied are largely psychological rather than physiological.

As already noted, much valuable evidence has accumulated about the biological basis of behaviour. However, physiological psychology is not yet sufficiently advanced to offer total explanations for memory, stress, learning, emotions and so on. Moreover the complexity of the physiological system and the countless environmental influences that may affect it make it difficult to predict behaviour and explain it in purely physiological terms. This complexity and the way in which factors interact make it difficult also to draw specific conclusions about one factor, for example genetic links with schizophrenia, without taking into account other factors, such as cultural or family influences. However, our knowledge is increasing and the insights gained are being applied – in medicine, in business and in everyday life. For example, the concept of stress has been widely studied as have the methods for coping with it. The use of psychoactive drugs has profoundly changed the treatment of mental disorders. Developments in areas such as psychoimmunology may have even greater impact in the future.

Some psychologists are afraid that overemphasising physiological links with behaviour may lead to reductionist explanations which override the value of psychological explanations. A more positive view would be to accept that physiological mechanisms underlie behaviour and should be studied. Insights from this research may be used to complement purely psychological observations and measurements, resulting in a more complete description and explanation of behaviour. (A more detailed examination of physiological psychology can be found in *Biopsychology* (in press) by Sheila Hayward.)

Self-assessment Questions

1. Briefly outline some of the issues which concern physiological psychologists.
2. What do you understand by the mind/body problem?
3. Briefly describe three pieces of research carried out by physiological psychologists.
4. What are the strengths and limitations of the physiological approach?

SECTION II THE PSYCHODYNAMIC APPROACH

The psychodynamic approach focuses largely on the role of motivation and past experiences in the development of personality and, hence, behaviour. It has arisen from **Freud's psychoanalytic theory**, a brief outline of which has already been given in Chapter 1. Freud's pioneering approach was the impetus of many similar theories, which share many of the same assumptions about human beings but which differ in conceptual detail. Therefore, it is appropriate to examine the wider context of psychodynamic theories rather than just Freud's theory

Post-Freudians

As has already been noted, many of Freud's original ideas have been adapted and modified by subsequent psychodynamic theorists, known as post-Freudians. Some of the ideas of Jung and Adler have already been outlined in Chapter 1. The work of three others, Anna Freud, Klein and Erikson, is briefly considered below. As was the case with Freud, much of the work of post-Freudians was centrally concerned with clinical problems and the treatment of mental disorders.

Anna Freud, Sigmund Freud's daughter, was part of the Continental school of psychoanalysis, though she came to Britain shortly before the Second World War, at the same time as her father. As part of the movement, starting in the 1930s, to apply a full psychoanalytic approach to problems of childhood, Anna Freud worked largely with older children and adolescents.

The publication of *The Ego and the Mechanisms of Defence* (A. Freud, 1936) encouraged a new tendency in psychoanalysis to attach more importance to the conscious mind, or ego, than had previously been the case. Anna Freud believed that the term 'psychoanalysis' could not be applied to any technique which focused attention on the unconscious mind to the exclusion of everything else. She also expressed the belief that her father had overstressed the influence of sexuality in early childhood and had neglected its importance in adolescence. She saw adolescence as a time when there is an upsurge in the activity of the libido (sexual energy) and young people experience renewed sexual feelings and strivings. The intensity of these inner drives, she contended, results in excessive emotional upset as the adolescent tries to cope with the resulting impulses and desires.

Melanie Klein was one of the leading figures in European psychoanalysis but, like Anna Freud, established herself in Britain in the 1930s. From her background as a nursery teacher she related much of Freud's psychoanalytic theory to the development of very young children. She developed a therapeutic technique for analysing children's play which made it possible for psychoanalytic principles to be applied to children as young as two to six years old. **Play therapy** is the term used to describe a means through which a psychoanalyst can use play to get in touch with a child's unconscious in order to help him/her deal with emotional difficulties.

In Klein's version of play therapy, simple play materials were used, for example male and female dolls, small models of familiar objects, such as cars, wheelbarrows or swings, and materials such as paper, string, clay and water. The child was allowed free access to play with all these objects and materials while the analyst knelt and attended to the content of the play. Occasionally she would offer an interpretation of the play to the child and would encourage **transference**; that is, she encouraged the child to transfer feelings towards the parents onto herself. Interpretations of the phantasy life of the child as revealed in play were given. Klein's methods offered new insights into development during the earliest years of childhood. Her views and methods dominated the mainstream of orthodox psychoanalysis in Britain. Prominent analysts such as D.W. Winnicott and John Bowlby, who were closely associated with the Tavistock Clinic where Klein worked, supported and were influenced by her views.

Erik Erikson began his psychoanalytic training with Anna Freud, whose interest in child analysis greatly influenced his work. In 1933, Erikson left Europe and began to practise as a child analyst in the USA. Though subscribing to much orthodox psychoanalytic theory, Erikson believed that Freud overemphasised the role of sexuality in the personality and neglected the importance of the social forces which influence development. He therefore proposed a series of **psychosocial stages** (rather than psychosexual stages, as proposed by Freud) through which an individual passes during his/her lifetime. In contrast to Freud, who particularly emphasised the importance of the childhood years for later personality, Erikson viewed the stages of development as covering the whole lifespan. Each stage was marked by a central crisis, the successful management of which would lead to the development and maintenance of a well-balanced personality.

Much of Erikson's clinical practice was carried out with troubled adolescents. His view that the conflict of 'identity versus role confusion' encountered during adolescence is the central crisis of all development, has received wide support amongst psychologists. Erikson has made a substantial contribution to the field of developmental psychology and in particular to the area of lifespan development where his theory is the single most important influence.

A more complete account of Erikson's theory can be found in Birch (*Developmental Psychology*, in press).

Evaluation of the Psychodynamic Approach

The psychodynamic approach attracts both wide acclaim and vigorous criticism. Freud's theory has made a monumental contribution to our understanding of the human personality. His emphasis on the importance of early childhood for later personality development and his attempts to account for individual differences in development have stimulated a great deal of research. His theory has also offered insights which have greatly influenced disciplines such as art, English literature and history. As already noted, psychoanalytic methods of treating mental disorders are widely used by many psychologists. Criticisms of the psychodynamic approach, starting with those levelled at Freud's original theory, can be summarised as follows:

- Though there is an abundance of research which claims to offer supporting evidence for psychoanalytic theory (for reviews see Kline, 1981, and Fisher and Greenberg, 1977), alternative explanations are often available to account for the findings. Not only can the theory not be reliably supported, it lacks **falsifiability**. In other words, it cannot be refuted – a serious violation of the scientific method according to Popper (1972) (see Chapter 4).

- Eysenck and Wilson (1973) have raised objections to psychoanalytic theory on a number of counts:

    (a) Freud's use of a limited sample composed mainly of adults who were suffering some psychological disturbance prevents generalisation of his theory to all human beings;

    (b) Because many of the processes described by Freud, for example instinctual drives and defence mechanisms, cannot be directly observed, the generation of precise and testable hypotheses is difficult

    (c) Freud's use of the clinical case-study method, unsupported by quantitative data or statistical analyses, renders his theory vague and difficult to verify;

    (d) Freudian theory is unable to predict an individual's development. It can be used only to explain something after an event.

- Criticisms have been made of Freud's over-emphasis on the role of biological factors in personality development. His insistence that the goal of all behaviour is to satisfy biological needs was not shared by other psychodynamic theorists such as Jung, Adler and Erikson. Whilst recognising the importance of biological factors, these theorists subscribed also to the *social* nature of human beings.

- Attention has been drawn to the problems encountered in trying to assess the effectiveness of psychoanalysis as a therapy, largely arising from the controversy over what constitutes a 'cure'. Eysenck (1952) reviewed five studies of the effectiveness of psychoanalysis and concluded that it achieved little that would not have occurred without therapy. However, using different criteria of the notion of 'cure', Bergin (1971) put the success rate of psychoanalysis at 83 per cent.

As we have seen, Freud's approach spawned many other psycho-dynamic theories of human personality. There are many similarities, but also many differences. One key similarity lies in the view that early childhood experiences crucially affect an individual's later personality. This 'similar-but-different' nature of psychodynamic models makes it difficult to determine which is the most accurate.

Because of the subjective nature of psychodynamic theories and their complexity, it is difficult to find effective ways of evaluating differences between them. Also, like Freud's theory, other psycho-dynamic models lack falsifiability and, in general, can describe but not predict human behaviour.

(Note that a more detailed account of psychodynamic theory appears in *Individual Differences* (1994) by Ann Birch and Sheila Hayward.)

Self-assessment Questions

1. Briefly explain what is meant by the psychodynamic approach.
2. Give an outline of the views or work of one of the post-Freudians.
3. What are the main strengths and shortcomings of the psycho-dynamic approach?

SECTION III   THE BEHAVIOURIST (OR LEARNING THEORY) APPROACH

Where physiological psychologists focus on genetics and an individual's biological make-up, behaviourists or learning theorists focus on the influence of the environment. They choose not to be concerned with the internal mechanisms which occur inside the organism. Questions likely to be explored are:

- Under what conditions might certain behaviour occur?
- What might be the effects of various stimuli on behaviour?
- How do the *consequences* of behaviour affect that behaviour?

Questions such as these are relevant to the behaviourist view that human beings are **shaped** through constant interactions with the environment. Put more simply, learning and experience determine the kind of person you become.

The behaviourist approach to psychological functioning is rooted in the work of associationists, Pavlov and Thorndike, and the early behaviourists, Watson and Hull, all of whom studied learning in the form of conditioning (see Chapter 1). Pavlov studied the conditioning of reflex responses, or **classical conditioning**, whilst Thorndike's work focused on the conditioning of voluntary behaviour, now referred to as **operant conditioning**, and later researched further by B. F. Skinner.

Behaviourism had a profound influence on the course of psychology during the first half of the twentieth century. Its offshoot, stimulus–response psychology, is still influential today. **Stimulus–response psychology**, studies the stimuli which elicit behavioural responses, the rewards and punishments that influence these responses and the changes in behaviour brought about by manipulating patterns of rewards and punishments. This approach does not concern itself with the mental processes which occur between the stimulus and the response. The work of B. F. Skinner on operant conditioning is central here; however, Skinner preferred to concentrate on the relationship between responses and their consequences because it was not always possible to determine which stimuli brought about which responses.

Skinner, in his *Behavior of Organisms* (1938), described experiments he conducted with rats and later with pigeons. For instance, he conditioned rats to press a bar in a 'Skinner box' in return for a reward of food. He was able to measure learning accurately under closely controlled conditions, varying the frequency of reward, or **reinforcement**, and sometimes applying irrelevant stimuli. Though he started his research with animals, Skinner worked towards a theory of conditioning which could include humans. This work is described in *Science and Human Behavior* (1953).

Some Practical Applications of the Behaviourist Approach

The influence of the behaviourist approach, with its emphasis on the manipulation of behaviour through patterns of reinforcement and punishment, can be seen in many practical situations, both in education and in psychotherapy. Below is a brief account of some of these practical applications.

Programmed Learning

Skinner applied the principles of operant conditioning to the formal learning situation. He developed a system known as 'programmed learning', in which teaching machines are sometimes used, although it can take the form of written self-teaching units. The material to be learned is broken down into a large number of small segments, or **frames**. The student works through the frames sequentially and is required to respond at the end of each one. Correct responses receive reinforcement in the form of **immediate feedback** and, if correct, the learner proceeds to the next frame. In this way behaviour is shaped. The sequence described above is known as a linear programme. A more complex sequence, known as a branching programme, can also be used.

Programmed learning was not adopted as widely as had been envisaged by Skinner. Reports of its effectiveness relative to conventional learning methods are variable.

Behavioural Therapies

Therapeutic techniques based on conditioning processes are usually referred to as either **behaviour modification** or **behaviour therapy**. Walker (1984) has proposed that techniques based on operant conditioning should be referred to as behaviour modification and that techniques which rely upon the principles of classical conditioning should be known as behaviour therapy. This distinction is used in the descriptions which follow.

Behaviour modification This is a technique which is used to change or remove unwanted behaviour. Its central principle, taken from operant conditioning, is that behaviour which has favourable consequences, that is, which is **positively reinforced**, is likely to be repeated and behaviour which is ignored is likely to die out. The desired behaviour is broken down into a sequence of small steps. Each step achieved is immediately rewarded, but gradually more and more of the required behaviour is demanded before the reward is given. This process is known as **behaviour shaping** through successive approximations.

Behaviour modification has been widely used in clinical settings with mentally handicapped children and adults and especially with autistic children. Typically a shaping technique is used. For instance, Lovaas (1973) developed a programme to modify the behaviour of autistic children from withdrawal to talking and social interaction. Appropriate responses were initially rewarded with sweets. Later, when the children became more responsive, cuddling was used as a reinforcement for 'good' behaviour.

Token economy systems are based on the principle of **secondary reinforcement**. Tokens are given in exchange for desirable or acceptable behaviours. These can then be exchanged for **primary** (or direct) **reinforcements**, such as sweets or extra outings.

There is evidence that well-organised token economy systems do promote desirable behaviour, particularly in an institutional setting. However, doubts have been raised about whether the effects are due to reinforcement or to other variables, and also about the long-term effectiveness of such programmes in the 'real world'. Also, in some situations involving token economies, ethical concerns have been expressed (see Chapter 5).

Behaviour therapy This is a term usually applied to techniques based on classical conditioning which deal with involuntary or reflex behaviour. It aims to remove maladaptive behaviours and substitute desirable ones. One example of such a technique is **systematic desensitisation**, which is mainly used to remove phobias. For example, a patient who had an irrational fear would first be taught to relax. Gradually the feared object would be introduced to the patient in a step-by-step process until the patient could tolerate actual contact with the object without anxiety. A second example is **aversion therapy**, which is used mainly to treat addictions or other unwanted behaviour. (See Chapter 6 for a consideration of some of the ethical issues surrounding the use of behavioural therapies.)

A more detailed examination of the principles and applications of classical and operant conditioning can be found in Malim *et al.* (1996).

Biofeedback

This is a technique which draws mainly on the principles of operant conditioning. Individuals are trained to control bodily processes such as heart rate and blood pressure, which are autonomic responses and not normally under voluntary control. Typically, patients are connected to a machine which gives a continuous reading of heart rate and blood pressure. They are trained to relax and are asked to try consciously to reduce one or both. When the readout falls to a given target level, a bell or tone sounds. The patients aims to maintain that level. The reinforcement for hypertensive patients in doing this is the knowledge that they are helping to improve their own health (see Mercer, 1986).

From a theoretical point of view, biofeedback demonstrates that the processes of classical and operant conditioning are more closely interleaved than was once thought, since it works on autonomic responses, thought to be the province only of classical conditioning.

Evaluation of the Behaviourist Approach

The behaviourist approach has been a dominant influence in psychology. It represents one of the 'hardcore' approaches which has contributed a great deal to our understanding of psychological functioning and has provided a number of techniques for changing unwanted behaviour. Its use of rigorous empirical methods has enhanced the credibility of psychology as a science. (See Chapter 3, for a discussion of behaviourism in relation to the scientific method.) Criticisms of the approach include the following:

- Its mechanistic views tend to overlook the realm of consciousness and subjective experience and it does not address the possible role of biological factors in human behaviour.
- Individuals are seen as passive beings who are at the mercy of their environments. This emphasis on **environmental determinism** leaves no room for the notion of **free will** in an individual. (A more complete discussion of the issue of free will and determinism appears later in this chapter.)
- Its theories of classical and operant conditioning cannot account for the production of spontaneous, novel or creative behaviour.

- Its basis in animal research has been questioned (see Chapter 6 on the use of animals in psychological research).
- One of the assumptions commonly made by behaviourists is that the principles of classical and operant conditioning apply to any response in any species. Laboratory studies using a wide range of species seemed to confirm this idea. However, researchers coming from **ethology** (the study of animals in their natural environments) have drawn attention to some of the biological limits of conditioning. This is concerned with the study of **species-specific behaviours** (behaviour characteristic of all members of a particular species) which are likely to be influenced by the genetic makeup of a species as well as by learning. (See Malim et al, 1996, for a discussion of the biological limits of conditioning).
- Clinical psychologists who adopt behaviourally-oriented therapies have been criticised for treating the probable symptoms of mental disorders whilst often ignoring possible underlying causes.(See Birch and Hayward, 1994, for an evaluation of the behavioural approach to therapy.)

Self-assessment questions

1. What, according to the behaviourists, is the most important influence on the development of behaviour?
2. Briefly explain how Skinner applied the principles of operant conditioning to programmed learning.
3. Describe one behavioural therapy based on the principles of classical conditioning and one based on the principles of operant conditioning.
4. Briefly evaluate the behaviourist approach.

SECTION IV   THE COGNITIVE APPROACH

The cognitive approach contrasts sharply with that of both the psychoanalysts, with their emphasis upon the importance of the unconscious mind, and the behaviourists, who focus largely upon the links between external events and behaviours. Cognitive psychologists believe that the events occurring within a person must be studied if behaviour is to be fully understood. These internal events, often referred to as **mediators**, since they occur between the stimulus and the behaviour, include perception, thinking processes such as problem-solving, memory and language. Unlike psychoanalysis and behaviourism, the cognitive approach does not espouse a single body of theory, and no single theorist has predominated in the way that Freud influenced psychoanalysis and Skinner behaviourism. What cognitive psychologists have in common is an approach which stresses the importance of studying the mental processes which affect our behaviour and enable us to make sense of the world around us. Thus cognitive psychologists may ask questions such as:

- How do we remember?
- Why do we forget?
- What strategies do we use to solve problems?
- What is the relationship between language and thought?
- How do we form concepts?

There is a general belief that cognitive processes operate not randomly but in an organised and systematic way. The human mind is therefore often compared to a computer and human beings are seen as information processors who absorb information from the outside world, code and interpret it, store and retrieve it.

The influence of the cognitive approach can be seen also in many other areas of psychology, the assumption being that some kind of mediational processes underlie behaviour. Thus one might talk about a cognitive approach to moral development or a cognitive theory of emotion. Within social psychology, a primary interest is in **social cognition**, the mental processes implicated in the way individuals perceive and react to social situations

Methods of Study

Clearly the processes that cognitive psychologists study are not directly observable: one cannot lift off the top of an individual's head and observe memory at work! However, it is recognised that insights into mental processes may be inferred from an individual's behaviour, provided that such inferences are supported by objective, empirical data. Therefore the experimental method, with its emphasis on objectivity, control and replicability, is often used. Some examples of experiments which may be encountered in the area of cognitive psychology are as follows:

- **Gregory** (1972) in his study of perceptual illusions investigated participants' perception of the Muller–Lyer figure and the Necker Cube. His findings indicated that, when the figures are removed from their flat paper background and represented as luminous figures suspended in the dark, they are perceived as three-dimensional. This finding contributed to Gregory's theory as to why people are 'taken in' by such illusions.

- **Neisser** investigated **feature detection theory** (FDT) in his research into **pattern recognition**. FDT maintains that patterns such as letters of the alphabet are made up of a number of basic features such as vertical lines, curves and diagonal lines. For example, the letter T may be analysed as one horizontal feature and one vertical feature. Recognition of letters involves the brain in detection of these basic features.

- In a series of well-known experiments, Neisser (1964) presented participants with tasks requiring them to search through lists of letters in order to locate a pre-specified letter placed in various different positions in the lists. He found that participants located the letter A much more quickly in lists made up of rounded letters such as O, Q and G than in lists containing angular letters such as N, E and W. This confirmed the hypothesis derived from FDT that, the fewer the common features between the target and non-target letters, the more quickly the patterns are analysed by the brain.

- **Loftus** has studied some of the effects of memory on **eye-witness testimony** (Loftus, 1980; Loftus and Hoffman, 1989). She has tested the hypothesis that memory is reconstructive in nature; that is, our memory for events is often unreliable in that we sometimes reconstruct the past in line with what we believe **could** or **should** have happened. This process, Loftus believes, can be greatly influenced in a court setting by the kinds of questions witnesses are asked.In one of her experiments, Loftus *et al.* (1980) showed three groups of participants a film of a car accident. One group were asked to estimate the speed of the cars when they hit each other. A second group were asked an identical question but with the words 'smashed into' substituted for 'hit'. The remaining participants were used as a control group and were not asked to estimate speed. Findings showed that the 'smashed into' group estimated speed as significantly higher than that estimated by the 'hit' group.

Models in Cognitive Psychology

As already noted, one of the difficulties facing cognitive psychologists is that of attempting to study processes which are not directly observable. Hebb (1949) proposed some clear guidelines as to how this problem might be partially dealt with. He suggested that, in order to study information processing by the nervous system, it was not necessary to have a precise knowledge of the brain and its functions. Until firm physiological evidence was available one could propose hypothetical (or possible) **models** of the way some aspects of the nervous system – for example that relating to memory – might operate. A model could then be tested by experimental or other means and in the light of research findings might be adapted or replaced by a new model.

The use of models in cognitive psychology has proved a valuable and fruitful means of gaining information. There follows a brief account of some models which have been developed and tested in cognitive psychology.

The Broadbent Filter Model of Selective Attention

This model represents an attempt by Broadbent (1958) to explain how the nervous system selects some stimuli to pay attention to while ignoring others. The model, which focused on the processing of auditory information, proposed that a filter exists, very early in processing, which is attuned to the physical features of the incoming stimuli. These are passed through for higher processing in the brain whilst other unattended information is filtered out and lost. (See Chapter 5 for further explanation of this model.)

Later models of selective attention were proposed by Treisman (1964a) and Deutsch and Deutsch (1963). The latter model was revised by Norman (1976).

Atkinson–Shiffrin Two-Process Model of Memory

Atkinson and Shiffrin (1971) proposed a model which illustrated the relationship between short-term memory (STM) and long-term memory (LTM) (see Figure 2.1). A central feature of this model was its emphasis on the role of **rehearsal**, which has two main functions: to maintain incoming information in STM, and to transfer information from STM to LTM. The notion of two

FIGURE 2.1
Atkinson–Shiffrin Model of Memory

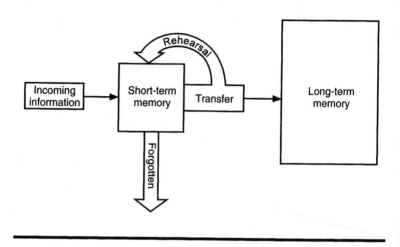

memory processes has received much research support. However other models have also been proposed, the most significant being that of the **levels** or **depths of processing model** (Craik and Lockhart, 1972).

Computer Simulation of Human Thinking

With the advent of the computer, many computer programmes have been developed which have attempted to model human thinking. This approach is known as computer simulation.

Perhaps the most famous of these programmes is the **General Problem Solver**, devised by Newell, Shaw and Simon (1958) and Newell and Simon (1972). This programme attempted to simulate the strategies used in human problem-solving. It proposed that much human problem-solving is heuristic; that is, it is based on the testing of intelligent 'hunches'. Newell *et al.* support this heuristic model with evidence derived from participants thinking aloud about the strategies used as they worked on problems.

As more sophisticated programmes have been devised in order to simulate human thinking a controversial debate has developed. Some critics question the whole premise of likening people to machines. Others argue that computers can do only what they are programmed to do, and that we do not yet know enough about the way the human brain works to be able to reflect its activity in computers.

Cognitive Development

A brief word should be said finally about the work of psychologists who have studied cognitive development. The most significant of these is **Jean Piaget**, who has made a monumental contribution to our understanding of the development of logic and concept attainment from childhood to maturity. **Jerome Bruner** and the Russian psychologist **L. S. Vygotsky**, have also made an outstanding contribution to an understanding of cognitive development in children. An account of these two theories and some of their practical applications can be found in *Developmental Psychology: from infancy to adulthood*, 2nd edn, by Ann Birch (in press).

Evaluation of the Cognitive Approach

The cognitive approach emphasises the importance of mediational processes, such as perception and thinking, which occur between a stimulus and a response. Research carried out by cognitive psychologists has aided our understanding of these processes. Practical insights have also been offered into such issues as how memory may be made more effective, how to improve problem-solving skills, and the merits and limitations of eye witness testimony in court. Criticisms of the cognitive approach include the following:

- A problem with the cognitive approach lies in its lack of integration. Though 'cognitive theories' exist in many different areas of psychology, no single, coherent theory links these areas into an identifiable framework. For example, in addition to theories of perception, memory and thinking, we refer to cognitive theories of emotion (though as yet an emotional theory of cognition has been largely ignored), cognitive dissonance and social cognition, but the descriptions and terminology used tend to vary in each area. This lack of integration may exist in part because of the lack of a single important theorist, as noted earlier.

- The information-processing metaphor drawn from computing and emphasising 'the human-being as a machine' has offended some psychologists. They point out that the computer analogy fails to recognise the most fundamental differences between humans and machines: for example, people forget, computers do not; people are emotional and irrational whilst computers are logical and unable to feel emotion. It must be remembered that the information-processing model is a metaphor and as such, it has limitations in explaining human behaviour.
- The wide use of laboratory experiments in cognitive psychology has been criticised, largely because findings are said to be 'artificial' and not in keeping with behaviour and events occurring in the 'real world'. It is suggested that people's behaviour may be influenced by the setting and by characteristics associated with the experimenter. (See Malim and Birch (1996) for a more complete evaluation of the experimental method.) Currently, however, there is a trend towards using more ecologically valid methods of study, particularly in the field of memory.

The cognitive approach is expanding rapidly within psychology. The trend towards 'cognitive science' is encouraging increasing dialogues among disciplines, including psychology, computer science, physiology and linguistics. It is possible that some exciting developments lie ahead.

(A more detailed examination of cognitive psychology can be found in *Cognitive Processes* (1994) by Tony Malim.)

Self-assessment questions

1. Why is the cognitive approach often referred to as an 'information-processing' approach?
2. Outline some of the questions explored by cognitive psychologists about human mental activity.
3. What do you understand by the term 'model' in cognitive psychology. Give an example.
4. Consider the main strengths and limitations of the cognitive approach.

SECTION V   THE HUMANISTIC (OR PHENOMENOLOGICAL) APPROACH

For many years psychology was dominated by two great schools: the psychoanalysts with their emphasis on instinctive, irrational human beings influenced by the contents of an unconscious mind and the behaviourists, who viewed humans as mechanistic beings controlled by the effects of the environment. Towards the middle of the twentieth century, a third great force appeared which offered a view of the human being as a free and generous individual with the potential for growth and fulfilment. This third force gave rise to the humanistic approach, some of the main tenets of which appear below:

- Humanistic psychologists believe that psychology should be concerned with the subjective, conscious experience of the individual; this is often referred to as a **phenomenological** viewpoint.
- They emphasise the uniqueness of human beings and their freedom to choose their own destiny.
- They regard the use of scientific methods as inappropriate for the study of human beings.
- A major aim of psychology, they believe, should be to help people maximise their potential for psychological growth.
- The humanistic view is optimistic. Humans are seen as striving to achieve their potential – to achieve the maximum personal growth within individual limitations.

Two leading exponents of the humanistic approach are Carl Rogers and Abraham Maslow.

Carl Rogers

Carl Rogers was a clinical psychologist and, like Freud, developed many of his views through his work with emotionally troubled people. During this work he observed that many psychological problems arise from what he called the **would/should** dilemma. This refers to the conflict between what people believe they ought to do (shoulds) and what they feel is best for them (woulds). For example, an individual may feel that he/she would like to get on with some important work at the office, but should spend more time with the family. The discomfort caused by the would/should dilemma results in anxiety.

Rogers's theory of the human personality started from the premise that people are basically good. Each individual is unique and has ;a basic need for **positive regard**; that is, to have respect and admiration from others. All people, Rogers believed, are born with the **actualising tendency**, a motive which drives us to grow and develop into mature and healthy human beings. Central to the theory is the concept of the self, the person's view, acquired through life experiences, of all the perceptions, values and attitudes that constitute 'I' or 'me'. This **perceived self** influences both the individual's perception of the world and of his/her own behaviour. The other aspect of self, according to Rogers's theory, is the **ideal self**, one's perception of how one should or would like to be. Thus a woman might perceive herself as successful and respected in her career but with certain shortcomings as a wife or mother (which might or might not be true). Her ideal self might demand that she be equally successful in both these spheres of her life. Good psychological health exists where the perceived self and the ideal self are relatively compatible. It is when there is a serious mismatch between the two or between the self and experiences of the real world that psychological problems arise.

Rogers developed a form of **client-centred therapy** in which the clients (not 'patients') have the power and motivation to help themselves, given the right circumstances. The facilitator (not 'therapist') attempts to create a warm, accepting atmosphere in which this can happen. Unlike the situation in other kinds of therapy, the facilitator is not an expert, authority figure and the therapy is non-directive. The aim is to help clients clarify their thoughts on problems to gain greater insight into them. This greater understanding helps the client to recognise his/her own strengths and limitations and is very often accompanied by an increase in self-esteem. Along with this, a clearer understanding of constraints which are real, as opposed to imagined or self-imposed, can eventually help the client to decide how to act. The key factor in Rogerian therapy is that the client becomes more in control of his/her fate and finds satisfactory solutions to problems. The facilitator does not offer a judgement on the appropriateness of the client's solutions.

Rogers and other humanistic psychologists often use a group setting for therapy. Group therapy, they believe, allows individuals to express their problems openly to others and the feedback they receive also provides valuable insights about how they are perceived by others.

Abraham Maslow

Both Rogers and Maslow believed that self-awareness and the ability to come to terms with oneself are necessary ingredients for psychological well-being. Both also see human beings as striving to achieve their potential – to achieve the maximum amount of personal growth possible within their individual limitations. However, where Rogers emphasised the importance of the self-concept, Maslow was greatly concerned with the motives that drive people. Maslow believed that there are two kinds of motivation:

- deficiency motivation, the need to reduce physiological tensions such as hunger and thirst, which may be seen as correcting inadequacies; and
- growth motivation, which has to do with the satisfaction of needs such as the need to be loved and esteemed; growth motives operate on the principle that, when no deficiencies remain, people have the need to develop beyond their present condition.

As Maslow studied motives in a wide variety of situations he noticed that they tended to fall into a specific pattern which could be arranged into a hierarchy (see Figure 2.2). Maslow's **Hierarchy of Needs** has become almost synonymous with his name. He believed the needs in the hierarchy to be inborn and present, at least initially, in all people. Lower needs, such as those for satisfaction of hunger and thirst, must be at least partially satisfied before needs further up the hierarchy become important. Maslow viewed the motive towards **self-actualisation** – the need to find self-fulfilment and realise one's full potential – as the pinnacle of achievement in the satisfaction of needs.

Victor Frankl

Rogers and Maslow are the best known exponents of the humanistic approach. However, another theorist whose basic assumptions fit within this approach is Victor Frankl. Born in Vienna in 1905, Frankl was initially greatly influenced by Freud's ideas about

FIGURE 2.2
A Representation of Maslow's Hierarchy of Needs (after Maslow 1959)

mental illness. Like Freud, he was exposed to the threat of the Nazis during the Second World War. Frankl spent three years trying to survive in a concentration camp, an experience which had a profound effect on his later theory. His best-known work, a book entitled *Man's Search for Meaning* (1992) prompted the development of a theoretical framework which he calls **logotherapy**. Logotherapy espouses a number of basic assumptions which are similar to those of other humanistic theorists:

- Like Rogers, Frankl believed in the freedom of individuals to control their own destiny, though he admitted that there are some circumstances which may limit this freedom. However, he believed that the real issue 'is not freedom from conditions, but it is freedom to take a stand towards these conditions' (Frankl, 1992, p. 132). Even within a concentration camp, individuals, he believed, had choice over their attitudes towards their experiences.

- Frankl believed that the meaning of a given set of experiences could only be truly determined by the person having the experiences. In order to understand an individual's behaviour, it is necessary to understand the meaning attributed by that individual. Thus, Frankl's beliefs can be said to be phenomenological.

Frankl places issues of meaning at the centre of his theory. He believes that a fundamental purpose in life is to find meaning in a world that seems meaningless. By meaning he meant a person's understanding of immediate experiences and the attitude he or she takes towards those experiences. He emphasised the need to focus on the here-and-now of experiences (unlike psychoanalysts who emphasise the individual's past).

In a therapeutic context, Frankl explains that the aim of logotherapy is to help patients to become fully aware of their own responsibleness. The therapist's role does not involve imposing value-judgments on patients, but should help them to discover their own values. This seems very like Rogers' client-centred therapy, though a key difference lies in Rogers' belief that certain kinds of values, for example that all people are basically good, are necessary in healthy human beings.

Frankl suggests three ways in which meaning in life can be discovered:

1. Through achievement.
2. Through a transcendent experience (for example, love or an appreciation of art).
3. By the attitude an individual takes when faced with unavoidable suffering (for example a terminal illness or experiences in a concentration camp).

The idea of finding meaning through suffering is a key theme in Frankl's theory.

Recovery Movement

This is a term which encompasses a number of approaches which share similar themes and assumptions. Its origins lie in the formation in 1935 of Alcoholics Anonymous (AA), a programme for the treatment of alcoholism. AA's philosophy of emphasising the possibility of a person's recovery with help from social and spiritual sources, has been adapted by many other groups, including Gamblers Anonymous and Overeaters Anonymous.

Some of the basic ideas which are central to the Recovery Movement include the following:

- There is a belief that no matter how traumatised an individual is, there is a hidden core within which will allow that person to grow and develop. This hidden core is sometimes referred to as **the inner child**. Through the inner child, an individual can re-experience the feelings and desires of childhood.
- The most serious sproblems that people experience arise from traumas that lead to feelings of **shame**. For example, a child growing up with an alcoholic parent will suffer a number of traumas. The most damaging of these is a sense of self-blame for the parent's problems, which often destroys the individual's sense of self-worth.
- Feelings of shame are closely connected to **guilt**, which may develop from the age of about four on, as a child develops moral concepts (Bradshaw, 1988).

The approach taken by AA to help sufferers of alcoholism combines self-help with social support. They are encouraged to view alcoholism as both a disease and a social problem. The solutions, it is believed, lie in the **twelve steps to recovery**. This begins with the individual acknowledging that at that point they are powerless over their problem (Step 1), seeking help from a Higher Power (Step 2) and ends with the individual resolving to practise the twelve steps and to share the message with others (step 12).

The Recovery Movement has become very popular over the past few years. Glassman (1995) argues that one must allow for the possibility that some practitioners within the movement have questionable credentials. However, he stresses that this should not detract from the usefulness of its theories. Like most other theories, for example those of Freud and Skinner, there is a belief that individual development is strongly influenced by the family. In suggesting that cultural pressures may work against feelings of self-worth and that most individuals are unable to resist those pressures, the Recovery Movement addresses the relationship of the individual to society in a way that most psychological theories do not.

Evaluation of the Humanistic Approach

The humanistic approach has served the valuable purpose of forcing psychologists to take account of the subjective experience of the individual and the importance of self-esteem and meaning in psychological functioning. Its insistence that the scientific method as presently conceived in psychology is an unsatisfactory vehicle for studying subjective experience has encouraged psychologists to look for more appropriate methods. In summary, humanistic psychology represents an important counterbalance to the more deterministic approaches which have dominated psychology for most of the twentieth century.

In a practical sense, humanistic psychologists have done much to advance methods of assessing self-concept and of developing therapeutic techniques which encourage self-respect and autonomy in individuals. The main criticisms of humanistic psychology centre on the following:

- That (as with psychoanalysis) its terminology is not clearly defined and therefore not easily testable. Data used to support the theories has tended to come from case studies and interviews, which, unlike experiments, do not use falsifiable predictions. However, Rogers himself has called upon psychologists to investigate some of his ideas. Also, he and his colleagues have contributed to psychotherapy research by tape-recording therapy sessions and making them available for analysis by researchers. Some empirical studies have been carried out using the Personal Orientation Inventory (Shostrum *et al.*, 1976) which claims to be a measure of self-actualisation.
- Differences in concepts and emphasis between humanistic theories are not easy to assess. For example, both Rogers and Maslow believed that there is a common set of values for healthy individuals, while Frankl rejects this view. Who is correct? The concept of shame plays a prominent part in the theoretical

framework of the Recovery Movement. How important is this concept?

- The client-centred therapy advocated by Rogers has some limitations. For example, it seems to be most successful with people who are more articulate and who are motivated to seek help. Clients who are withdrawn or seriously disturbed may need more direct help in changing their behaviour.
- Some have criticised the values espoused by humanistic psychologists. The view has been expressed that the theories of Rogers and Maslow place too much emphasis on the well-being of the individual at the expense of concern for the welfare of others (Wallach and Wallach, 1983). The same could be said of Frankl's logotherapy.

Self-assessment Questions

1. Outline the most important ways in which the humanistic approach differs from other approaches.
2. Briefly describe the main aspects of Rogers' theory of human personality.
3. Give a brief account of Maslow's 'hierarchy of needs'.
4. Explain what Frankl meant by 'logotherapy'
5. Outline some of the principles which are central to the Recovery Movement.
6. Evaluate the humanistic approach.

SECTION VI   WHICH APPROACH?

The details of the five approaches outlined above will become clearer as you encounter them in greater depth in your wider study of psychology. The conflict of ideas and beliefs between these different approaches may seem confusing and you would be forgiven for asking 'Which is the right approach?' However, it is important to realise that no one approach contains the whole truth about psychological functioning. Each focuses on different aspects of human behaviour or experience and, as such, may be seen as complementary rather than competing. Indeed, many psychologists working in practical situations feel free to select from different approaches those ideas which seem most helpful to the particular situation in which they are operating.

Psychology is a young discipline relative to other sciences. As such, it has no global **paradigm**, or single accepted theory, about the nature of human beings in the way that biology, for example, is influenced by Darwin's theory. Until this is possible in psychology, the scope and variety of the many different approaches allows us to adopt different **levels of explanation** in order to explain human functioning.

Levels of Explanation

It is possible to describe and explain an aspect of human functioning in many different ways. The following example should help to illustrate this fact: the simple act of shaking hands when you meet an old friend could be described and explained from many different perspectives:

- It could be reduced to an account of the neural and muscular activities which occur (physiological approach).
- It might be seen as an activity which is the result of previous conditioning processes; that is, it has been associated with rewards or reinforcement and is triggered by an appropriate stimulus, in this case meeting an old friend (behaviourist approach).
- It could be argued that thought processes are important. Your purpose in shaking hands is to demonstrate to your friend that you remember him well and still hold him in high esteem (cognitive approach).
- Psychodynamic explanations could be introduced. Physical contact with someone you previously found attractive may affect your emotional state (psychoanalytic approach).
- The need for acceptance and approval by others may be seen as an important variable (humanistic approach).

Many other perspectives or levels of explanation might also be employed. For example, social and cultural factors most certainly play a part in the act of shaking hands. Whilst some psychologists concentrate their efforts on one particular approach, many others are happy to draw upon a number of different levels in their attempts to describe and explain human behaviour and experience.

Self-assessment Questions

1. What is the value of having many different approaches to the study of psychology?
2. Think of your own example which may illustrate the use of different levels of explanation

FURTHER READING

W. E. Glassman, *Approaches to Psychology*, 2nd edn (Buckingham: OU Press, 1995).

J. Medcof and J. Roth (eds), *Approaches to Psychology*, 2nd edn (Milton Keynes: Open University Press, 1988).

REDUCED TO MANAGEABLE PROPORTION
HE'S MUCH EASIER TO STUDY !

skill were rated significantly higher on feeling free than on being free.
- Feeling free seemed to be related to situations where individuals perceived themselves as free and *liked* the situation.
- The most frequent examples of situations where individuals did not feel free were those involving outside constraints, unpleasant feelings and conflict and indecision.

Arguments for Free Will

- Valentine suggests that the main argument for the existence of free will lies in the idea of **moral responsibility**. If we accept that people are responsible, at least some of the time, for their own moral actions, we cannot deny the existence of free will. Koestler (1967) said that whatever one's philosophical stance on the issue of free will and determinism, in everyday life it is impossible not to accept the notion of personal responsibility – and responsibility implies freedom of choice.
- An important factor which cannot be dismissed when considering free will is based in **subjective impressions** – people *feel* they have freedom of choice over their lives. However, Valentine (1992) argues that subjective impressions are notoriously unreliable and do not guarantee truth however firmly they may be held.

Arguments against Free Will

- A major problem faced when trying to justify the existence of free will lies in the difficulty of formulating an adequate definition of what we mean by it. As we have seen above, there are a number of different definitions and this makes it difficult to give a coherent account of the concept.
- A second drawback is that if we take an extreme stance on the notion of free will, it is difficult to justify the scientific approach to the study of behaviour. The scientific approach makes the assumption that events in the world are not random but ordered and thus determined (see Chapter 4, Section I). Also, the more that is learned about factors that determine behaviour, the less likely it is that humans have total freedom over their actions.

Determinism

This follows loosely from the work of the seventeenth-century philosophers Locke, Berkeley and Hume, who believed that human behaviour is the result of forces over which one has no control. This applies to factors both within and outside the person.

Internal causes (**biological determinism**) include a biological need state (for example, hunger or thirst), instinctive energy or genetic endowment. Classical psychoanalysis is an example of biological determinism. Sociobiology, which explains all individual and social behaviour in terms of the selection of genes in evolution, represents an extreme form of biological determinism. External causes (**environmental determinism**) may include learning experiences or stimuli in the environment. An example might be radical behaviourism. All behaviour thus has a cause and cannot have happened any other way.

Points arising from this approach include the following:

- The approach is compatible with scientific method, and is one of the central assumptions of this method. Determinists assume that human behaviour is orderly and obeys laws, and so is explainable and predictable. A person's current behaviour is the result of what went before and the cause of what is to come. When you know a person's history and current situation you can predict what that individual will do next.
- If you can predict behaviour you can also control it. Knowing a person's history and current state, it is only necessary to arrange circumstances to obtain the desired reaction. (Skinner described a Utopian society created along these lines in *Walden Two*, 1948.)
- If behaviour is determined by events outside one's control then the idea of responsibility vanishes. Neither criminal nor benevolent acts are the result of free choice, so that notions of praise and blame are worthless. To punish or reward people for certain behaviour may therefore be a pointless exercise. This has important implications for the penal system. An environmental determinist might see criminals as victims of circumstances beyond their control: it is not the criminal that needs changing but the environment. Imprisonment and various other forms of punishment might be seen to be appropriate as providing new learning experiences aimed at producing more socially desirable

behaviour. If one believes in free will, punishment becomes retribution, because the criminal act is the result of free choice.

Arguments for Determinism

- The scientific approach is based upon determinism. (See Chapter 4, Section I.)
- Science is a successful route to knowledge.
- Therefore determinism seems to make sense – it has face validity.

Arguments against Determinism

- The assumption that one can ever arrive at a complete description of the current state of a person is probably not justified. To do this takes time, during which the individual has moved on.
- It is a false assumption that accurate predictions are possible. Even physicists have to build 'uncertainty factors' into their laws. If physicists have this problem, where does that leave psychologists with their notoriously unpredictable subject matter of human behaviour? They may argue in their defence that it is not the inherent nature of the subject matter but their own lack of skill in making precise measurements which makes it difficult for them to make accurate predictions.
- Determinism is unfalsifiable. If determinists cannot find a cause for human behaviour they assume, not that a cause does not exist, but that they have not been able to discover one yet. For example, an advocate of free will (FW) might challenge a determinist (D) to predict what FW will do next. FW can prove D wrong by choosing not to do as D predicts. But this does not invalidate D's position because D's prediction has added another variable. FW has behaved in a different way from the way he would have done had he been ignorant of FW's prediction.

Soft Determinism

This view holds that behaviour is determined by the environment, but only to a certain extent. While a person can choose between a number of courses of actions, there is only free will if there is no coercion or compulsion. Where there is consistency between a person's wishes and actions, there is an element of free will. A hard-line determinist would argue that there is no element of choice: all behaviour is caused by events outside one's personal control.

A soft determinist approach sees the problem as one of freedom v. coercion; a hard determinist approach sees the problem as one of freedom v. causation.

Summary

The free will side of the argument needs to see a person as actively responding to forces rather than being passive in the face of them. The cause of behaviour is likely to be located within the individual. Concepts such as cognition, reason and judgement would be used when a person decides how to deal with an environmental or physiological demand.

Soft determinism seems to have more face validity than either hard-line determinism or pure free will. In a society which advocates personal responsibility, hard-line determinism is unacceptable and free will is difficult to define satisfactorily. If there is inconsistency between a person's desires and actions, a sense of freedom can still be achieved by changing one's desires or one's actions so that they are in line with each other.

The argument in psychology is likely to be between soft and hard determinism rather than between free will and determinism. Unless some aspects of behaviour are determined, the scientific approach cannot be justified:

> The scientist can ignore the free will/determinism question if he wishes, with the proviso that there is one extreme position – that of complete indeterminacy – which he cannot hold since it is inconsistent with his activities. No regularities, no science. The scientific view of man must therefore hold that man's behaviour is, at least to some extent, lawful and predictable.
>
> (Wertheimer, 1972, p. 31)

Free Will and Determinism in Theory and Practice

Psychoanalysis

In classical psychoanalysis the cause of behaviour is located within the individual. Behaviour is driven by powerful instinctual forces of which the individual is largely unaware. These forces are largely sexual and aggressive. The behaviour which results may be either constructive and self-preserving or destructive or even self-destructive. Behaviour originates from within, but the individual has little free choice about how to behave. Determinism holds that no behaviour is without a cause; psychoanalytic explanations therefore score highly. One of the attractions of Freudian theory is that it can deal with aspects of behaviour and experience which other approaches find hard to explain – dreams, slips of the tongue, sense of humour and the wide appeal of great works of art are examples. Accidents also may sometimes be explained by arguing that they are unconsciously motivated. If you fall off your bicycle on your way to take your psychology exam and sprain your wrists there may be said to be an unconscious connection! Freudian theory can explain the development of personality, sex role, morality and various mental disorders. The determinist approach also has implications for psychoanalytic therapy. Every detail which the analysand is urged to divulge (thoughts, dreams, wishes: seemingly disconnected, meaningless trivial or inoffensive details) is seen as a possible window on the unconscious mind, which determines behaviour. The impression of freedom in the psychoanalytic situation is an illusion.

More recently ego psychologists, such as Karen Horney, Anna Freud and Erik Erikson, have challenged this extreme determinist view. They see the goal of analysis as 'ego strengthening'. This puts individuals more in command of their fate by making them more able to deal with the demands of reality. Horney even suggested self-analysis.

Behaviourism

Radical behaviourism is an example of environmental determinism. It is theoretically possible to predict and control behaviour by means of a full knowledge of a person's genetic limitations, past experiences and current situation. All behaviour is rational (it obeys laws) and people are therefore fundamentally alike.

Skinner (1971) rejects free will as an illusion. Only by recognising that behaviour is environmentally determined is it possible to harness the environment to create and maintain socially acceptable behaviour. In our society poorly defined, inconsistent and uncontrolled reinforcement contingencies give an illusion of freedom. We need to recognise that behaviour is already controlled; the control needs to become more systematic if Western societies are not to head for self-destruction. Freedom does not mean self-determination but freedom from aversive control. Skinner believed this can be achieved through the careful use of positive reinforcement, with minimal use of negative reinforcement and punishment.

Some critics of the behaviourist view argue that determinism and free will can be seen in the processes of learning known as *classical* and *operant conditioning*. In the former the organism is passive. The conditional stimulus produces an automatic conditional response in a machine-like manner. Clearly such behaviour is determined. In operant conditioning the organism could be seen as having free choice over which response to make. (Pavlov's dogs had no choice but to salivate to the sound of a bell but a rat in a Skinner box can choose whether or not to press a lever.) Skinner rejects this distinction, arguing that operant behaviour is determined by a history of reinforcement which affects the probability with which responses will occur. Some responses to a stimulus will have been reinforced more often than others and so are more likely to recur.

Behaviourism can also explain seemingly altruistic behaviour in animals. If conditioning determined behaviour, organisms would act only in their own interests and not be altruistic. Wertheimer (1972) gives the example of pigeons playing ping-pong. A hungry pigeon can be trained by behaviour-shaping techniques to peck a ping-pong ball off the opposite side of a miniature ping-pong table for the reinforcement of a few seconds' access to some seed. The bird, once trained, can be placed opposite an equally well-trained partner. The pigeons peck the ball to and fro until one fails to return it. Then a few seconds elapse in which the winner can feed. Then the game begins afresh. The birds become more skilled, the rallies lengthen and the opportunities for feeding diminish. At this point the birds are likely to allow the ball to fall off the table, thus allowing the other to feed. This seems to be co-operative, insightful, unselfish and therefore free behaviour. Skinner, however, argues that this is not the case. Relatively more frequent reinforcement results from allowing one's partner to win. Sharing pays better than selfishness.

Therapies influenced by the environmental determinism of radical behaviourism include:

- Systematic desensitisation for the treatment of phobias.
- Modification of problem behaviour in children.
- Treatment of self-injurious behaviour through aversion therapy.

- Development of self-care in the mentally ill by the use of token economies.
- Cognitive behaviour therapy, such as Ellis's rational emotive therapy.

The stereotyped picture of the behaviour therapist is of one who controls a passive client, but many modern behaviour therapies encourage the active participation of the client, aiming to teach self-control and coping. One example is systematic desensitisation for phobic behaviour. Clients develop their own hierarchy of feared situations and learn to face these with the support (not the control) of the therapist. They might also arrange their own reinforcements for positive behaviour.

Biofeedback is another example of therapy where the client is in control. A physiological measure such as pulse rate or galvanic skin response (GSR) is taken, amplified and continuously fed back to the person visually or audibly. Clients learn to control their own physiological responses. Reinforcement is the knowledge of progress made. This is useful in the treatment of headaches and nervous tension, for example. (See Section I of this chapter for an account of the behaviourist approach.)

Humanistic Psychology

This is often said to be the nearest one can get to free will in psychology. Humanistic psychologists have a problem with scientific method because it is based on the assumption of determinism and reductionism. Humanistic psychologists advocate study of the whole person and are especially critical of experimental method in psychology and of the behaviourist tradition of studying animal behaviour and then extrapolating this to humans. They view humans as unique and reject a method which removes freedom and dignity from experimental participants: if we can view animals in experiments as objects, how long will it be before we start to see humans in the same way?

Rogers's client-centred therapy reflects the view that we are in charge of our own lives and responsible for our own personal growth. Both client and facilitator are free agents. If the client chooses to allow his life to be determined by forces outside himself he is still, paradoxically, acting freely. (See Section I of this chapter for an account of the ideas of humanistic psychologists.)

Summary

Free will and determinism are not mutually exclusive. While humanistic psychologists lean towards free will, but still accept that there are constraints on behaviour, determinists accept the existence of 'uncertainty' factors. It is possible to take an entirely environmental approach and see behaviour as externally controlled or else to argue that control comes from within the individual, exercised by internal biological forces (hence nature–nurture debates). If we see free will and determinism as extremes on a continuum, then the question to be asked is not whether behaviour is free or determined, but where on the continuum it lies.

Self-assessment Questions

1. Distinguish between free will, determinism and soft determinism.
2. Explain where psychoanalysis, behaviourism and humanistic psychology stand on the free will–determinism issue, and show how this is reflected in their therapeutic approaches.

SECTION III THE HEREDITY–ENVIRONMENT ISSUE

The heredity–environment issue (often referred to as the nature–nurture debate) in psychology concerns the role of genes and environment in determining behaviour. Historically, the heredity or nature side of the controversy is associated with the nativists, who argued that behaviour is (for the most part) determined by innate or inherited factors. Environmentalists, or empiricists, were associated with the environment or nurture side. They argued that behaviour is mainly determined by experience.

The empiricist position was that the baby's mind at birth is like a blank state (*tabula rasa*) on which experience will write. Behaviour which is acquired as the baby grows is the result of experiences, especially learning. Therefore changes in the environment produce changes in the individual. Within their physical limitations, anyone can become anything, providing the environment is right.

The nativist position was that individuals are born with an inherited 'blue-print'. Behaviours which are not already present at birth will develop as though they were on a genetic time-switch; that is, through the process of maturation. The environment has little to do with individual development and there is little anyone can do to change what nature has provided.

It follows from these two views that learned behaviours are within our control; innate ones are not, unless they are modified through genetic engineering. The question of what psychologists might be able to control and what is beyond their control occurs in many areas of research. Examples include the origin of language, personality, mental illness, aggression, gender differences and intelligence. However, it is the purpose of this section to deal with the general problem of heredity and environment rather than with specific issues. The reader may be familiar with research in some of these areas and should consider its validity in the light of what is to come.

Changes in the Emphasis of the Heredity–Environment Question

The heredity–environment debate is older than psychology itself and is still as vigorous as ever. Its emphasis has altered over the years. These changes were discussed in a classic paper by Anne Anastasi (1958) and can be summarised as follows.

Which One?

At its most extreme, the nature–nurture debate asked which of the two, heredity or environment, was responsible for behaviour. Anastasi argued that to ask the question in an 'either/or' form was illogical. One could not exist without the other. Both heredity and environment are absolutely necessary for the person to exist; therefore both must exert an influence on the person.

How Much?

If it is accepted that both nature and nurture play a part in determining behaviour, how much is contributed by each? Thus the either/or question is replaced by an assumption that the two forces operate in an additive, but still separate, way: $X + Y =$ behaviour. In Anastasi's opinion, such an attitude is as illogical as its predecessor. Even if we consider that, say, 80 per cent of intelligence is due to nature and 20 per cent to nurture, that 80 per cent still has to exert its influence in an environment and the 20 per cent can only be expressed through the organism. To ask 'How much?' is simply to ask 'Which one?' in a slightly more complicated way. It is still illogical.

In What Way?

If neither of the previous two questions is useful, the obvious answer is to consider that genetics and environment interact. The argument is as follows:

- Genetics and environment exert an influence on each other such that $X \times Y$ = behaviour. A useful analogy is the area of a rectangle. The rectangle cannot exist unless both length and width are present, yet its area is altered by changes in either of them. Similarly behaviour is determined by both heredity and environment.
- Different environments acting on the same genetic pattern would result in different behaviours. Similarly the same environment would produce different behaviours from individuals who were genetically different.
- Genes never determine behaviour directly; they only do so via the environment. Likewise the environment does not directly affect behaviour but only via the genetic make-up of the individual.
- It is thus much more logical to accept that nature and nurture interact. This raises the inevitable question, 'In what way do they interact?' How do changes in one affect the influence of the other? This is the question which now occupies psychologists.

What is Meant by Heredity and Environment?

Defining heredity and environment is not as simple as it appears. Lerner (1986) offers a solution by suggesting that we should think of environment as having different levels. (These ideas he borrowed from Riegel, 1975/6.) Anastasi elaborated her ideas further by suggesting that the influence of heredity and environment can vary from very powerful to relatively weak. The ideas of Lerner and Anastasi are summarised as follows.

Levels of the Environment (Lerner, 1986)

The inner–biological level This refers to the environment experienced by the individual *in utero*. The influence exerted by the individual's genes can be modified by the physiological state of the mother, for example if she smokes, consumes alcohol or other drugs, has an unbalanced diet or contracts a disease, such as rubella.

The individual-psychological level   Another influence on the unborn child is the mother's psychological state. She may experience stress, which can affect the foetus differently according to when, during pregnancy, the stress is experienced.

The physical–environmental level   After birth the child may be subjected to unfavourable environmental influences, such as pollutants, additives in food, excessively noisy surroundings or overcrowding. Alternatively physical–environmental influences could be favourable.

The sociocultural–historical level   People experience unique environments which vary according to where and when they were born. The environment will be affected by the current state of scientific knowledge about what is good or bad for you. For example, educational and health-care practices change with our knowledge of the effects of diet, pollution and lifestyle.

Because of socio-historical influences, cross-sectional and longitudinal investigations into heredity–environment issues are fraught with problems. Researchers are unlikely to find consistency in their results when studies are carried out on different samples, in different places and at different times.

The Continuum of Heredity (Anastasi, 1958)

If it is accepted that heredity's influence on behaviour is always indirect (via the environment), how does this influence operate? Anastasi considers that the influence of heredity operates along a 'continuum of indirectness', meaning that, at one extreme of the continuum, influences are 'least indirect' while at the other they are 'most indirect'. She gives examples of indirect influence from four points along the continuum.

Hereditary influences which resist environmental change   These are at the least indirect' end of the continuum. However, they are not entirely independent of environmental influences because heredity needs an environment in which to express itself. Down's syndrome is a good example of this level of influence. Given our current state of knowledge, it remains a problem which cannot be 'cured'. However, future scientific advances in chromosome technology might enable scientists to deal with such genetic abnormalities antenatally.

Hereditary defects that can be changed by the environment   These move a little further towards the 'most indirect' end of the continuum. Babies born with hereditary defects such as deafness and/or blindness fall into this category. Such defects can retard social and cognitive development considerably unless special training is given. Dramatic examples of this are provided in the stage-play and film, *Children of a Lesser God*.

Inherited susceptibility   It is conceivable that individuals inherit predispositions to develop certain diseases, disorders or capabilities which will only appear if the environmental conditions are favourable. Examples might be heart disease or some mental disorders, such as schizophrenia. At this point on the indirectness continuum, two people with the same genotype could be influenced quite differently by different environments.

Social influence   Towards the 'most indirect' end of the continuum lie social influences on heredity. An example of this lies in social stereotypes. People may be stereotyped on the basis of inherited physical characteristics, such as hair colour, body-build or sex. This could lead to certain expectations about the abilities and behaviours which go with the stereotype. For example, if someone who is genetically female encounters a stereotype which holds that females are not very academic, it is likely that she will encounter a different educational and social environment from one in which no such stereotype exists. She may even grow into the expectations which society has of her through a mechanism known as the self-fulfilling prophecy. In this way hereditary influences can be altered by social forces.

The Continuum of the Environment (Anastasi, 1958)

Environment also can exert different degrees of influence on behaviour (at whichever of Lerner's levels we choose). Anastasi sees environment as influential according to a continuum of breadth.

This means that environmental influences, operating via the person, can have very narrow and specific effects or very broad and general effects on behaviour. Anastasi offers two types of environmental effect.

Organic effects The environment can bring about physiological (organic) changes in a person through either damage, disease or enrichment. Long-term use of alcohol, for example, can bring about a variety of physiological changes which have a very broad effect on behaviour. A disease such as polio can have very general effects. Other diseases, such as chicken pox, have relatively narrow and short-term effects. Enrichment of diet in children may have very broad effects on their intellectual functioning, though this may only affect specific aspects of intelligence-test performance.

Stimulative effects Stimulative effects exert a direct influence on behaviour which, again, can be broad or narrow. Broad stimulative effects include such things as social class, through which a person may be exposed to experiences different from those in other social classes, in terms of lifestyle, expectations, opportunities and material wealth. Narrow stimulative effects involve relatively short-term experiences, such as receiving a particular type of schooling or being fostered by a particular family. (The reader might like to consider educational enrichment programmes such as 'Project Headstart' in the light of these ideas.)

Do we Construct our own Environment?

An alternative view of the nature of the environment, which goes against what is proposed in mainstream developmental psychology, is to consider that people may construct or contribute to their own environments (Scarr, 1992). Scarr proposes that children construct reality from the opportunities which exist in their environment and this constructed reality has a considerable influence on variations among children and individual differences between adults.

Eliciting Responses

One way of considering how individuals may influence their own environments is to think about how certain behavioural or psychological characteristics may elicit particular responses from other people. An individual's behaviour or biological characteristics may call forth particular responses from other people, which can be illustrated in a number of ways:

- **Temperament** Babies vary in a number of temperamental characteristics; for example how active they are, how responsive to others, how easily upset. Some theorists have proposed that it is these characteristics in infants which influence the nature of their relationships with parents and other people. For instance, Belsky and Rovine (1987) have suggested that children with different temperamental characteristics present differing challenges to their caregivers, and these in part determine those caregivers' responses to them. Happy, easy-going babies are more likely to elicit positive responses than are more 'difficult', discontented children.
- **Gender** It is well-documented that people tend to react differently to boys and girls on the basis of their, often stereotyped, expectations of masculine and feminine characteristics. To quote just one example, in a study by Rubin, Provenzano and Luria (1974) parents were asked to describe their new-born babies. Even though boys and girls were very similar in health and in size and weight, boys were generally depicted as more alert, stronger and better co-ordinated than girls. Girls were described as smaller, softer and less attentive than boys.
- **Aggression** Rutter and Rutter (1993) describe how aggressive children think and behave in ways that lead other children to respond to them in a hostile manner. This in turn reinforces the anti-social child's view of the world as negative and hostile, and a self-perpetuating spiral of anti-social behaviour follows. Thus, aggressive children tend to experience aggressive environments partly because they elicit aggressive responses in others

(See Gross (1995) for a discussion of other ways in which individuals may influence their own environments.)

The Heredity–Environment Issue in Perspective

The writings of Lerner and Anastasi cited above show just how complex the heredity–environment issue has become. To add to this complexity, Lerner points out that, potentially, there are an infinite number of different environments. In addition, it is estimated that there are over 70 trillion potential **genotypes** (genetic types). (Even identical twins who share the same genotype have different environments from the start, since they occupy different points on the placenta.) Further to this, recent genetic research seems to suggest that genetic endowment does not place fixed limits on an individual and that even some genetic characteristics are flexible. Given that this infinite number of environments will interact with the enormous number of potential (and possibly flexible) genotypes to produce behaviour, it might be tempting to give up research into such a vast problem at this point! However, it is still possible to go on to consider the second question in the nature–nurture debate: 'How do heredity and environment interact?'

How Do Heredity and Environment Interact?

In trying to answer this question, Anastasi and others have used the concept of **norm of reaction**. Rather than seeing the genotype as a kind of blue-print for development, Anastasi prefers to think of it as something which sets upper and lower limits. There are a number of potential outcomes for individuals within the range of their genetic limitations and this is the 'norm of reaction'. Which one eventually develops will depend on the interaction of their genes with a particular environment.

A famous example provided by Hebb (1949) on intelligence illustrates the norm of reaction idea. The genetic upper and lower limit to intelligence makes up Intelligence A. Intelligence A interacts with the environment so that some or all of it is realised. This is known as Intelligence B. However, the usefulness of 'norm of reaction' is limited. For example, there is no way of measuring Intelligence A or B. Intelligence tests are not the answer as they can only assess a portion of Intelligence B. (This portion is known as Intelligence C – see Figure 3.1 from Vernon, 1969.) Also they may attempt to draw on parts of intelligence A which have not yet developed. However in many aspects of behaviour, including intelligence, there is often no way of assessing what potential could be expected even when the genotype (which could be flexible) is known. It has to be accepted, therefore, that in most cases the norm of reaction, as an explanation of heredity–environment interaction, is limited.

FIGURE 3.1
The Hebb/Vernon Model of Intelligence

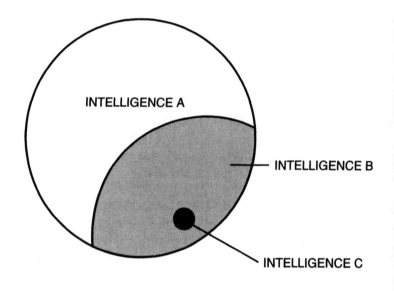

Conclusions

In conclusion a number of points may be made:

1. Given the potential variability in genotypes, coupled with the infinite variations in environment, the inevitable conclusion is that no two individuals (even identical twins) are alike.
2. It follows from (1) that it is nonsense to look for general laws of behaviour which are couched in environmental terms (as in radical behaviourism, for example). Instead it would make more sense to look for individual laws which can explain a person's unique developmental pattern. Nativists must at least accept the influence of the 'norm of reaction' and even, perhaps, the idea of flexible genotypes. An added dimension comes from the con-

structionist view that individuals do not simply respond passively to their environments. They actively play a part in creating and shaping their own experiences.

3. An item of animal research will serve to illustrate the complexity of the current state of affairs. Various strains of pregnant mice were subjected to a variety of environmental stressors, such as swim tanks, noise and so on. Their offspring were then compared with the offspring of controls. The experiences of the mother while pregnant had different effects on the behaviour of the offspring but these effects varied according to both the genotype of the mother and that of the offspring. Here the mother's genotype interacted with her environment and that influenced the prenatal environment of the offspring, which interacted with its genotype to produce the final behaviour (De Fries, 1964).

4. If the insights from De Fries's study were thought of in human terms, individuals' behaviour is also likely to be influenced prenatally. They will also experience different social, cultural, domestic and scholastic environments. How does this affect something like educational policy? According to the norm of reaction argument, each person needs individual attention in a uniquely tailored environment. However, in practice, it is more usual to adopt the view that everyone deserves the best, no one should have more advantage than another and what is best for one is best for all. Passionate arguments develop about selection and streaming in education and about which school a child should attend. It should be borne in mind that a so-called 'better' environment is not ideal for everyone. This is, of course, just one narrow application of the nature–nurture question. The reader will doubtless think of many others.

5. Recent developments in genetics now suggest that the idea of a 'norm of reaction' must be modified and that genetic endowment is more flexible than was previously thought. Rigid upper and lower limits to development may not exist.

Self-assessment Questions

1. Identify three stages in the development of the heredity–environment debate
2. How do heredity and environment interact?

FURTHER READING

W. E. Glassman (1995) *Approaches to Psychology* (Buckingham: OU Press).

R. Gross, *Themes, Issues and Debates in Psychology* (London: Hodder & Stoughton, 1995).

E. R. Valentine, *Conceptual Issues in Psychology*, 2nd edn (London: Routledge, 1992).

I'M SORRY, MISS PRETTY, BUT YOU'RE NOT THE WHITE MAN FOR THE JOB.

Controversies in Psychological Research

4

At the end of this chapter you should be able to:

1. explain what is meant by the terms 'science' and 'scientific method';
2. discuss the use of scientific method in psychology;
3. consider alternatives to the scientific approach to psychology;
4. explain what is meant by cultural bias in psychological theory and research studies;
5. identify ways in which racial and gender bias may affect psychological theory and research studies; and
6. suggest ways in which cultural bias may be overcome.

The sections in this chapter covers two major controversies in psychological research. The first concerns whether it is appropriate to think of psychology as science. The second is to do with forms of cultural bias in psychological research and how they may be overcome.

SECTION I PSYCHOLOGY AND SCIENCE

Introduction

To many people the term 'science' is something which can only be applied to the life or physical sciences such as biology, chemistry or physics. They are unlikely to place psychology with such subjects. If asked to justify reasons for excluding it, they may argue that psychological subject matter is not scientific, that psychologists do not collect information in a scientific way and that they do not have scientific theories. As a result, it can come as a surprise to learn that psychology shares many characteristics with the natural sciences. In fact, psychologists often do adopt a scientific approach and feel that they are well-justified in defining psychology as the scientific study of behaviour.

The purpose of the first part of this section is to explain what science is. We will then explore some of the problems psychologists encounter when they adopt a scientific approach. We can then go on to consider whether science and scientific method are appropriate in psychology. The section closes with a brief account of some of the new developments in this area.

Routes to Knowledge

The scientific approach is just one way of acquiring knowledge about the world. Peirce (1951) describes three others:

1. *The method of tenacity.* Tenacious believers convince themselves of 'truths' by frequent repetition of them. They are adept at dealing with information which contradicts their beliefs, perhaps reinterpreting it to suit themselves. Festinger *et al.* (1956) encountered this when they infiltrated a quasi-religious group who believed themselves to be in touch with extra-terrestrials from the planet Clarion. The group had been warned of the day on which the world was to end and they were expecting to be rescued by means of flying saucers. When disaster did not strike, some members of the group were disillusioned and left. Others convinced themselves that their faith had saved the world so that the incident simply served to strengthen their commitment. Such a route to knowledge is obviously error prone!

2. *The method of authority.* In this case, something is true if it comes from a credible authority. The authority may be the Bible, the Prime Minister, parents, television or 'an expert'. Belief in authority as a source of knowledge is based on trust. The authority is not necessarily wrong but it could be unreliable since its own source of information could be at fault or it could be swayed by its own interests and values.

3. *The method of intuition* (the *a priori* method). This is the 'stands-to-reason' or 'common-sense' method. If enough people agree that something is true then it must be so. (For example in the Dark Ages it stood to reason that the Earth was flat since everyone agreed that if it were not they would have fallen off!) Critics of psychology sometimes say that much of psychological

knowledge is common sense. At times, common sense does prove to be accurate but psychologists have shown that it is not always to be trusted. For example, we would expect group decisions to be relatively sensible ones but research has shown that group decisions are often more risky than those made by individuals – a phenomenon known as the 'risky shift' (Stoner, 1961). Common sense can be extremely misleading.

So how does science differ from these routes to knowledge? To answer this question it is necessary to look in detail at the characteristics of the scientific approach.

What is Science?

The word 'science' is derived from the Latin 'scire' meaning 'to know'. Science is just another way of gathering knowledge and it has its own way of answering questions and solving conflicts between different explanations. It coexists with the other three routes to knowledge and, at the moment, is favoured by many psychologists. However, if psychology is to be regarded as a science, it must share with other sciences certain:

- aims;
- assumptions;
- ways of carrying out research; and
- ways of building and modifying theories.

The Aims of Science

The four main aims of science are:

1. *Description.* The most basic scientific aim is to achieve an objective description of events. This differs from everyday descriptions in the precision of the methods used. Scientific description should be as free as possible from biases arising from personal values and interests, but this is an ideal as human observers can never achieve complete objectivity.
2. *Prediction.* This arises from good, objective description which reveals patterns and thus makes prediction possible. If scientists can make accurate predictions, the status and credibility of their knowledge is enhanced. For example, psychologists may

regularly observe that children who enjoy watching a lot of violent programmes on television also tend to be highly aggressive in their own behaviour. The prediction could then be made that the more exposure a child has to violent TV programmes, the more aggressive that child will be. Research may then verify or refute this prediction.

3. *Understanding.* If prediction turns out to be reliable, the scientist can go on to study the relationship between cause and effect. It may be that exposure to TV violence and aggressive behaviour go together, but why is this so? It could be either that children are imitating what they see, or alternatively it may be that naturally-aggressive children choose to watch more violence on TV. These two explanations could be tested out to see which receives more support thus leading us to a much sounder understanding of the processes involved.

4. *Control.* Accurate prediction and thorough understanding put the scientist in the position of being able to arrange for an event to happen and thus control it. For example, if we can show that aggressive behaviour is the result of imitation then it should be possible (but not necessarily ethical) to control it by changing children's TV diet.

The Assumptions of Science

Scientists make four key assumptions about the natural world:

1. *Order.* Scientists share the belief that events in the world are not random and haphazard. The implication of this is that it is possible to discover regularities and patterns (order) which will eventually lead to the formulation of laws. Thus some psychologists assume that it is possible to discover laws of behaviour.

2. *Determinism.* If there is order in events then it makes sense to assume that they are causally related. Psychologists who accept this view usually talk about behaviour being determined either environmentally or biologically or through an interaction of both. The ultimate implication of this is that no psychological event is irrational. It will always have an underlying cause which will eventually be detected.

3. *Empiricism.* 'Empiricism' is derived from a Greek word meaning 'experience'. Scientists prefer empirical data; that is to say, information gathered through direct sensory experience rather

than by introspection, faith or hearsay. Empirical data are publicly observable so they can be used to settle disputes about the superiority of one belief over another. Thus, inconsistent observations should eventually be discarded and consistent ones retained.

4. *Parsimony.* This refers to economy of explanation. A good parsimonious explanation does not go beyond the available empirical evidence. It applies to a wide variety of participants and contains very few contradictions. Behaviourism is often held up as a good example of a parsimonious theory whereas psychoanalytic theory is not.

Characteristics of Scientific Method

Scientific method is not just concerned with how data are collected. Of equal importance is the manner in which theories are constructed and modified. Most importantly, the methods of data collection should be objective and the theories should be systematically tested and refined.

Objectivity   A feature of scientific method is that data are collected in an unbiased, objective way. The laboratory experiment features as the clearest example of the scientific approach in this respect but it is not the only scientific method. Other methods can be scientific if they take an objective approach. There are three main ways in which objectivity can be maximised:

1. *Control.* This is best illustrated if we take the example of the laboratory experiment in which the experimenter manipulates an independent variable (IV), observes and measures the effects of that manipulation on a dependent variable (DV) and holds all other variables constant. A rigorously designed experiment 'purifies' the effect of the IV on the DV and makes the intervention of unwanted influences less likely. For example, a test of the effect of alcohol (IV) on driving ability (DV) would need to include many controls to ensure that the only variable that was affecting driving ability was alcohol rather than, say, previous driving experience or drinking history.
2. *Operational definition.* This means that the scientist must define exactly what particular terms mean so that they can be measured and quantified. Psychologists may find themselves devising

measures of aggression or anxiety or attachment strength in order to avoid ambiguity and satisfy this aspect of objectivity.

3. *Replicability*. One way to check the objectivity of findings is to see if they can be repeated. Scientific research is painstakingly reported so that scientists can check each other's findings. If similar results are yielded with thIe same or different participants and in different contexts then they are more convincing and can be used to construct a body of knowledge, or theory.

The Use of Theory

A psychological theory is a general system for explaining the underlying principles of behaviour. The process of gathering knowledge leads ultimately to the construction of theories. How this is done is the second hallmark of scientific method.

Research and theory stimulate each other through the processes of induction and deduction. The first step in building knowledge is **induction** which involves creating theories from observing regularities in empirical data. Information is summarised and integrated into a coherent whole. **Deduction**, on the other hand, involves deriving testable statements from theory. These are known as hypotheses (hence the term hypothetico-deductive method). The induction/deduction process is cyclical and self perpetuating. The scientist uses the theory as a guiding framework for research so that the investigations are done in a systematic way. A theory is never static; it is refined and changed all the time on the basis of empirical evidence. A scientist would never talk of proving a theory – only of supporting it. Evidence may eventually cause it to be substantially modified, or even abandoned. Theories are not truths, only probabilities. Figure 4.1 illustrates the induction/deduction process, or the hypothetico–deductive method of theory formation.

The implication of this is that psychology can only be scientific if its theories qualify through being testable (and so refutable), parsimonious, and a fertile source of new hypotheses. Refutability, in Popper's (1972) view is a hallmark of a scientific theory. He argues that we should adopt a critical attitude to theories and attempt to refute them as it is all too easy to interpret data in ways that support our predictions. Good scientific theories emerge from the testing process as valid and reliable. This in turn improves their powers of prediction and therefore their practical value. As we shall see, psychological theories do not always meet these stringent criteria.

FIGURE 4.1.
The Hypothetico–Deductive Method of Theory Formation

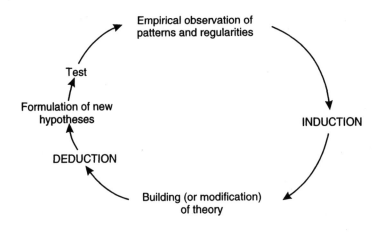

Applying Scientific Method in Psychology

If it can be argued that psychology is a science then psychologists can apply scientific method as a means of gathering information, but this is not a problem-free approach.

The overwhelming difficulty for psychologists in using scientific method lies in their subject matter – other human beings. Both participants and researchers are known to introduce various forms of bias into the research situation. So well-known is this source of bias that it has become a research area in its own right known as 'The Social Psychology of the Experiment'. The special nature of psychological research makes the aims of scientific method (control, operational definition and replicability) so much more difficult to realise. This, in turn, creates problems in the formulation and testing of theories.

The Social Psychology of the Experiment

Research in this area has tended to focus on the experimental method. This is not to say that the pitfalls described do not apply to other methods. All research is affected to a greater or lesser extent by the situation in which it takes place, the participants involved and the experimenters.

The influence of the situation   Human participants are often affected by the knowledge that they are being observed. Orne (1962) said that they are influenced by **demand characteristics** by which he meant cues in the experimental situation which might alert the participants to the hypothesis being tested, for example the physical set up of the experiment or the experimenter's behaviour. Orne and Evans (1965) found that out of 18 participants, 15 were prepared to pick up a snake which they were told was poisonous, plunge a hand into a container of fuming 'nitric acid' to retrieve a coin, and then throw the 'acid' in the face of an experimenter – actions which would be extremely unlikely outside the experimental situation. What is more, participants may maintain that they suspected no deception. Tedeschi *et al.* (1985) calls this 'a pact of ignorance' – participants who think they have 'caught on' to the experimenter's hypothesis do not let the experimenter know, either in order to save face, or so as not to 'spoil' the experiment. The experimental situation can alter participants' behaviour in so many ways that the goal of objectivity is not achieved, neither is the participants' behaviour a good indication of how they would behave normally (that is, there may be a lack of ecological validity).

The influence of the participant   Participants can affect the objectivity of research in two ways according to who they are and how they behave:

1. A recurrent criticism of psychology is that it is the science of the white, male, American undergraduate (or failing that, of the laboratory rat). Tedeschi *et al.* (1985) cite a number of surveys covering the years 1969 to 1979 and found that, in each year, a minimum of 70 per cent of social psychology research projects used college students. This severely limits the generalisability of the findings. Also important is the idea that many participants are volunteers. Ora (1965) found that volunteers are more easily influenced, moody, in need of approval, aggressive and neurotic than were non-volunteers. Again, the generalisability of research data obtained from such people would be limited.

2. The second factor which reduces the suitability of scientific method in psychology concerns participants' behaviour. Weber and Cook (1972) identified four roles which participants being studied might adopt:

- The faithful participant tries to react to the situation as naturally as possible. This may be deliberate, or just borne out of disinterest.
- The co-operative participant tries to discover the hypothesis being tested so that they can do their best to help prove it.
- The negativistic participant tries to discover the hypothesis in order to disprove it.
- The evaluatively apprehensive participant believes that the experimenter is capable of uncovering some hidden truth about them and does what they can to avoid being evaluated negatively.

Of these four roles, the faithful participant is clearly the most desirable, but it is not always possible to know which stance is being adopted. As a result, the objectivity of research is threatened once again, and with it the suitability of scientific method for collecting knowledge about humans.

The influence of the experimenter   Rosenthal (1969) has conducted a number of classic pieces of research into the influence of the experimenter on research results and has discovered three problems:

1. *Biosocial or physical characteristics* of the experimenter such as age, sex, race and appearance. Participants' prejudices and stereotypes may well affect the way they respond to different experimenters.
2. *Psychosocial factors* which have to do with the experimenter's social skills in dealing with participants. The experimenter may be friendly and supportive so that participants are at ease and feel co-operative. On the other hand, they may find the experimenter off-putting.
3. *Experimenter expectancy effects.* Experimenters who have a hypothesis in mind may end up validating it simply because of their belief about how the results will turn out. The hypothesis then becomes a self-fulfilling prophecy. It is assumed that the

experimenter unwittingly influences the results, not that it is a deliberate action.

The Standing of Psychological Theories

As stated earlier, part of the scientific approach has to do with theory building and modification. Psychology is unusual among sciences in that it can often explain the same thing from a number of theoretical viewpoints. These differ in terms of how closely they fit the scientific standard. Four approaches are outlined below (see Chapter 2 for more detail on some of these):

1. *Introspection.* In the early days of psychology, data were gathered in the form of introspections made in carefully controlled conditions – an approach advocated by Wundt (1879). In spite of attempts to control things such as stimuli and instructions to participants, it proved very difficult to achieve the aims of operational definition and replicability. Introspection also failed because the data were not empirical.
2. *Psychoanalytic theory.* The psychoanalytic approach of Sigmund Freud (1856–1939) has had similar problems in adopting scientific method .The subject matter – the workings of the unconscious mind – is neither empirically observable nor easily defined. Psychoanalytic theory also runs into difficulties with control and replicability. It assumes order and determinism, but the assumptions of parsimony and empiricism are less easily met. Although it has been claimed that psychoanalytic theory can be tested experimentally (and many attempts have been made to do so), opponents of psychoanalytic theory argue that it is not suitable for scientific testing as it is often irrefutable – the theory can account for apparently contradictory research evidence.
3. *Behaviourism.* Possibly the most successful application of scientific method to psychology has been achieved by the behaviourist school (Watson, 1919). Behaviourists rejected earlier approaches advocating instead publicly observable behaviour as the proper subject matter for psychology. Behaviourist research was, and still is, characterised by rigorous control, operational definition and replicability. The four assumptions of science – order, determinism, empiricism and parsimony – are accepted as central. Behaviourist theories are a source of readily testable hypotheses because the subject matter lends itself to

testing. For all its shortcomings, as a source of scientifically researched data, the behaviourist approach has few equals in psychology.

4. *Humanistic psychology.* The humanistic approach takes conscious experience as its focus of attention and so shares similar problems to those of introspection and psychoanalysis. Scientific testing is not easy at least in part because there is no coherent humanistic theory to work from. Nevertheless, Carl Rogers, a founder of the humanistic school, made great strides towards more systematic testing of humanistic ideas. In particular, he developed Q-sort techniques (devised by Stephenson in 1953) as a way of assessing the effectiveness of the his own 'client-centred therapy'. However one of the central tenets of the approach is that scientific method is not the best route to knowledge about humans and that the only meaningful way to understand them is to see the world from each person's unique perspective. Since one person's inner world is not open to public scrutiny, observations could never be empirical. Humanistic psychologists also reject the idea of determinism in favour of free will, preferring to see humans as exercising choice over their actions, in which case assumptions of order and parsimony are untenable. Finally, humanistic psychologists reject experimentation as a means of finding out about humans, seeing it as dehumanising and reductionist.

Conclusions

To summarise the arguments outlined here, a science aims to describe, understand, predict and control. It also makes assumptions of order, determinism, empiricism and parsimony. Its methods have particular characteristics and its theories are constructed systematically.

So is psychology a science? The answer to this question is not straightforward and is closely linked to how we define science. If it is defined by its aims then, on the whole, psychology is scientific. If it is defined by its assumptions, then some schools of psychology fit the mould more comfortably than others.

Even if it is assumed that the aims and assumptions of science are appropriate in psychology, then there are still difficulties in conducting research objectively because of the special nature of the subject matter. However, it is important to remember that psychologists are not alone in the problem of achieving objectivity. All scientists are human beings, and it is in their nature to select and interpret information, consequently their personal values and biases will always intervene regardless of their subject matter. If psychology fails the science test on the grounds of insufficient objectivity then so do other sciences.

Turning finally to the way in which theories are built and tested, it can be said that some psychologists do take a scientific approach but this is not equally true for all schools of psychology. Different schools focus on different types of subject matter, some of which are more easily operationally defined and tested than others. Schools also differ in their approach to research methods. The humanistic school, for example, regards tightly controlled experimentation as unsuitable for understanding human experience. Others, such as the behaviourists, regard it as essential.

The philosopher Kuhn (1962) says that an essential characteristic of a mature science is that it has a uniting **paradigm** – something which psychology lacks. (A paradigm is a set of assumptions about what should be studied and how – it is a common global theory or perspective such as Darwinism in biology.) In fact, Kuhn says that, until psychology has a paradigm, it is not science but pre-science. If this is the case, then it is too soon to ask questions about the applicability of the scientific approach to psychology. There can be no clear answers as long as it incorporates so many differing schools of thought. Behaviourism is, perhaps, the closest psychology has ever been to having a uniting paradigm (Valentine, 1982).

New Developments in Psychological Research Methods

Some psychologists do seem to value the traditional scientific approach more than others. It is interesting to note that when Sigmund Freud was a young man in the latter part of the nineteenth century, the scientific route to knowledge was relatively new and caused great excitement. Freud's theory, amongst others, was eventually criticised for not being amenable to scientific testing. Ironically, we are gradually moving towards a situation where the suitability of the scientific route to understanding human behaviour is being questioned – a change Freud might well have welcomed!

Some psychologists have long argued for a shift away from hard-line quantitative research, such as experimentation, to approaches that are more qualitative and these fit less comfortably with traditional scientific aims and assumptions. Quantitative approaches tend to emphasise the empiricist paradigm (which involves measurement and statistical analysis) and take the view that it is possible to understand the world in an objective and dispassionate way. Those who favour more qualitative approaches are critical of empiricism for many reasons. They say:

- it produces findings which lack ecological validity (for example as in some laboratory studies of memory);
- it values objectivity and distance from the participant (which, in fact, is impossible to achieve as every research situation is a social situation);
- it takes people out of their social context (and so giving a narrow and artificial view of people's experiences from the rather patronising perspective of the 'experimenter' controlling 'subjects');
- it operationalises terms to reduce them to something measurable (thus losing their full meaning for the participant on whom the researcher's meanings are imposed).

New Paradigm Research

An emphasis on qualitative methods is characteristic of new paradigm research which offers a number of alternatives to the traditional empirical approach. New paradigm researchers generally:

- see the researcher and participant as collaborators in research rather than as 'controlling experimenter' and 'responding subject';
- prefer more open-ended, detailed analysis of what people say, write or do arguing that, in order to understand them, we have to appreciate that they construct their own view of the world in a way which has meaning for them based on their social, cultural and historical background;
- utilise the more familiar techniques of the case-study, certain kinds of observation, role-play or interview but also use other techniques of gathering information, such as 'action research' and discourse analysis.

The issues raised by new paradigm researchers have important implications for the question about the suitability of scientific method in psychology because, as we have seen, science is more allied to traditional empiricism. Nevertheless, quantitative and qualitative methods have co-existed for a long time in psychology and both have a great deal to offer. Perhaps a more positive and productive solution to the question of the scientific status of psychology would be to acknowledge the value of mixing the best of the different paradigms together and taking a pluralist or eclectic approach to understanding human behaviour. This would surely be preferable to adopting an adversarial stance and trying to argue that one approach is better than the other.

Self-assessment Questions

1. What routes to knowledge are there apart from the scientific one?
2. What are the aims and assumptions of science?
3. What are the characteristics of scientific method?
4. How are scientific theories built and modified?
5. What is meant by 'the social psychology of the experiment'?
6. Compare two psychological theories in terms of their scientific status.
7. Explain why Kuhn thought psychology was still pre-science.
8. Briefly explain what is meant by 'new paradigm' research.

SECTION II   BIASES IN PSYCHOLOGICAL RESEARCH

Introduction

Critics of psychology say that, far from being an unbiased, value-free and objective science, it is profoundly Eurocentric (Howitt and Owusu-Bempah, 1994). By this they mean that it is steeped in cultural values which are part of American and European life and that these values shape psychological theories and research studies. There is also the view that psychologists, unwittingly or otherwise, hide their cultural bias behind science. In other words, although they appear to take a cool and objective view of human behaviour, the so-called 'universal' theories that result are, in fact, invented in their own culture. Furthermore, the Eurocentric standards in these theories tend to be seen as 'normal' and 'natural' so that cultures which do not share them are viewed as somehow failing to measure up. Because biases like these can arise, it is important to remind ourselves that science cannot give us absolute truths. Scientific knowledge is a social creation which could be seen as serving the needs of the dominant groups in society. In psychology, those groups are American and European.

There is a growing awareness of 'culture boundedness' in psychology and, with it, a clearer realisation of some of the serious shortcomings of the discipline. Berry (1983) commented that some American psychology was so culture-bound that it should not be employed in cultures outside the United States, not even in Canada. Howitt and Owusu-Bempah go further. They say 'Psychology has not simply colluded in the denial of the needs of culturally and racially diverse groups, it has trained psychologists unfit or incompetent for work in a multi-cultural society' (1994, p. 140).

Clearly, this is a situation which psychologists must address since the consequences of bias are too important to ignore. But where do they start? A good place to begin would be to examine what is meant by 'culture'. The next step would be to identify some of the biases resulting from a culture-bound view. Only when psychologists begin to understand what they are dealing with will they be in a position to act constructively to counteract bias. In this section we will follow this route, ending with the issues of race and gender as specific examples of culture bias in psychology. As we go along, a useful general point to bear in mind is that over-arching much of psychology is the Eurocentric view that science should be favoured as the main route to knowledge and this, in itself, is a form of bias.

Culture and Psychology

One reason why psychologists compare cultures is that they see it as a way of addressing the 'nature–nurture' debate. The reasoning behind this is that if they can find certain behaviour patterns are 'universal' regardless of environment, then that behaviour is more likely to be 'human nature'. Behaviour patterns which differ between cultures are seen as 'culturally relative' and more open to the effects of environment. In practice, this is an issue which is very hard to resolve since research across cultures is fraught with theoretical and technical difficulties.

First psychologists must be clear about what is meant by 'culture'. Moghaddam *et al.* (1993) take a wide view. They say it is the 'human-made part of the environment' and that it can be both objective and physical (for example everyday objects and structures, works of art) and subjective and psychological (for example beliefs, identities and values). They make the important point that humans both shape their culture and are shaped by it. Another useful approach is taken by Triandis (1990) who talks of 'cultural syndromes'. By this he means that a culture consists of a particular combination of beliefs, values, attitudes, norms and behaviours, and that these distinguish it from other cultures. Brislin (1993) adds that such syndromes are:

- passed down the generations;
- taken for granted and not generally discussed;
- apt to arouse strong feelings within the culture if cultural values are violated;
- apt to lead to clashes with people who have sharply contrasting cultural syndromes.

Triandis (1990) and Hofstede (1980) have, between them, suggested a number of general ways in which cultural syndromes might vary and these appear in Figure 4.2. In addition, there are many ways in which members of different cultures may express the elements of the syndrome even when they 'score' similarly on them, so it is important that psychologists take this into account. Furthermore, as Brislin (1993) reminds us, culture is not static. Individuals within a culture may vary in how committed they are to its values at different times in their lives, and cultural values can be flexible or even change significantly over time. It is also important to remember that the similarities between what we would casually call 'different' cultures often outweigh the differences. All of these things make the effects of culture particularly difficult to research simply because of the problems they present to psychologists attempting to obtain truly comparable samples from different cultures.

So we can see that studying different cultures does not necessarily mean travelling the world and seeking out remote groups of people untouched by Western ways. In explaining this, Much (1995) draws a distinction between traditional cross-cultural psychology and the newer 'cultural psychology'. The traditional approach involved devising theories and measuring instruments in the home culture and then imposing them on another culture in the hope that cultural universals would eventually be discovered. Cultural psychology, on

FIGURE 4.2
Some Dimensions of Cultural Difference

Dimensions	*Notes*
● Individualism–collectivism	● Individualism is more common in Western cultures and collectivism in Eastern cultures. The first is characterised by individual responsibility and achievement, the second by group responsibility and support
● Power distance	● Cultures differ in the prevalence and nature of power-relationships where some individuals or groups may be deferential to others
● Masculinity–feminity	● Masculine cultures (e.g. Japan) emphasise work, achievement, strength and effectiveness. Feminine cultures (e.g. Sweden) emphasise quality of life, interpersonal relationships, nurturing and care
● Tight–loose	● A tight culture is one in which norms are strictly defined. In a loose culture a great deal of freedom would be acceptable
● Uncertainty avoidance	● This refers to the degree to which a culture tries to plan for the future and maintain stability
● Cultural complexity	● This can be defined by the number and diversity of roles occupied by people in the culture. (Certain individuals may have very clearly defined roles, e.g. the Pope.) Complex cultures also seem to lay great emphasis on time
● Emotional control–expressiveness	● This refers to whether it is more usual to express emotions openly or to exercise restraint
● Contact–no contact	● This is to do with the culture's rules of proximity (physical distance) between individuals, e.g. how close individuals permit others to get and how status and relationships affect this

Source: Based on Triandis (1990) and Hofstede (1980).

the other hand, does not assume that there is an 'intrinsic psychic unity' about humankind that is seeking to be discovered. Instead it lays emphasis on different social systems as the source of variation between people. Thus, modern cultural psychologists may find similar cultures to their own in other parts of the world, and very different cultures on their doorstep.

Sources of Cultural Bias in Psychological Theory and Research

A brief consideration of the dimensions of culture shown in Figure 4.2 will give an idea of the kinds of values that shape Eurocentric psychology. It has grown up against a complex cultural background which tends to emphasise individualism, power-distance, masculinity and uncertainty avoidance, and which is relatively tight, distant and emotionally inexpressive. This affects how research questions are framed, how research findings are interpreted and how theories are constructed and modified, but, most importantly, it seems to set the standard against which all other cultures are compared. The widely influential theories of Freud, Piaget and Skinner can all be considered Eurocentric by these criteria even though there has been some success in applying them across cultures.

There are many ways in which cultural bias can be perpetuated in psychology, but here we will consider just three. They concern choice of research participants, choice of methods and how findings are communicated to a wider audience.

1. Choice of Research Participants

It is generally well-known that much American psychology is based on studies using readily available, white, undergraduate students who can be invited, induced or expected to act as research participants. Undergraduates could hardly be thought of as widely representative of other Americans, let alone other cultures, nevertheless participants of other types rarely appear in the research literature. In fact, in a content analysis of 20 years of publications in six of the American Psychological Association's journals, Graham (1992) found that less than 4 per cent of the 15 000 published articles were about African Americans. In addition, there had been a drop to 2 per cent in the final five years covered by the study. This selectivity may happen simply because participants other than undergraduates take more time, effort and money to recruit. Alternatively, it could be that cultural research is often very 'socially sensitive' and so tends to be avoided. On the other hand, it could signify lack of interest by the researcher based on the view that different cultures are not important.

2.   Choice of Methods

The distinction drawn by Pike (1967) between 'emics' and 'etics' helps to explain why the methods, derived from particular theories and used to study different cultures, are likely to be a source of bias. To take an 'etic' view is to study a culture from the outside using criteria common to the 'home' and the studied culture. The 'emic' view studies it from the inside, perhaps using participant observation or by devising measures within the culture, often in collaboration with one or more of its members. Problems arise when measures devised on the basis of Eurocentric psychological theory (for example certain IQ tests) are 'exported' to other cultures and treated as though they are 'etics' when they are, in fact, 'emics'. Their use outside the home culture then becomes an 'imposed etic' which could render the measure, and any theoretical conclusions drawn from the resulting data, largely or completely invalid. The 'etic'/ 'emic' distinction can thus explain why certain findings cannot always be replicated outside the home culture. (Examples in psychology include Milgram's *Obedience to Authority* research (1974) and Sherif *et al.*'s (1961) *Robber's Cave* studies into inter-group conflict.)

One danger in failing to recognise that they are using an imposed etic is that researchers may simply bend their findings to fit their theoretical, and hence cultural, view (for example explaining IQ differences in terms of genetics). A possible solution would be to take the 'emics' of the two cultures to be studied and use what they have in common to arrive at a 'derived etic' which is equally valid in both cultures (for example a culture-fair IQ test). This, of course, is easier said than done.

3.   Communicating Findings to a Wider Audience

One important way in which bias can be perpetuated is in psychological publications. Eurocentric psychology has a 'written tradition' – it likes to communicate its findings in writing. However, before publication, books and research papers are 'filtered' by the dominant culture so that anything which is not mainstream or which does not fit the prevailing view may be selected out. The content of what remains is highly Eurocentric. Smith and Bond (1993), for example, analysed two widely available social psychology textbooks, the first by Baron and Byrne (1991) and the second by Hewstone *et al.* (1988). They found that the books contained 94 per cent and 68 per cent American studies respectively, even though the second one is a British textbook written by a team of European authors. Overall, Smith and Bond estimate that 64 per cent of psychological research world-wide is American and much of this will predominate in published material. A related source of bias in written matter, as we shall see, is that particular views of others can be perpetuated in the choice of words. This is important simply because Eurocentric psychology markets its literature so successfully all over the world.

Cultural bias in psychology has a long history. So long, in fact, that Bulhan (1985) likens the actions of psychological researchers to the political colonialists of the past. Just as, throughout history, members of dominant cultures have seen it as their right to invade other cultures and help themselves to valuable raw materials, so psychologists have practised 'scientific colonialism'. By this he means that they too have invaded any other culture which interests them and helped themselves to valuable raw data to use for their own gain. At its worst, this can grow into a kind of auto-colonialism where the colonised culture 'actively participates in [its] own victimisation' (Bulhan, 1985, p. 44) and hands its power over to the invader. If this does not happen, the invading culture will eventually seek to impose its own values on the colonised culture. Political colonialists do this by 'Westernising' other cultures while Eurocentric psychologists either ignore, marginalise or 'Europeanise' them.

Racial and Gender Bias in Psychology

So far, we have seen a number of general biases that arise in Eurocentric psychology and how these can affect the nature of psychological knowledge. A further important consequence of adopting a particular cultural view is that certain ways of grouping or categorising people will be seen as appropriate. The dominant view in Eurocentric psychology is that it is meaningful and useful to separate people in terms of race and gender. The unfortunate result of this is that it encourages psychologists to emphasise differences between races and sexes, compare them to each other and make value judgements about them. Black people and women in particular have not done well out of such comparisons. Indeed, it has been argued that they have been rendered virtually invisible through being ignored, marginalised or Europeanised. In the sections which follow we will see some of the results of these biases and consider how the situation can be resolved.

Racial Bias in Psychology

The culture out of which Eurocentric psychology has arisen tends to make three main classifications of race based on superficial appearance. These are African, Mongoloid, Caucasoid (or black, yellow and white to which some add a fourth category of American Indian or red). There is a persistent myth that these 'races' are biologically very different. This view persists in spite of clear evidence that genetic differences between them are minuscule. In addition, to apply simple categories like these to people is to both take them out of their cultural context and to ignore individual differences. They come to be seen as 'all the same', as 'different from the (white) norm' and ultimately 'less worthy'. Since it is most likely that it is the predominant white standard against which people are judged, 'non-white' groups will almost invariably be found wanting. The discrimination which often results has led Howitt and Owusu-Bempah (1994), amongst others, to accuse psychology of being not only culturally biased but also racist.

Old racism　The racism of psychology has a long history. Howitt and Owusu-Bempah give many examples of what they call 'old racism'. This is based largely on assumptions about the importance of alleged biological differences between races, particularly genetic ones. Such a view was fuelled by 'bad gene' theorists who were opposed to racial mixing on the grounds that so-called inferior genes in certain races would dilute the quality of the gene pool in other races and destroy their culture. Some of the results of this idea are plain to see. Hiding behind 'science', and using IQ testing (an imposed etic) to provide 'objective' evidence, psychologists have colluded in discriminatory immigration and education policies and even in eugenics and 'ethnic cleansing' such as that carried out by Adolf Hitler and, more recently, in former Yugoslavia. Sadly, in spite of its name, 'old racism' is not a thing of the past, but is alive and well (for more about the controversial uses of IQ tests, see Chapter 6, Part II).

New racism Howitt and Owusu-Bempah say that, although some of the more outrageous, overt expressions of 'old racism' may have disappeared from psychology, racism is still there but in a subtler form. This 'new racism' is expressed in a number of ways, for example:

- thinking of racism as characteristic only of extreme groups;
- denying that racism is a problem;
- being 'colour blind' (that is, thinking that to acknowledge that racism exists simply perpetuates it);
- seeing people who are the victims of racism as responsible for their own misfortune.

It is also practised in a number of ways:

- by formulating theories and asking research questions which perpetuate boundaries between races, for example hereditarian views of intelligence and inter-group conflict theories of prejudice;
- by 'filtering' the content of research journals and textbooks to reflect the views of the dominant culture;
- by choice of words in written material which suggest that other races are not only 'different' but also 'deficient'; for example primitive, tribal, savage (that is, like animals) or non-Western (that is, an undifferentiated mass) or 'culturally deprived' (not as good);
- by failing to support research interests that might further an understanding of other cultures;
- by failing to appoint psychologists from outside the dominant cultural group;
- by exercising 'tokenism'; for example appointing a few black psychologists but relegating them to marginal research areas.

So Howitt and Owusu-Bempah show that racism still features in modern psychology and has yet to be actively and effectively confronted and eradicated. Even replacing racism with racial tolerance does not go far enough since it only amounts to 'the best that bigots can achieve' (Howitt and Owusu-Bempah, 1994, p. 17) and is about as constructive as replacing a headache with a toothache. The authors are in no doubt about the seriousness of the problem. They warn that racism is, possibly, 'psychology's most versatile and persistent theory. . . From the perspective of its victims, racism inhibits human growth, limits productive living and causes death' (ibid., p. 37).

Gender Bias in Psychology

In relation to race, we saw how applying a Eurocentric standard can lead to discrimination against certain groups. Just as the culture of psychology is dominated by white standards, so it is dominated by male standards. The problem with this is that women, like certain racial groups, are in danger of suffering discrimination as a result of being viewed as 'all the same', 'different from the (male) norm' and 'less worthy'. Race, as we saw, is a convenient label and more of a social invention than a biological reality. The same applies to gender. Male and female may be physiologically distinguishable, but psychologically similarities between the sexes far outweigh the differences. Nevertheless, clearly differentiated social categories prevail. To help emphasise that anatomy is not necessarily destiny, psychologists like to draw a distinction between biological sex (male and female) and psychological gender (masculine and feminine).

Many of the themes raised in connection with racial bias reappear when we consider gender bias. In both cases the use of white, masculine theories and methods amounts to an imposed Eurocentric 'etic'. In the case of females, Matlin (1993) suggests this renders invisible many things that are important in their lives such as:

- exclusively female experiences, for example pregnancy and menopause;
- almost exclusively female experiences, for example rape and sexual harassment;
- how females fare in male-dominated domains, for example certain workplace settings.

Much of the literature in this area focuses on the damage gender bias can do to women, but it is important to remember that it can work both ways and be disadvantageous to both men and women.

In considering the effects of gender bias we can borrow from Howitt and Owusu-Bempah's ideas about racism and talk of 'old sexism' and 'new sexism'. We are, hopefully, seeing a decline in blatant examples of old sexism which sees women as biologically predisposed to be witches, mothers or sex objects. However, we must guard against more subtle forms of new sexism, which is simply old sexism in disguise, and be active in eliminating it. As with racism, it is not enough to think of sexism as:

- characteristic only of extreme groups;
- not a problem;
- something to be ignored (because to raise it as an issue only perpetuates it);
- women's fault.

And again, like racism, sexism can be practised in a number of ways:

- by formulating theories and asking research questions which perpetuate boundaries between the sexes, for example by using Freudian theory as a basis from which to test the detrimental effect of working mothers but not of working fathers; or by starting from the assumption that it is legitimate to look for sex differences (as opposed to comparisons);
- by filtering what is published in research journals and textbooks to reflect the stereotyped view of male and female and to emphasise differences, for example failing to publish research which shows similarities rather than differences or which identifies variables other than gender as a source of females' disadvantage (the 'file-drawer phenomenon');
- by choice of words when describing women and what they do, for example use of the generic masculine (he) to denote both sexes; in embedded figure tests where women typically take longer than men to locate a hidden shape, they are called 'field dependent' (the label for males is 'field independent'). Why not call women 'context aware' and men 'context blind'?
- by failing to support research interests which concern women, for example experiences of menstruation or childbirth;
- by failing to appoint or promote women academics;
- by exercising 'tokenism', for example appointing a few women but then marginalising them and/or their research interests.

In relation to gender bias in the psychological theories (which of course underpin research) Hare-Mustin and Maracek (1990) distinguish between alpha bias and beta bias:

- Theories with alpha bias exaggerate differences between men and women.
- Theories with beta bias minimise the differences.

Neither approach is particularly helpful because the first tends to perpetuate sex stereotypes and the second tends to make women invisible by applying male standards to all. To overcome this, Hare-Mustin and Maracek suggest we adopt a 'constructivist standpoint'. By this they mean we should recognise that men and women seem different only because that is the social reality we have created about them. This 'reality' is based on the pervasive myths and folklore of our alpha-biased culture and its falsity can be demonstrated many times in research.

Worell and Remer (1992) also provide a useful classification of psychological theories to show how they might lead to gender bias in research. These are shown in Figure 4.3. **Freudian psychoanalytic theory** stands out as an excellent example of all of these kinds of bias yet its influence is still great:

- It is androcentric because it explains the experiences of both males and females from a male viewpoint.
- It is gendercentric because it sees development of males and females as taking different routes (for example the Oedipal and Electra conflicts in the phallic stage of development).
- It is ethnocentric because of its Eurocentric background.
- It is heterosexist because it sees heterosexism as normal and homosexuality or lesbianism as abnormal.
- It is both intrapsychic and deterministic seeing behaviour as determined by the operation of instincts.

Erikson's (1963, 1968) theory of **psychosocial development** and **Kohlberg**'s (1975) theory of **moral development** can be seen as androcentric, ethnocentric and intrapsychic. However, neither of them is deterministic as both are lifespan approaches. Erikson's theory could be seen as somewhat gendercentric and heterosexist because of the differences it sees in the developmental paths of males and females. Kohlberg's theory tends not to address the heterosexism issue, being more concerned with cognitive development. Neither is it gendercentric – men and women follow the same route except that females allegedly do not progress as far as males. Worell and Remer's solution is to suggest that we examine all

FIGURE 4.3
Types of Bias in Psychological Theories

Types of bias	*Explanation*
• Androcentric	• The male view is seen as legitimate for explaining experiences of both sexes
• Gendercentric	• Males and females are seen as developing along different paths
• Ethnocentric	• American-European or 'Eurocentric' bias manifested in, for example, viewing the nuclear family, or specific roles for men and women, as normal
• Heterosexist	• Seeing heterosexism as the normal and desirable state and other sexual orientations as deficient
• Intrapsychic	• Attributing behaviour to internal factors. In effect, this blames people for their behaviour; e.g. women's subjugation is due to their own inherent weaknesses
• Deterministic	• Emphasising the importance of early experience for 'fixing' behaviour patterns at a young age

Source: Worell and Remer (1992).

psychological theories for evidence of the six types of bias and transform them into a Feminist Theory format which is beneficial for both males and females. Characteristics of the **feminist approach** and some ways of transforming biased theories are as follows:

1. *Gender free*. Dispose of androcentric and gendercentric theories by concentrating on the similarities between males and females. Avoid stereotypes and sexist language and emphasise the role of socialisation, rather than biological processes, in affecting behaviour.
2. *Flexible*. Dispose of ethnocentrism and heterosexism by using concepts that apply to everyone regardless of age, culture, race, sexual orientation or gender.

3. *Interactionist*. Drop the intrapsychic emphasis and devise an approach which sees behaviour as having multiple causes, both individual and environmental.
4. *Lifespan*. Dispose of deterministic ideas and see development as a lifelong process with options for growth and change at any age.

Many feminist theorist are optimistic about the progress that is being made to eradicate gender bias. The psychology of women, for example, has now become institutionalised and is an option in many degree courses. Crawford and Unger (1995) write 'The new psychology of women and gender is rich and varied. Virtually every intellectual framework from Freudian theory to cognitive psychology [and] . . . virtually every area of psychology, from developmental to social, has been affected' (p. 39). But there is still much to do.

What Can be Done about Racial and Gender Bias?

Howitt and Owusu-Bempah warn that racial bias and the resulting racism must be rooted out completely. It is wholly unsatisfactory, they say, simply to replace it with 'tolerance'. The same reasoning can be applied to gender bias. It might seem sensible, therefore, to establish alternatives such as Black Psychology or Psychology of Women but, unless handled with care, these may simply create new and different divisions. Howitt and Owusu-Bempah also comment that, apart from in its extreme forms, racism appears to be harder to identify than sexism and that this may be one reason why women have had relatively greater success in challenging sexism. So what can be done? Since bias seems to operate on at least three levels – individual, institutional and cultural – any attempt to bring about change would need to address all of these.

1. The Individual Level

On an individual level, psychologists should strive to:

- become sensitive to their own and others' biases;
- empathise with the victims of bias;

2. The Institutional Level

On an institutional level, bias can be tackled in many ways. Howitt and Owusu-Bempah (1994) suggest ten ways to combat racial bias in particular. These have been adapted to show how they can be applied equally well to tackling gender bias in psychological institutions:

1. Examine the policies and practices of the institution paying special attention to racism and sexism. Publish anti-racist and anti-sexist materials.
2. Adopt and implement equal opportunities policies; for example the British Psychological Society (BPS) ethical guidelines for research with human participants (1993) contains notes on avoidance of sexist language (but not, as yet, of racist language).
3. Scrutinise the curriculum in psychological education and training to make it more relevant to a multi-cultural society.
4. Evaluate and monitor the professional practice of members of the institution.
5. Commit the institution to equality, perhaps through a formal ethical requirement.
6. Join with other organisations (for example medical, educational) to combat bias.
7. Prepare and equip students and practitioners to provide an unbiased service in a multi-cultural/multiracial society.
8. Provide anti-racist/sexist resource materials for teachers and practitioners to help raise self-awareness.
9. Provide journal editors and committees with guidelines to help them monitor research papers for unacceptably biased content. Amongst other things, such committees should be alert to the use of 'imposed etics' and insist that researchers either adopt an 'emic' approach or strive to employ derived 'etics' which have equivalence of meaning in the home and studied culture.
10. Take steps to recruit disadvantaged groups to the profession, for example through publicity and educational materials and the provision of grants.

3. The Cultural Level

On a cultural level, bias is infinitely harder to tackle because of the sheer scale of the problem. The Eurocentrism of psychology is pervasive and deep-rooted, and it can be politically very sensitive to attack the status quo, but this should be no excuse for inactivity. As we have seen, it is possible to work away at the problem on a number of other levels and to create clear standards to aspire to. It is also important to realise that significant change is likely to come about both slowly and painfully. Nevertheless, as Howitt and Owusu-Bempah remind us, we have a moral obligation to work to reduce all kinds of bias in psychology since not to do so is tantamount to complicity.

Self-assessment Questions

1. What do psychologists mean by 'culture'?
2. What is meant by 'Eurocentric bias' in psychology?
3. Outline three ways in which Eurocentric bias might be perpetuated.
4. Give examples of racial and gender bias in psychology.
5. Suggest at least six ways of combating racial or gender bias in psychology.

FURTHER READING

R. D. Gross (1995) *Themes, Issues and Debates in Psychology* (London: Hodder & Stoughton) chs 6, 8 and 11.

D. Howitt and J. Owusu-Bempah (1994) *The Racism of Psychology: Time for Change* (Hemel Hempstead: Harvester Wheatsheaf).

M. Matlin (1993) *The Psychology of Women* (New York: Harcourt Brace Jovanovich).

J. Worrell and P. Remer (1992) *Feminist Perspectives in Therapy* (New York: Wiley).

I SAY, TREATED HUMANELY, IT'S PERFECTLY ETHICAL TO STUDY THEM.

Ethics in Psychology 5

At the end of this chapter you should be able to:

1. identify ten areas of concern in the BPS ethical guidelines for research with human participants and comment on each one;
2. analyse ethical issues raised in the studies of obedience by Milgram and Zimbardo;
3. comment on psychologists' everyday experience of applying ethical guidelines;
4. identify some ethical issues raised by psychotherapy in general and behavioural treatments in particular;
5. explain what is meant by and give examples of 'socially sensitive research';
6. consider some of the dilemmas psychologists face when conducting socially sensitive research;
7. describe the kinds of research psychologists conduct with animals and comment on its incidence; and
8. analyse practical and ethical issues raised by animal research in psychology.

SECTION 1   ETHICS IN PSYCHOLOGICAL RESEARCH WITH HUMAN PARTICIPANTS

One of the primary aims of psychology is to improve the quality of human life and to do this it is necessary to carry out research with human participants. They are a vital resource. Without them there would be no psychology and no advances in knowledge. If psychologists are to enjoy the freedom they need to conduct research, they must take great care that they do not create an atmosphere where people are unwilling to take part in psychological research. Above all else, however, psychologists have a duty to respect the rights and dignity of research participants. Consequently they must maintain high ethical standards whatever their field of research or practice.

111

This means that they must abide by certain moral principles and rules of conduct and these serve to protect research participants, the reputation of psychology and the psychologists themselves.

The British Psychological Society (BPS) regularly publishes and revises general ethical guidelines concerning the use of human participants in research, the most recent in 1993. The Society also publishes guidelines about the use of animals in research and about professional and ethical conduct in various areas of psychological practice. However, as with all guidelines, there is room for interpretation and there will always be a point at which the psychologist has to exercise judgement since no code of ethics can take care of all possible situations. Figure 5.1 summarises the main points of the BPS guidelines concerning research with humans, and offers some extra information about how psychologists might deal with any problems that may arise. These issues can be more conveniently arranged under two headings: 'Risks' and 'Informed Consent'.

Risks

1. The most obvious form of risk a participant is likely to encounter is some form of **psychological stress** such as fear, anxiety, embarrassment, guilt or loss of self-esteem. Psychologists have an ethical obligation to avoid causing these as far as possible and to protect participants from unforeseen risk. This may mean abandoning or redesigning the research.
2. A less obvious form of risk arises from **coercion** of participants to take part in research. This is especially important when participants are not self-selected volunteers and are offered payment or other perks for their co-operation. Participants may feel obliged to take part in the research because of these.
3. **Deception** is another form of risk. It may be necessary to withhold information from participants for a variety of reasons, for example it could make a nonsense of the experiment if participants knew the hypothesis being tested. If there is no alternative to deception, and the research is important enough to warrant it, then the researcher should be careful to debrief the participants afterwards in order to ensure that there has been no lasting harm.
4. Finally, if **breaches of confidentiality** or privacy have occurred, measures must be taken to ensure the anonymity of participants and, if it is possible, give them the option to withhold their data.

FIGURE 5.1

A Summary of the 1993 BPS Ethical Guidelines for Research with Human Participants and Some Comments on their Use

GUIDELINES	EXPLANATION	COMMENTS
• General	• In all cases, investigators must consider the ethical implications and psychological consequences for the participants in their research. This should be done for all participants taking into account ethnic, cultural, social, age and sex differences	• The best informed judges of whether a piece of research is ethically acceptable will probably be members of the population from which the participants are to be selected. It is not always possible to do this if, for example, the participants are children or intellectually-impaired in which case people acting for them would be consulted
• Consent	• Whenever possible, investigators should obtain the consent of possible participants in a research project. This usually means 'informed consent', that is, the investigator should explain, as fully as possible, the purpose and design of the research before proceeding	• In some cases this will mean advising participants that the research procedures involve discomfort or other risks which they would not normally encounter. In such cases, the researcher must seek the guidance of colleagues before asking for consent
• Deception	• Psychologists must avoid deceiving participants about the nature of the research wherever possible. However, there will occasions when to reveal the research hypothesis to participants would make the research pointless and so deception would be considered	• Deception should not be used if there is an alternative procedure to the one proposed. If deception is being considered, safeguards include consultation with others about its acceptability, e.g. individuals similar to the proposed participants, colleagues and various ethical committees (for example, those set up by the BPS). Sometimes, it is possible to ask participants if they would accept deception until after the research is completed. At all times, it should be considered how participants are likely to be

	affected by finding out later that they have been deceived
• Debriefing	• This is more than just informing the participants of the nature of the research and the findings after the study is over. It must take the form of 'active intervention'; i.e. the psychologist must be prepared to discuss the procedures and findings with participants and endeavour to ensure that they leave the research situation, as far as possible, in the state in which they entered it	• Intention to debrief participants later is no excuse for exposing them to unacceptable levels of risk, neither is the inability to debrief them (e.g. as in some observational research)
• Withdrawal from the investigation	• Investigators must inform participants of their right to withdraw, without penalty, at any stage of the research. They should be prepared to remind participants of this right and to stop any procedure which appears to be causing discomfort	• This may be difficult to achieve (e.g. with children or in observational research) but it should still be attempted. After debriefing, participants have the right to withdraw their data and see it destroyed in their presence
• Confidentiality and privacy	• Participants are protected by law (The Data Protection Act 1984) in that they have the right to expect that any information provided by them will be treated confidentially and that their identities will not be revealed	• Failure to observe confidentiality would quickly ruin the reputation of research psychologists; nevertheless, they have a duty to break this guideline if they discover a situation where human life is in danger, e.g. if a suicide threat had been made. This guideline may also be broken if a participant gives full and knowing consent to their identity being revealed (preferably after seeing a written account of the research report)
• Protection of participants	• This refers to protection of participants from mental or physical harm during psychological investigations. Risks greater than those likely to be encountered in everyday life should be avoided. Participants should also be asked to reveal any medical conditions, or other problems,	• Discussion of results with participants must be done with the utmost care and sensitivity. Test results, for example, may be poorly understood by the layperson and this could cause undue anxiety. Participants should also be informed about how to contact the investigator should

	which might put them at special risk. If encroachments of privacy are likely the participant must understand that they do not have to reveal anything private or personal	some unforeseen consequence of the research arise either immediately after the investigation or later on. The researcher is then obliged to correct or remove the problem

- Observational research
  - In observational research, individuals cannot always give informed consent; nevertheless it is still important to respect people's privacy and well-being especially as, in some cases, it will not be possible to obtain informed consent or provide a debriefing
  - Observations should be made only in those situations where people would normally expect to be in public view and not where they expect to be unobserved. Covert participant observations present a particular problem here especially as they raise further issues of deception and confidentiality

- Giving advice to participants
  - If, during an investigation, a researcher becomes aware that a participant has a significant psychological or physical problem, there is an obligation to reveal this to the participant and to attempt to help them obtain professional advice should they wish it
  - This is a sensitive issue. Few research psychologists are expert enough to make on the spot diagnoses. On the other hand, if a participant does seek advice from the researcher, it is only acceptable to give it if it were agreed beforehand as part of the research design and the psychologist is appropriately qualified

- Monitoring colleagues
  - Investigators share a moral responsibility to maintain high ethical standards and should monitor their own work and that of colleagues
  - This applies at any level of research from GCSE upwards. All research projects need to be carefully assessed on ethical grounds before proceeding

Source: Adapted from BPS, *A Code of Conduct for Psychologists*, 1993.

Sometimes, the latter would not be possible, for example Humphreys (1970) was able to conduct research into homosexual acts in public toilets by acting as a lookout for the participants. While the breach of privacy is obvious, it could be argued that the participants had, in a sense, granted the researcher permission to observe them.

Informed Consent

Informed consent is a second key issue in research because it is not always desirable to inform participants fully, nor is the researcher always in a position to do so, for example if the research is into new areas. Even with the best of intentions, the researcher may fail to inform participants fully because they are told too little or they fail to understand. In some research (for example Zimbardo's prison simulation study) it is not possible to inform potential participants in full because the researcher cannot know in advance how things will progress.

If the researcher feels that it is necessary to proceed without obtaining informed consent there are two further possible courses of action. One is to run a pilot study and interview participants afterwards about how acceptable they found the procedure. Alternatively, role-play could be used where fully-informed participants act-out the procedures. The latter was used by Zimbardo (1973) in his famous prison simulation exercise.

Examples of Ethically Questionable Research

The reader will probably be familiar with some examples of psychological research which have been attacked on ethical grounds and which have been defended on the basis of their contribution to knowledge. Social psychology is particularly rich in examples (although there are many others, for example in developmental psychology, bio-psychology and psychometrics). Solomon Asch's (1956) classic conformity experiments are well-known, and there are a number of 'bystander apathy' experiments. These all involved some deception of the participants and, in some cases, considerable stress, but could be justified on the basis of what was learned about group influence. Accounts of such research can be found in most introductory social psychology texts.

Milgram's Research on Obedience

In the context of ethical issues, the most frequently quoted are Stanley Milgram's *Obedience to Authority* research (1974) and Philip Zimbardo *et al.*'s (1973) prison simulation. Detailed accounts of these are easily found (for example see Gross, 1992) so only the briefest details are necessary here.

Milgram's research centred on the extent to which people would obey authority. Volunteer participants were recruited and tested individually. A cover story was necessary to lead them to believe that, during the experiment, it was necessary to give increasingly painful electric shocks to another person who was out of sight in the next room. As the voltage of the shocks increased, the other person made sounds indicating increasing distress until eventually there was an ominous silence.

The fact that 65 per cent of the participants were prepared to continue to give shocks to others to the end of the voltage scale surprised Milgram, especially as the learner had made no response after a certain shock level. However, many of the participants were clearly upset by the experiment and showed reactions ranging from nervous laughter to full-blown uncontrollable seizures.

After the experiment was over, Milgram went to great lengths to debrief the participants. He reunited them with the learner to convince them no harm had been done. He held post-experimental interviews and reassured participants that their reactions were not unusual and he followed participants up afterwards to check that no long-term damage had been done. In spite of all these precautions, Milgram's work has come under attack as we shall see.

Zimbardo's Prison Simulation Study

Zimbardo *et al.*'s intention was to conduct a two-week-long study of social and situational factors affecting reactions to prison life. Young male volunteers were screened to ensure that they had no psychological problems. Those that were chosen were randomly assigned to role-play the prisoners or guards in a mock-up prison in the basement of one of Stanford University's buildings. None of the participants had any training for these roles. Each received $15 a day for taking part and no deception was involved.

Events in the prison were monitored continuously. In a very short time, the prisoners attempted a rebellion but this was crushed by the guards. After this, the prisoners became increasingly passive and the guards more aggressive. In less than 36 hours one of the prisoners was released because of uncontrolled crying, fits of rage, disorganised thinking and severe depression. Other had to be released over the next few days because of a variety of stress symptoms. Zimbardo *et al.* stopped the project after only six days because of its effect on the prisoners. Like Milgram, Zimbardo subsequently found himself defending his case against complaints that his research was unethical.

Weighing-up Costs and Benefits

When questions are raised about ethical aspects of research, it is usually necessary to weigh-up the costs (such as risks to the participants, the researcher and the reputation of psychology) against the benefits (for example important theoretical or practical advances).

Can Milgram's research be defended in terms of costs and benefits? Certainly his findings appear to be significant, but what of the ethical question? Concerning this, **Baumrind** (1964) has been a vociferous critic.

Baumrind's criticisms centred mainly on whether enough was done to protect the participants from harm. Milgram had found it necessary to deceive them and to put them through procedures which many found stressful, that is causing pain to another person. He verbally 'prodded' them to go on when they expressed a wish to withdraw.

In reply, Milgram argued that he could not have known in advance how far participants would be prepared to obey his instructions nor the degree of discomfort this would cause them. He felt that they were given ample opportunity to withdraw if they wanted to. Before the experiment, he had 'piloted' the procedure by asking 14 psychology students and 40 professors to estimate what a sample of 100 participants would do. They estimated that most participants would stop about halfway through and only one or two would go right to the end. Admittedly, Milgram did not ask people like the participants he eventually used but he had tried to anticipate problems.

Secondly, Milgram defended his case on the basis of the debriefing procedures he followed afterwards. The participants were reassured that they had not delivered electric shocks to the 'learner' and they had a long discussion about what had happened with the 'learner' and the experimenter. All participants were reassured that the feelings they had experienced were similar to those of other participants. Later, all participants were given a detailed account of the procedures and the results.

Of particular interest were the responses to a post-experiment questionnaire which participants filled in. This gave them a chance to express their feelings about having taken part. 84 per cent said that they were 'very glad' or 'glad' to have taken part; 15 per cent were 'neutral' and only 1.3 per cent said they were 'sorry' or 'very sorry' to have taken part. 80 per cent of participants thought that there should be more research of this kind, and 74 per cent claimed to have learned something of personal value. In fact, a year after the experiment, Milgram received a letter from one of the participants who said that he had learned how important it was not to harm another person even if this meant disobeying authority.

In the end, Milgram seems to have satisfied himself that the means of his research justified the ends, and he was careful to follow ethical guidelines when events took an unexpected turn. What is more, the majority of his participants seem to have benefited from the experience in the longer term.

Zimbardo (1973) also found himself defending his case after publication of his study. He responded with an assessment of the costs and benefits involved in the research. He acknowledged freely that participants role-playing 'prisoners', even though they were carefully selected for their stability, suffered 'psychological humiliation, anxiety, perhaps a loss of innocence and extremely unpleasant memories' (p. 249). On the benefit side there was an advance in social–psychological knowledge which raised people's consciousness about prison conditions. There were a number of publications and a great deal of publicity which, subsequently, put enormous strain on Zimbardo's time and personal resources.

Like Milgram, Zimbardo *et al.* dealt carefully with the participants after the study using intensive individual interviews, encounter-group sessions and follow-up surveys. They were satisfied that the suffering experienced by 'prisoners' was restricted to the somewhat artificial situation. They also claim that many of the participants felt that the experience had been a valuable source of personal insight.

Zimbardo also felt that some participants benefited from dealing with the moral dilemmas posed by the research findings. (In

Kohlberg's view (1975) this is the best way to raise an individual's level of moral reasoning.) Subsequently, some volunteered to work in local prisons and most became interested in prison reform. They also gained financially, and were able to use the experiences in their college courses. Some also enjoyed the notoriety of appearing in *Life* magazine!

Zimbardo felt that his findings were not artefacts of an unusual research setting but, instead, revealed important forces at work in institutions. Far from being worried by criticism, he asserted that responsible psychologists welcome and expect evaluation of their work and methods as a necessary and desirable part of what they do. Both Zimbardo and Milgram also realised that they were conducting 'socially sensitive research' (see later) and were prepared to take responsibility for the consequences of their findings as far as possible.

Ethical Guidelines in Use

So what is the experience of psychologists in the real world of psychological research and practice? The BPS has guidelines and disciplinary procedures which can be used to consider complaints against its members and these may result in a charge being dismissed or a psychologist being reprimanded, expelled from the Society or encouraged to re-train. This only applies in extreme cases, so how do psychologists handle the less extreme day-to-day problems? In 1995, Lindsay and Colley surveyed 1000 randomly selected members of the BPS and asked them to describe an incident that they, or a colleague, had experienced in the last year or two that was ethically troubling. 172 respondents produced usable returns and these gave 263 incidents. 17 per cent described issues of confidentiality, especially where non-disclosure of information could put another person at risk. 10 per cent of incidents were connected with research and were mainly to do with the issue of informed consent.

Lindsay and Colley thought that applying the ethical guidelines raised one set of dilemmas but they also identified an unforeseen dilemma concerning psychologists' worries about whether they could do an adequate professional job in the face of financial cuts and lack of teaching resources. This, of course, is not covered by any code of ethics. Lindsay and Colley also noted that 37 per cent of the respondents said that they had no ethical dilemmas in their work and query whether this reflects the truth or simply a lack of awareness of ethical issues.

Approaching the real-world situation from another angle, Lindsay (1995) examined the nature of the first 58 complaints reported to BPS investigatory panels in 1993–4 and found that most concerned client-related professional psychology. (Only eight were research related.) This may seem like a small number but it is increasing, and the fact that there were any complaints at all underlines the point that guidelines are only recommendations. Applying them is not always straightforward nor is it any guarantee that psychologists, their clients or research participants will be completely protected. Finally, not all the complaints made against psychologists can be dealt with by the BPS since not all psychologists are members. At the very least, perhaps, potential clients could check that any practising psychologist they may encounter is registered with the BPS as a chartered psychologist (C. Psychol). This will confirm that the psychologist is genuine and properly qualified, and it will allow a client to refer any complaints they may have against the psychologist to the BPS who will investigate and take the necessary action.

Self-assessment Questions

1. Summarise the main points of the BPS guidelines for research with human particicpants and comment on each one.
2. Assess the ethical standing of two pieces of psychological research.
3. Comment on psychologists' everyday experience of ethical issues.

SECTION II   THE WIDER RESPONSIBILITIES OF PSYCHOLOGISTS

In this section, we will consider two of the ways in which psychological research may have wider implications:

- When it is applied in clinical settings.
- When it is into socially-sensitive subject areas.

If one of the main purposes of psychological research is to gain greater understanding of behaviour in order to improve the quality of human life, psychologists must, at some point, put their ideas into practice. The main settings in which they do this are educational, occupational and clinical. Ethical issues raised in psychometric testing are especially relevant in the first two settings, and these are discussed in Chapter 6 along with other controversies surrounding the use of psychometic testing. Here we will concentrate on applications of psychological research in clinical settings, using behaviourist techniques as a specific example, before going on to discuss the possible consequences of carrying out socially-sensitive research.

Applications of Research in Clinical Settings

People seeking help with psychological problems are often especially vulnerable. They may be emotionally upset. Their relationships with others may be under strain and they may be concerned about what seeking help says about their ability to cope. There is also the double handicap of both having a psychological problem and having to deal with other people's attitudes towards it which are not always well-informed, positive or helpful. Furthermore, this vulnerability should lead us to question whether the troubled person would really be able to give informed consent to a therapist.

In an attack on psychotherapy in general, Masson (1992) expressed doubts about whether psychotherapies were effective and concern about the financial, emotional and sexual power therapists could be seen as having over their clients. In defence of psychotherapy, Holmes (1994) argued that psychologists were no better or worse in these respects than other professionals such as medical doctors or lawyers. Nevertheless, he recommends that all types of psychotherapy need regulatory bodies, standards and codes of practice and procedures for expulsion of the minority who do abuse their power. Currently, many different kinds of treatment are available. Clients may be confused about

- the qualifications of who is treating them;
- why certain procedures are being carried out;
- what to do if they have a complaint about any aspect of treatment.

Behavioural Techniques

One group of therapeutic techniques that people may be offered arises from the behaviourist approach to psychology. Behaviourist approaches (often distinguished from non-behavioural psychotherapies) are based on principles of learning gained from research with animals. One of the main assumptions of behaviourists is that many problems are the result of learning maladaptive habits. These are learned in the same way as adaptive behaviour and can be unlearned given the appropriate treatment. In spite of the demonstrable success of this approach, some critics accuse behaviourists of being manipulative, coercive and controlling, conditioning people against their will into behaviour patterns which they would not necessarily choose. How far is this image of the behaviourist psychologist justified?

Some writers find it useful to distinguish between **behaviour therapy** (based on Pavlovian or classical conditioning) and **behaviour modification** (based on Skinnerian or operant conditioning principles). Behaviour therapy includes relatively uncontentious techniques such as systematic desensitisation for phobias and the use of electric alarm blankets for the treatment of persistent nocturnal enuresis. Ethical questions are more likely to be raised where pain or sickness is involved as in **aversion therapy**.

Aversion therapy   A well-known example of the power of a type of behaviour therapy called aversion therapy is provided by Lang and Melamed (1969). (This study is described in connection with applications of animal research, p. 139.) In this case there is little doubt that aversion therapy saved the child's life. It is the means by which it was done that is in question. A more contentious use of aversion therapy is its potential to treat other conditions such as homosexuality and this takes us into the realms of socially-sensitive research (see pp. 126–33).

Token economies   Stated simply, behaviour modification uses the idea that behaviour can be shaped and changed by the controlled use of reinforcement and punishment. One of the best known applications of behaviour modification is the 'Token Economy'.

In 1968, Ayllon and Azrin introduced an economic system into a ward of schizophrenics whereby tokens could be earned for desirable behaviours such as general hygiene, self-care, and work on the ward. Tokens could be saved and exchanged for such things as TV viewing time, cigarettes and sweets, clothes or cosmetics. The principle behind this was that desirable behaviours would increase because they were rewarded. While it was no cure for schizophrenia, the frequency of social and self-care skills in long-stay patients did improve considerably. Not only does the behaviour of participants change, but often, the morale and enthusiasm of staff improves when they begin to see the beneficial effects of their efforts in implementing a programme.

What is ethically problematic about techniques which are so obviously beneficial? Objections centre on four concerns:

1. **The use of punishment or pain.** It has been argued that punishment only has a temporary suppressive effect and, as it produces negative reactions in the learner, it is important to have controls against its use. To guard against the free use of electric shock (such as in aversion therapy), Miron (1968) suggested that psychologists should first try the shock on themselves! This is a form of 'countercontrol' (Skinner 1971). (However, punishment is part of everyday life and to treat problem behaviour without it would not teach the patient much about how to cope in the real world.)

2. **Deprivation.** In some behaviour modification procedures, it is necessary to deprive the experimental participant of reinforcers in order to encourage them to respond. Reinforcement becomes dependent on the appearance of certain behaviours as in token economies. Token economies fell foul of the critics when some of them appeared to infringe basic human rights, for example when attendance at church, food or privacy were made contingent upon the performance of desirable behaviours. While such extreme measures may not be used today, the behaviourists argue that the level of reinforcement on a programme may be higher than that normally experienced by a patient, and that not to use such techniques may deprive that person of the chance of rehabilitation.

3. **Free will.** The criticism that behavioural techniques remove people's freedom to act as they wish is a problem for all deterministic approaches. Radical behaviourists would answer that it is not a question of imposing restrictions where none existed before. Their theoretical position is that all behaviour is controlled. The ethical problem is not whether behaviour should

be controlled but who should presume to take control of another and for what ends. In their eyes, behavioural techniques simply make systematic use of the processes already at work in everyday life and people's alarm at their methods results from recognition of how powerful this can be.

This does not mean that behaviourists are not concerned about the possibility that their methods could be used to exploit others. Accordingly, many behavioural therapists now turn much of the power to the client. For example, in systematic desensitisation the client would construct their own hierarchy of feared situations with the therapist's help and then have considerable control in the pacing of exposure to them. There are also strict codes of conduct for therapists. All these things help towards 'countercontrol'.

If the wider ethical implications of behavioural therapies are considered, then in terms of costs and benefits they fare well. In certain areas of disorder such as sexual dysfunction, enuresis, nervous tics and habit disorders, treatment is very effective. It can alleviate suffering, improve the quality of life and even save lives.

4. **Cure**. Behavioural therapies are often attacked as ethically unsound because they define 'cure' as disappearance of the problem behaviour. (To psychologists who see problem behaviour as a symptom of something more deep-rooted, all the behaviourist has done is to cover the real problem up.) Radical behaviourists can answer this in three ways:

- If it is accepted that the problem is the product of faulty learning, new learning does eradicate the whole problem.
- If the whole problem has not been cured, it should reappear in the form of a new symptom but symptom substitution seems to be comparatively rare.
- If behaviour is determined by experiences in the environment, then problem behaviour is the result of a faulty environment. It is society, not the individual, which needs to change. This is ultimately a political issue raising new ethical concerns about whether people are simply being treated so that they fit in better with an oppressive social system.

Of course, behaviourist techniques are not the only ones available and they are often mixed, to good effect, with other approaches (for example as in cognitive behavioural therapy) to suit the client. In all cases, however, the consequences of cure can be far-reaching and the change in the client may have implications that affect their spouse, family and others.

Conclusion

There are many other types of treatment, not fully discussed here, where still more ethical concerns are important. For example, consider the problems involved in various kinds of biomedical intervention such as electrical stimulation of the brain, the use of psychoactive drugs and psychosurgery. Some would argue that these are strictly in the realm of psychiatry but the boundaries between psychology and psychiatry can be fuzzy especially as the conditions treated manifest themselves psychologically.

Psychological knowledge could not advance without a certain amount of risk both to the researchers and their participants or to clinical psychologists and their patients. If in the end, as Hawks (1981) asserts, psychologists are working towards the ultimate goal of prevention of psychological problems, rather than cure, ethical risks are a relatively small price to pay along the way.

Ethical Issues in Socially Sensitive Research

Writing for the *American Psychologist* in 1988, Sieber and Stanley used the term 'socially sensitive research' to describe:

> . . . studies in which there are potential social consequences or implications, either directly for the participants in research or the class of individuals represented by the research. For example, a study that examines the relative merits of day-care for infants versus full-time care by the mother can have broad social implications and thus can be considered socially sensitive. Similarly, studies aimed at examining the relationship between gender and mathematical ability also have significant social implications.
>
> (p. 49)

As Gross (1992) reminds us 'we should regard every psychology experiment as an ethical situation' (p. 51), but some areas of research, such as those in the quote, pose particular problems. Socially-sensitive research is more likely than most to attract a great deal of interest from psychologists, the media, and hence the general public. There are plenty of examples where psychologists and their families have been threatened (as in the case of some animal researchers) or ostracised (as in the case of researchers into race and intelligence) as a result of their work. Howitt (1991) adds:

> . . . Psychological research touching on important social issues will rarely have a calm passage. Tackling questions which are not simply difficult, but controversial, involving moral as well as other questions, will hardly enamour psychologists to each other, let alone the rest of the community.
>
> (p. 149)

It is understandable, then, if psychologists choose to sidestep the issue altogether by refusing to carry out research of a socially-sensitive nature. However, to avoid such research completely would leave them simply studying 'safe' areas and ignoring the thornier issues where their work could, perhaps, have an important and beneficial effect. Sieber and Stanley say:

> . . . Sensitive research addresses some of society's most pressing issues and policy questions. Although ignoring the ethical issues in sensitive research is not a responsible approach to science, shying away from controversial topics, simply because they are controversial, is also an avoidance of responsibility.
>
> (1988, p. 55)

Examples of Socially Sensitive Research

Psychology is rich in examples of socially sensitive research. Studies of racial or gender differences, child-rearing practices, the impact of aging or health-related issues such as drug abuse or sexual behaviour are just a few examples from many. Milgram and Zimbardo's research, discussed earlier, are also relevant here. Concerning negative social consequences for the individual participants, both researchers felt confident that there had been no long-term negative effects. Indeed, in some cases, change for the better had occurred. However, the studies could be considered to be socially sensitive in the wider effect they had on people who were more generally anxious about the implications of the findings. If ordinary people would do such extraordinarily unpleasant things in research situations what hope was there that any of us would behave humanely in the real world?

Other well-known socially sensitive research includes:

- **Bowlby**'s (1951) view that 'Mother love in infancy and childhood is as important for mental health as are vitamins and proteins for physical health' had a profound effect on social policy concerning child-care. He argued that, ideally, a child up to the age of 5 years, should have the unbroken, loving care of its mother or permanent mother substitute. During World War II, the role of women had changed considerably as they joined the work-force in large numbers to help the war effort. State nursery care helped many of them to cope with the practicalities of single parenthood while their partners were in the forces, or with widowhood if their partners were killed. After the war, many men were unemployed and it could be argued that women were under pressure to hand their jobs over. Bowlby's findings were timely in this respect. Although they undoubtedly did a great deal of good in improving aspects of child-care, they also encouraged the belief that a woman's place was at home with her children. Sadly, the guilt and pressure this has caused both working mothers and fathers continues to this day and child-care facilities in the UK remain inadequate. However successful a mother is at mixing career and home-life, the confusion that persists will probably lead her to feel that wherever a woman's place is, it is probably in the wrong.

- **Freud**'s influence on Western thinking has been profound and many of his ideas have crept into our everyday language. He was one of a number of influential psychologists who emphasised the importance of early experience, especially the role parents played in helping or hindering the infant or child as it moved through various stages of psychosexual development. These ideas placed a huge responsibility on parents who would find themselves wondering what they had done wrong if the child subsequently developed problems. Another influence from Freud's theory has been the perpetuation of the idea that women suffer from 'penis envy'. This resulted in women being seen as incomplete and inferior compared to men and driven to recover their lost penis preferably through giving birth to a male child. Finally there is the possible damage done by emphasising infantile and childhood sexuality which could have us believing that the accounts of some sexually abused children are based on fantasy.

- Any research which links intelligence with **genetic factors** can have far-reaching consequences for different social classes or races. **Burt** used studies of identical twins who had been separated early in life and reared apart to support his ideas that measured intelligence was largely affected by genetics rather than experience. His thinking greatly influenced recommendations made in the Hadow Report (1926) for selection at 11 years old for different types of education, that is in grammar, secondary modern or technical schools. Generations of children have been affected by the so-called 11+ examination even though a controversy has long raged about whether Burt invented some of his data and manipulated it to achieve the desired results. Other psychologists, such as Eysenck (1973) and Jensen (1969), who have argued for a biological basis to differences in IQ test performance, are treading in similarly socially sensitive areas.

Cautionary Notes about Socially Sensitive Research

1. One alarming aspect of socially sensitive research findings is that their influence can be difficult to dislodge even when there is little evidence for them or a wealth of evidence against them. One possible reason for people's immovability in this respect is that research can sometimes fit well with the prevailing *Zeitgeist* (intellectual mood of the times) and so tell people, including psychologists, what they are ready to hear. Their subsequent actions, for example in changing social policy, are then somehow legitimised by scientific research even though the reliability of that research may be less than perfect.

2. On the other side of the coin, psychologists can sometimes interpret socially-sensitive research findings in ways that are not readily accepted. This is particularly likely to happen if the psychologist's (ideally) academic, objective view is not in tune with the institution for which research is being carried out. Levy-Leboyer (1988) illustrates this with an example of a psychological study carried out for the French telephone department into vandalism of public telephones. The telephone company believed most vandalism was caused by young criminals intent on stealing from those payphones that were likely to contain the most money. The psychologists' research gave a different picture.

Instead they suggested that the busiest phones, often due to being full, were most likely to break down and not return money. These were consequently most often damaged because it was the only way people (of all kinds) could express their frustration. The psychologists suggested phone booths should contain maps showing the nearest alternative phone and instructions about where to go for reimbursement. However, the telephone department disagreed with these findings (perhaps because they did not fit with their prevailing views about young vandals). They subsequently invested in strengthening the payphones and introducing a phone-card system.

3. Sieber and Stanley say that although existing ethical principles warn psychologists to be cautious when conducting socially-sensitive research, there is no code of conduct explaining exactly how to be cautious or deal with the consequences. For example, although Milgram and Zimbardo would have realised they were researching into sensitive issues and were ready for some of the consequences, it is debatable whether they were fully prepared for the strength of reaction their findings caused. Mindful of the risks psychologists run in conducting such research, Sieber and Stanley identified ten ethical issues which are especially pertinent in socially sensitive research. In an attempt to help psychologists remain vigilant they also suggested ways in which the issues could cause problems. These are presented in Figure 5.2.

Conclusion

Sieber and Stanley advise that, in general, research psychologists must always be acutely aware of their role in society and work hard to make explicit such things as their theoretical background and limits to the generalisability of their research when they publish it. They should also attempt to keep open clear lines of communication with the media and policymakers in order to minimise distortion or abuse of research findings however difficult this may be.

Scarr (1988) concludes on a similar note. She argues that psychologists cannot afford to avoid socially sensitive research, even if they discover socially uncomfortable things. There is a desperate need, she says, for good studies that highlight, for example, race and gender variables. Her point is that, if we hide from such findings, we will never be in a strong position to tackle any of the inequalities that can be so damaging to certain groups of people. In his well-

FIGURE 5.2
Ethical Issues in Socially Sensitive Research and Reasons to be Cautious

Ethical issue	*Reasons to be cautious*
● Privacy	● The risk here is that some research may be used to shape public policy, e.g. AIDS research could, perhaps, lead to later breaches of privacy through requiring by law that certain people be tested for HIV
● Confidentiality of data	● Breaches of confidentiality about, for example, being found to be HIV-positive could have serious social and economic consequences for the individual due to general lack of understanding about how HIV is transmitted between people. Consider, for example, the consequences of breaching confidentiality of a participant who confesses to having AIDS but not telling their partner
● Sound and valid methodology	● Findings based on unsound or invalid methodology may find their way into the public domain where the flaws and carefully qualified conclusions drawn from them may not be as fully appreciated as they might be between researchers. Such findings may be unwittingly or cynically used to influence public policy (possibly as in the Hadow Report – see text)
● Deception	● This really refers to self-deception in which research may lead people to believe in a stereotype formed from hearing about certain findings, e.g. hearing that boys are more able at maths than girls could lead girls into deceiving themselves that this is generally true of all girls including themselves
● Informed consent	● It is always important for the researcher to obtain fully-informed consent from participants but this is especially important in socially sensitive research.
● Justice and equitable treatment	● Research interests, techniques or findings should not result in some people being treated unfairly, e.g. through creating unfavourable prejudices about them or withholding something potentially beneficial, such as a particular experimental drug or educational technique, from some but not others
● Scientific freedom	● This must be weighed against the interests of wider society. Many scientists agree that science advances through open discussion and competition of ideas. Censorship of scientific activity is usually thought to be unacceptable but there are some kinds of research which should be, and are, carefully monitored

Figure 5.2 *continued over*

• 'Ownership' of data	• This is a complex and largely unresolved issue which involves trying to decide who can have access to scientific data. Scientists generally welcome openness, but in the wrong hands or if poorly understood, certain findings, especially socially sensitive ones, could be potentially explosive and used to manipulate, coerce or subjugate people
• Values and epistemology of social scientists	• This refers to scientists' theoretical beliefs (and personal beliefs) about human nature and how best to understand it. Psychologists must recognise that their research is not value free and that this may be reflected in the kinds of research question they ask, how they conduct research and how they interpret findings. To even ask the question 'What is the effect of race on IQ?' is to assume that race, IQ and any connection between them are of importance. The research by Levy-Leboyer, described in the text, illustrates how different values can cause people from an academic or business background to carry out and/or interpret research differently
• Risk/benefit ratio	• While most people would agree that it is unacceptable to carry out research where the costs outweigh the benefits, risks and benefits may be that much harder to assess accurately in socially sensitive research so it is more than usually important that they are carefully considered

Source: Adapted from Sieber and Stanley (1988).

known book *The Social Animal*, Aronson (1992) ends a brief discussion of 'the morality of discovering unpleasant things' (p. 422) by agreeing that such research should not stop or be conducted secretly. Instead, he recommends that the public are carefully educated about socially sensitive research findings so that they are empowered to be vigilant about their abuse.

Howitt (1991) is, perhaps, less optimistic and more cautious. He agrees that it is important for psychologists to be well-intentioned and careful, but thinks that they should recognise their limitations. He argues that psychologists can only give us a particular view of human nature and that such a view is affected by historical times and prevailing social values. For these reasons, it is impossible for psychological research to be objective, value-free and somehow capable of revealing the absolute truth. Its basis in research may give the illusion of objectivity but, ultimately, it may be no more valid than any other way of interpreting events. Psychologists should not, therefore, seek to impose a collective professional view on others about socially sensitive issues from a supposed scientific 'high ground'. He argues that psychologists are not yet in a position to influence social policy which is probably why there is no recognised set of principles to guide socially-sensitive research. Nevertheless, he senses positive change ahead as psychologists become more aware of their wider social responsibilities and concludes by saying that:

. . . With the changes in the priorities of psychology, pressure may increase for a new sort of ethic – a social ethic, rather than an individual one orientated towards the individual research participant. (p. 161)

Self-assessment Questions

1. What is meant by the term 'socially sensitive research'?
2. Identify two research areas which could be thought of as socially sensitive and explain your choice.
3. Outline three cautions that psychologists conducting socially sensitive research should observe.
4. What are the views of Scarr, Aronson and Howitt on socially sensitive research in psychology?

SECTION III PSYCHOLOGICAL RESEARCH AND THE USE OF ANIMALS

Introduction

If we consider the strength of feeling that surrounds the use of animals in research, it can come as a surprise to learn that the existing legislation (Animals: Scientific Procedures Act 1986), which protects living vertebrates, is the first since 1876. During the 1980s, the promise of this new legislation gave a fresh impetus to debates about the use of animals in research and the arguments rage on to this day in psychology as well as in other disciplines.

It is important to be aware that most psychologists do not carry out research with animals, and neither are they involved in using animals for product-testing, farming or exhibition in zoos. In addition, not all animal research in psychology involves intrusive experimental methods. These points are not meant to imply that psychologists can dodge their responsibilities to animals and, as we will see, they have not tried to do so. Nevertheless, psychological research with animals has received its share of adverse publicity and the reader is encouraged to examine some of the readily available anti-vivisectionist and animal-liberation literature and to consider their claims in the light of what is presented here.

The following questions will be addressed:

1. What kinds of research do psychologists conduct with animals and what is its incidence?
2. What practical issues are raised by animal research in psychology?
3. What ethical issues are involved?
4. How are psychologists attempting to resolve these ethical issues?

The Type and Incidence of Animal Research in Psychology

One way to test the type and incidence of animal research is to survey psychological research publications. Accordingly, in the US, Coile and Miller (1984) reviewed all the articles published in the American Psychological Society's journals in the preceding five years. Of the 608 articles examined, only 7 per cent reported research primarily on animals, and no instances of the kind of research condemned by animal rights campaigners were found. Of course, published research does not cover all research but the authors still maintained that there is far more abuse of animals on farms and in zoos than in any research facility.

In the UK, Thomas and Blackman (1991) used a different method. They surveyed all the 67 university and polytechnic departments known to offer first degree courses in psychology and compared their findings with similar data collected by the British Psychological Society in 1977. Sixty-two of the departments responded to their questionnaire. Between 1977 and 1989 the numbers of vertebrates used in these departments dropped from 8536 to 3708 – a decline of 43 per cent – and the number of departments using animals dropped from 39 to 29. There was also a sharp decrease in experimental work on animals and a corresponding increase in observational studies. (As a matter of interest, in 1989, 92 per cent of the animals used were rats or mice, 6 per cent were pigeons or other birds and 1 per cent were monkeys.) Thomas and Blackman call this decline in animal research disconcerting since animal models have proved so useful in psychology. They add that it is causing 'a fundamental shift in psychology's subject base' (p. 208). They doubt whether this is due to new legislation or the actions of pressure-groups. Instead they suggest it is due to a shift in research interests. Indeed, Furnham and Pinder (1990) reported that although young people's attitudes to animal experimentation were generally positive they were unwilling to do such research themselves. Thomas and Blackman conclude that undergraduates should be exposed to a positive and reasoned case in favour of animal research.

A quick look through any general psychology text book will yield a wealth of examples of the kinds of animal research that interest psychologists. See, for example, work by Blakemore and Cooper (1970), Brady (1958), Harlow (1959), Lorenz (1937), Savage-Rumbaugh (1990) and Goodall (1978). These examples cover a wide variety of methods and research interests, ranging from experimental analysis of brain function through to social behaviour in the natural environment, and all have made important contributions to psychology.

Practical Issues in Animal Research

On what Practical Grounds do Psychologists Justify their Use of Animals?

Broadbent (1961) justifies the use of animals in psychological research in three main ways:

1. If it is assumed, as in Darwin's view, that all species are biologically related to each other through evolution, then it can be argued that their behaviour patterns are also related. Just as human anatomy (for example the nervous system) can be understood by reference to other species, so can human behaviour. In many respects, humans differ from other animals in complexity only, so much can be learned about them by reference to other species.
2. Many laboratory experiments that are carried out on animals would not be permitted with humans for ethical reasons. Examples are controlled interbreeding experiments (for research into genetic correlates of behaviour), various kinds of deprivation (social, maternal, perceptual, sensory), and brain and tissue research.

3. One of the standard techniques of science is to study simpler systems in order to understand more complex ones. If we accept the notion of continuity between animal species (as in 1) then studies of the behaviour and nervous systems of animals could reveal a great deal about humans.

To these three points, two more can be added:

4. Animals make convenient subjects for several reasons. They reproduce rapidly so the effects of early experience and selective breeding can quickly be assessed. Heredity and environment can be precisely controlled in nature–nurture research, and emotional involvement with animal subjects is less likely than with humans so the experimenter's objectivity is improved.
5. Animal experiments can be useful in the early stages of research as a means of generating hypotheses for subsequent testing on humans. Alternatively, research findings which are only suggestive or correlational in nature with humans could be tested experimentally on animals in order to isolate cause and effect.

On what Practical Grounds can Animal Research be Opposed?

Practical objections have two main themes. The first concerns whether it is reasonable to transfer (extrapolate) findings from animals to humans and the second concerns objections about the nature of the research methods used.

Anti-extrapolationists emerge from a number of camps.

1. Some argue that the human condition is unique, that is that humans are qualitatively different from animals as well as quantitatively different. **Humanistic psychologists** subscribe to this view as do those who disagree with Darwin's theory of evolution or who object on religious grounds. Koestler (1970) wrote that to transfer findings from rats to humans was to commit the sin of **ratomorphism**, that is to see humans and rats as being very alike when in fact they are very different.
2. Others argue that there is a danger that researchers may be unable to adopt an objective view of their animal subjects so that they attribute them with human qualities for which there is no real evidence – this is known as **anthropomorphism**.

3. Animal-rights campaigners may well draw on cases where extrapolation of findings about drugs from one species to another has been inappropriate. The implication of this is that, if physiological reactions to the same chemical differ so much between species, how can we be confident in transferring findings about behaviour from one to another?
4. Some would argue that unique human attributes such as language and the relatively greater openness to learning and flexibility of human behaviour make comparisons between humans and animals less valid.
5. Finally, it could be argued that the need to extrapolate could be avoided altogether if psychologists made full use of all the opportunities open to them. For example there are plenty of cases of naturally occurring deprivation in infants and children so why subject laboratory animals to deprivation (as in Harlow's research with monkeys)?

Regarding research methods, there is a pay-off to be considered between laboratory-based research and field research. One objection to laboratory experimentation concerns the degree of control exerted over events. There is no doubt that the precision thus achieved is a strength of the method, but it is also its greatest weakness because it leads us to doubt whether laboratory experiments have **ecological validity**. In other words, we should question whether the results would be meaningful in the real world. Field experiments might have greater ecological validity but, although realism is gained, control is lost. It is also tempting to think that studying animals in their natural environment is more acceptable than laboratory-based research, but Cuthill (1991) expressed concern that some techniques of field research could, if not properly controlled, seriously threaten the survival of a species, for example where animals are captured and recaptured for tagging or when decoy or dummy animals are used to test the animals' responses or when the mere presence of observers is disturbing. Even unintrusive naturalistic observation could affect certain species so it needs to be carried out with the utmost sensitivity.

Practical Applications of Animal Research in Psychology

In 1985, Neal Miller published a detailed article describing research on animals which he considerd to be valuable. This was, at least in part, a response to various animal-rights groups who, he said, could mislead people with 'grossly false statements' about animal research. Rather than help animals, he said their actions impede research which is beneficial to both animals and humans. He suggested that their energies could be more usefully directed towards fighting for the conservation of endangered species or towards raising funds for refuges for abandoned or mistreated animals.

Miller noted the many ways in which animal research has benefited animals. For example, a better understanding of the behaviour of animals which damage crops or carry disease has led to the development of deterrents (for example specially designed 'scarecrows', Conover 1982) thus doing away with the need for lethal control. Animal research has also helped in the preservation of endangered species and has done much to promote the health of domestic pets. It has also led to improvements in animal husbandry, animal welfare in zoos and on farms, and in conservation of animal species and their habitats.

From a psychological point of view, research into animal learning stands out as being of great practical use to humans. Some examples will serve to illustrate this contribution:

- *Treatment of nocturnal enuresis.* In 1938, Mowrer and Mowrer used principles derived from Pavlov's experiments on classical conditioning in dogs to develop an alarm blanket for the treatment of persistent night-time bedwetting (nocturnal enuresis) in children. Apart from the obvious benefits to be had from the disappearance of the enuresis, Mowrer and Mowrer found that the children improve in other ways too. Teachers, for example, noted improvements in various aspects of such children's personality and behaviour even though they were unaware that the children had been enuretic.
- *Life saving.* Pigeons have been trained to detect coloured life rafts against the background of the sea using operant conditioning techniques derived from Skinner's work (Simmons, 1981). Pigeons can be trained to peck discs of different colours to earn food rewards and they will generalise this training to new situations. In tests, their keen vision enabled them to detect 85 per cent of life-raft targets compared to the 50 per cent detected by helicopter crews.
- *Behaviour change in educational settings.* Teaching machines, programmed learning and token economies, all derived from

operant conditioning principles, have been successfully used in educational settings.

- *Behaviour change in clinical settings.* (See Section II.) Walker (1984) draws a distinction between behaviour therapy (based on classical conditioning), and behaviour modification (based on operant conditioning). Both are derived from experiments using animals and have been used to explain and treat some kinds of mental disorder.

  The classic case of Little Albert (Watson and Rayner, 1920) who was conditioned to fear a white rat, spawned a variety of behaviour therapy techniques for the treatment of phobias including systematic desensitisation and flooding (implosion). Another technique derived from classical conditioning is aversion therapy. Lang and Melamed (1969) described how this had been used to save the life of a nine-month-old baby who was malnourished and dehydrated through persistent ruminative vomiting (regurgitation and rechewing of food). After all other treatments had failed, the therapists trained the infant to develop a conditioned aversion to vomiting by applying a series of one second long electric shocks to his calf whenever he showed signs of regurgitation. The infant learned not to vomit in order to avoid the shock, and subsequently he made a complete recovery.

  Behaviour modification also has many applications in clinical settings. In one case described by Isaacs, Thomas and Goldiamond (1969), a schizophrenic man, who had been mute for years, was gradually trained to speak again by using behaviour shaping procedures with chewing gum as a reinforcer. Token economies used in clinical settings are another good example of operant conditioning principles in practice.

- *Animal helpers.* Pfaffenberger (1963) was able to improve on the efficiency of guide dogs for the blind by selective breeding and by applying research findings concerning the most sensitive periods for learning in a puppy's life. Willard (1985) has trained Capuchin monkeys to be home helps for disabled and paralysed people. Monkeys can learn to serve drinks with a straw, place a magazine on a reading stand, open and close doors, operate lifts and carry out a variety of other tasks for the reward of food or fruit juice dispensed by the disabled person.

Miller concludes that there is a strong financial and moral case for continuing to back animal research and others would agree. The work of Lorenz (1937) on imprinting, for example, is linked to the well-known work by Harlow (1959) on deprivation of maternal contact in infant monkeys. More recent developments from this have led to improvements in the care of premature babies for whom contact comfort is now known to be an important factor in improving their survival rate. Green (1994) uses the examples of diseases that are on the increase and whose nature and progress could be better understood through animal research. Alzheimer's disease is one such condition which is increasing in incidence due to growing numbers of elderly people. It leads to long-term degeneration and affects not only the sufferer but the sufferer's family and carers. AIDS is another example where the effects are not confined to the affected individual. Although these are, strictly speaking, physical rather then psychological conditions, their impact reaches beyond the physical to psychological and social aspects of a person's life.

Ethical Aspects of Animal Experimentation

The view that all animal research should be banned is an example of what Michael Eysenck (1994) calls 'moral absolutism'. Another moral absolutist view would be that there should be no restrictions whatsoever on animal research. Both of these extremes would be difficult to live with and both seem to close the door to further debate. This is why psychologists often find themselves preferring 'moral relativism', that is the view that, after weighing up various arguments, some research is permissible and some is not.

Adopting a position of moral relativism, in 1985, the British Psychological Society and Experimental Psychology Society jointly issued some guidelines (most recent edition 1993) to assist in the planning of experiments on animals. In general, they say researchers have an 'obligation to avoid, or at least minimise, discomfort to all living animals.' The guidelines are summarised in Figure 5.3. As we saw in the earlier discussion of ethical issues in research with humans, these are only guidelines and they can only take us so far. There will often come a point where professional judgement has to be made, especially where there are 'fuzzy' areas (for example whether in some research the 'ends justify the means'). Some of the main contenders in recent debates are Gray, Ryder and Singer.

FIGURE 5.3
A Summary of Guidelines for the Use of Animals in Research

1. *Regard for the law.* New legislation following the Government bill 'Animals (Scientific Procedures)' was passed in 1986. Its purpose is to control the use of animals in all kinds of scientific research including psychology, and it is the first review of such legislation since 1876. In the UK, The Universities Federation for Animal Welfare (UFAW) Handbook (1987) was, until now, the only set of guidelines in general use. It is the duty of all animal researchers to be familiar with the most recent legislation and abide by it

2. *Ethical considerations.* If the research necessitates that animals should be confined, constrained or stressed in any way, the experimenter must be sure that the means justify the ends. If the knowledge to be gained is trivial, alternatives should be favoured

3. *Knowing the species.* In order to avoid distressing animals unduly, the experimenter should have a sound understanding of how the species being studied responds to different situations. Some species may suffer more from a particular research situation than others, in which case the one least likely to suffer should be preferred. In any case, distressed animals do not make good subjects so it is in the experimenter's best interests to care for them properly

4. *Numbers of animals.* Experimenters should have a sound knowledge of experimental design such that the minimum number of animals can be used to maximum effect. Statisticians may be able to advise on techniques of analysis which can give meaningful results from the fewest number of subjects

5. *Endangered species.* For obvious reasons, endangered species should not be used unless the research is a serious attempt at conservation

6. *Animal suppliers.* Experimenters should take care to use reputable suppliers so that breeding, housing and transport of animals is handled competently. If animals have to be

trapped in the wild then it should be done as humanely and as painlessly as possible

7. *Caging and social environment.* This should take into account the social habits of the species. Some are distressed by being isolated, others will be distressed by being caged together

8. *Fieldwork.* Researchers observing animals in the wild must disturb them as little as possible otherwise their breeding patterns may be upset and their survival threatened. If capture is necessary, for marking or attaching transmitters, then a good knowledge of what the species can tolerate is necessary. Capture and recapture may be too stressful for the animal and certain kinds of marking intolerable

9. *Studies of aggression and predation including infanticide.* Even though pain and injury may occur to animals in the wild, this is little excuse for staging it in the lab. so any research into aggression and predation should be done through field studies. If staging of encounters is absolutely necessary, then the use of models or animals behind glass screens should be considered. In any case numbers should be kept to a minimum

10. *Motivation.* In some experiments, animals may be motivated to behave by being deprived of food. Again, the needs of individual species should be understood. What amounts to a short period of deprivation for one could be intolerable to another. In addition, unchecked food intake is harmful to some animals

11. *Aversive stimuli and stressful procedures.* These procedures are illegal unless the researcher has a Home Office licence and other relevant certificates. To get these the researcher has to justify the method, show that other techniques are unsuitable and show that suffering is kept to a minimum. It must be demonstrated that the animals' suffering is justifiable in terms of the scientific contribution of the research

12. *Surgical and pharmacological procedures.* Again a Home Office licence and the necessary certification is required. The researcher must be experienced in this field and be able

to train others appropriately. The researcher must know how to use anaesthesia techniques and how to prevent post-operative infection in vertebrates. If drugs are to be used, the researcher must be aware of their behavioural effects and toxicity levels and should conduct pilot studies where these are unknown

13. *Anaesthesia, analgesia and euthanasia.* A Home Office licence and certification is also necessary here. The researcher must know how to use anaesthesia techniques and analgesics (post operatively). If a subject suffers severe and enduring pain, euthanasia, as set in the UFAW handbook, should be used

14. *Independent advice.* If the researcher is in any doubt about an animal's condition during the research, the advice of an expert should be sought. Ideally this would be a qualified veterinary surgeon with no vested interest in the research

15. In general researchers have an 'obligation to avoid, or at least minimise, discomfort to all living animals'.

Source: A summary of the joint proposals of the British Psychological Society and the Experimental Psychology Society, most recent edition 1993.

- Gray (1991) makes the case that to unnecessarily inflict suffering is wrong, nevertheless we sometimes have a special duty to protect our own species. This duty starts with our closest kin and then spreads to other humans and then to other species. He argues that the resulting behaviour is at least partly biologically-based.
- This obligation to our own species creates a perplexing imbalance of interests. For example, it is possible to think of a number of cases where great pain and suffering in humans could be avoided if experiments (even painful ones) were carried out on animals.
- Although Gray accepts that some procedures could cause such immense suffering to animals that they should never be done, he still maintains that we have a moral justification to do other research where the ends justify the means. The dilemma comes in deciding at which point this is true.

Arguing against animal research:

- **Ryder** (1990) attacked Gray's views as 'speciesist' (discrimination and exploitation based upon a difference between species), and aligns it with racism and sexism.
- **Singer** (1991) supported Ryder and added that, although there could be a biological basis to speciesism, as Gray had suggested, this did not excuse us from our moral obligations to other species as we are not bound to behave according to our biological make-up.

Towards a Resolution of the Debate

A number of issues have been raised in an attempt to contribute to a resolution of this debate:

1. Costs and Benefits

Bateson (1986) says that costs and benefits of animal research should be considered by people on both sides of the debate. He suggests that a committee made up of research scientists, animal welfare representatives and disinterested parties should consider three important issues in deciding whether a research proposal should be accepted. (Although these proposals relate to medical research they can easily be related to psychology.) The issues are:

- certainty of medical benefit;
- the quality of the research;
- the degree of animal suffering involved.

If the first two are high and the third low, then the research would probably be permitted. See Figure 5.4. The committee's most important function would be in deciding how to proceed in different circumstances, for example when animal suffering was likely to be high but the quality of research and the certainty of medical benefit were also high.

2. Animal Suffering

At this point in the debate we are still skirting issues such as how we assess the degree to which an animal suffers in a research. Bateson

FIGURE 5.4
The Bateson Model

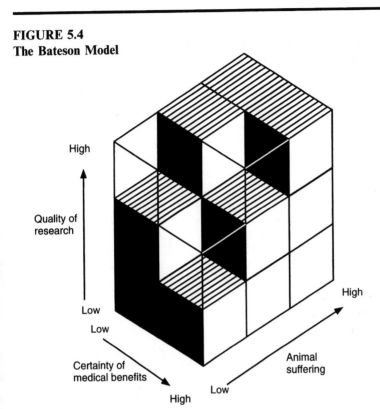

Source: Bateson (1986), with permission.

(1991, 1992) again attempted to resolve this. He used findings from the Institute of Medical Ethics working party's investigations into animal suffering to develop several criteria to help researchers to judge whether the species they intended to study could feel pain. In summary, these are:

- Does the animal have anatomical, biochemical and physiological mechanisms similar to those in a human that are known to be related to the experience of pain?

- When stimulated in particular ways, does the animal behave in a similar way to humans who are thought to be in pain?
- Do analgesics (painkillers) alter this behaviour?

By comparing various species on these criteria, Bateson arrived at the conclusion that insects probably do not feel pain but that animals on the same evolutionary level as fish and octopuses and above probably do. If this is the case, we are then left with the problem of pitting animal and human suffering against each other.

3.   Sentiency

Offering an alternative criterion to 'suffering', Ryder (1991) suggests that 'sentiency' should be the basis of our decisions. (By sentiency he means that a creature is capable of 'sensing', feeling and having consciousness.) Unlike Bateson, however, Ryder is not prepared to compromise and thinks that sentient animals should not be used in research at all.

4.   Deservingness

Green (1994) offers a further consideration, that is, how 'deserving' humans might be in benefiting from animal research. He gives a range of examples to illustrate different grades of deservingness. (Note that, in all these cases, animal research could help us to understand and alleviate human suffering but in none of them are animals responsible for the human's plight.) Green's examples are concerned with:

- Problems that seem to be self-inflicted such as in smoking and lung-disease;
- Problems arising from how human society is organised, for example in ways that encourage problems such as stress-related disorders or depression. Such problems are self-inflicted in a wider sense;
- Disorders that are not self-inflicted, for example Alzheimer's disease.

Unfortunately, all of the four considerations described raise further problems. In Bateson's model, for example, quality of research design may be relatively easy to judge but assessment of animal suffering and certainty of medical benefit is much more difficult. Similarly, there are problems in deciding how to judge suffering, sentiency and deservingness and we are not yet able to do so with real certainty. However, if animal research is halted until we can decide, the consequences could be catastrophic and we would find ourselves back in a position of moral absolutism. Morton (1992) suggests a compromise in that reports of research using animals always include accounts of any anticipated or unforeseen adverse effects so that they can be avoided or minimised in future research. Morton realises that this leaves researchers vulnerable to attack but thinks that openness allows for broader consent from people who are not engaged in research.

Closing the Gap between Animals and Humans

The arguments outlined so far focus on seeking dividing lines between species so that we can continue with research. Dawkins (1993) is critical of such approaches and calls them 'regrettable'. She says they support the idea of the 'discontinuous mind' which promotes the view that there is a yawning gulf between humans and others species, even closely related ones such as gorillas. Dawkins and others prefer to work towards closing the perceived gaps between species thus making animal research less acceptable. Vines (1993, 1994) agrees with Dawkins and adds that some sort of consciousness in both birds and mammals is discernible through their behaviour, but its role and nature remain a 'profound mystery' (p. 31). This mystery needs to be unravelled so that we can re-examine our conventional exploitative relationship with other animals.

One consequence of such approaches is the *Great Ape Project* – the brainchild of Professor Singer (see Singer, 1993; Singer and Cavalieri, 1993). Singer is supported by a group of 34 biologists, philosophers and writers whose purpose is to bring the great apes (gorillas, chimpanzees and orang-utans) into the human fold and give them the same moral rights including protection under the law. Three principles have been derived and these make up the Declaration of Great Apes:

- The right to life;
- Protection of individual liberty;
- Prohibition of torture.

Naturally, not all human rights extend to the great apes because of their different interests, but even to acknowledge those listed above would mean an end to the use of great apes in experimentation and as exhibits in zoos. In support of this, Singer quotes research into chimpanzee behaviour by Goodall (1978) and into chimpanzee language by Savage-Rumbaugh (1990), both of which help to close the gap. (Indeed, humans share 98.4 per cent of their DNA with both the common and pygmy chimp, a little more than with the gorilla.) Ironically, it is research with great apes that is likely to help the *Great Ape Project* along, and if we ever arrive at a solution we then have the problem of what to do with the research animals. As BBC's Horizon programme 'Chimp Talk' (1993) showed, the aging Washoe will need sensitive care for the rest of her life. The best that can now happen is that research with great apes is phased out and that the reasoning behind this leads to the phasing out of other animal research as well.

Conclusion

We have seen that any kind of animal research, whether it is experimental or naturalistic, can affect animals in undesirable ways, yet to stop all animal research could be detrimental to both humans and animals. There are some alternatives to the use of animals in medical research, such as tissue research and in vitro techniques, but much of the content does not apply to psychological research which tends to focus on the intact, living individual. There is some scope for computer simulations of behaviour, particularly in the field of cognition, but again these do not suit all areas of enquiry.

Finally, it is worth considering the implications of the rationale which ultimately underlies all animal research: that human life is more valuable than animal life. A dangerous extension of this rationale is to argue that some human lives such as those of the terminally-ill, the intellectually-impaired and life prisoners, are less valuable than others. During World War II, unscrupulous scientists used the 'value of life' argument to justify research on prisoners, and sometimes their own military forces, into surgical procedures, germ warfare and human endurance. Ironically, some of the findings from this research could prove immensely useful to humankind but the means by which it was gained are so repugnant that it is unlikely that they will ever be released. The dilemma about animal research remains and, as there are few viable alternatives at present, it is likely to be with us for some time.

Self-assessment Questions

1. Outline practical arguments for and against the use of animals in psychological research.
2. Give three examples of animal research which have been of benefit to humans.
3. List 10 of the 15 ethical guidelines on animal research issued by the BPS.
4. Outline the views of Gray, Ryder and Singer on animal research.
5. Comment on the worth of 'cost–benefit analysis', suffering, sentiency and deservingness in helping to resolve ethical questions about animal research.
6. Describe some of the ways in which psychologists have tried to close the gap between animals and humans.
7. What alternatives are there to animal research?

FURTHER READING

S. Fairbairn and G. Fairbairn (1987) (eds), *Psychology, Ethics and Change* (London: Routledge & Kegan Paul).
R. D. Gross (1995) *Themes, Issues and Debates in Psychology* (London: Hodder & Stoughton) ch. 10.

WHAT HAVE YOU GOT ?

Controversial Applications of Psychological Research

6

At the end of this chapter you should be able to:

1. explain what is meant by the terms 'advertising' and 'propaganda';
2. outline some of the findings from the Yale studies of persuasion and describe two more recent models of persuasion;
3. describe some of the persuasion techniques used by advertisers and propagandists;
4. consider some ways in which people can resist persuasion;
5. consider the ethics of persuasion;
6. provide examples of 'psywar' research;
7. explain why 'psywar' research is such a contentious area;
8. explain the term 'psychometric testing' and say what it is used for;
9. describe some examples of psychometric tests; and
10. consider some of the controversies surrounding the uses of psychometric testing.

Introduction

There is an increasing awareness within the psychological community and amongst the general public of the power of psychological knowledge to affect people's lives and bring about change. As we have seen in connection with clinical applications of research and with animal research (see the previous chapter) this knowledge can be of great benefit to people. This chapter considers two further areas of psychology where the application of psychological knowledge is particularly controversial. The first section examines the application of psychological research to advertising, propaganda and warfare, and the second section considers controversies surrounding the use of psychometric tests (such as those used to measure intelligence or personality). In each case, there is great potential for good but also for harm. Psychologists are in a strong position to let people know about these influences so that they can understand what is happening and make informed decisions for themselves about how to act.

SECTION I   ADVERTISING, PROPAGANDA AND WARFARE

Advertising and Propaganda

Advertisers and propagandists are both in the business of persuasion. They have a great deal in common in terms of the techniques they use to persuade although their underlying motives may be different. In addition, they are both phenomena of the twentieth century, cashing in on the growth of mass communication. 'Advertising' is a term usually applied to attempts at 'mass-selling' of products, services, information or ideas via the mass-media. The term 'propaganda' became widespread during World War I and, in most people's minds, it conjures up images of being fed biased ideas through the use of lies, manipulation and deception. Pratkanis and Aronson (1991) give a wider definition. They say it is:

> ... mass suggestion or influence, through the manipulation of symbols and the psychology of the individual. Propaganda is the communication of a point of view with the ultimate goal of having the recipient of the appeal come to 'voluntarily' accept this position as if it were his or her own. (p. 9)

Not all propagandists are necessarily dishonest or malevolent. Some of them firmly believe in the worth of their message and look on their attempts to persuade as helpful to others. For example, there is the view that education is a form of propaganda. Through the National Curriculum, we are, after all, giving schoolchildren a particular body of knowledge which has been deemed worthwhile. Certain religious groups who try to persuade others to join them might also consider their actions to be in people's best interest. However, in both these cases, the message is one-sided. Pratkanis and Aronson urge us to remember that not all persuasion qualifies as propaganda. Some persuasion comes about through open, balanced and honest debate from two or more different viewpoints in which case it is educational in the true sense.

We are bombarded daily with attempts to persuade us to buy a product, vote a certain way, adopt a particular health behaviour or make donations to charity. Persuasion, in all its forms, is a part of modern life and the explosion in communications means that we now live in a world that is so 'message dense' that our limited capacity, information-processing, cognitive systems are over-loaded. At the same time, people are growing more knowledgeable and cynical about others' attempts to persuade. We can all think of examples of misleading advertisements, dishonest politicians, unnecessary health scares or cases where charity funds have disappeared. Knowing this, advertisers and propagandists are faced with having to develop ever more ingenious ways of attracting our attention and changing our behaviour. The existence of campaign managers, image consultants, PR companies and market research organisations are testimony to how seriously persuasion is taken these days. It is big business and it pays.

Techniques of Persuasion

Immediately after World War II, prompted by an interest in wartime propaganda and persuasion, the US Government gave its support to an extensive programme of research at Yale University. Amongst the questions the government wanted to answer were 'Are some messages more persuasive than others?' and 'Are some people more persuasible than others?' The psychologists at Yale accordingly developed the 'communication model of persuasion'. This model views persuasive communications as depending on the action of four main variables at different stages in the communication process. The model can be summed up as asking 'Who says what by what means to whom?' The variables are:

- Communicator variables;
- Message variables;
- Channel variables;
- Audience variables.

In any persuasive communication, these variables exert differing amounts of influence on the persuasion process. Persuasion can succeed or break down because of any one of these or through the combined action of more than one. It is worth looking briefly at some of the early research into this model because of its important influence on later work.

Communicator Variables

These are often relatively superficial characteristics of the communicator, for example:

- Communicator **credibility**. In a simple test of this. Hovland and Weiss (1951) asked participants to read an article advocating the building of nuclear powered submarines. (This was before they actually existed.) Some participants were told that the message they were reading was by the respected physicist J. R. Oppenheimer, others were told the message was from the Russian newspaper *Pravda*. Oppenheimer was seen as a more credible source to these participants who were consequently more persuaded to his view.
- **Physical attractiveness**, **expertise**, **trustworthiness** and **prestige** also seem to be important communicator variables and, at times, these can over-ride the credibility of the message. Advertisers know this when they employ celebrities to help sell their products even if the connection is tenuous. (At the time of writing (April 1996), Liz McColgan is appearing regularly on our television screens promoting Shredded Wheat. The timing is no accident. She has just won the London Marathon.)

Message Variables

The content of persuasive messages has been varied in a number of ways, for example to induce fear, to include one or two-sided arguments and to contain repetition:

- Leventhal (1970) found that **fear-arousal** could aid persuasion but only if it were handled carefully. Too much fear can cause people to 'switch off'. A recent example in the UK, which follows Leventhal's recommendations, concerns the campaign to promote 'safe sex' as a protection against AIDS. The message must arouse some fear by making people feel they really are at risk. It must also make it clear that failure to follow the given advice could result in dire consequences. Having thus gained people's attention and worried them sufficiently, it is then vital to offer them a 'do-able' response (that is, always use a condom) which will reduce the fear. Persuasion is then more likely.

- Hovland *et al.* (1949) published a study reporting the effects of **one or two-sided messages** on American soldiers who were still involved in World War II. Germany had been defeated but the Pacific war against Japan looked set to continue for some time. In these circumstances it was necessary to convince the soldiers of the struggle ahead. Some were given a one-sided message stressing Japan's strength. Others heard a two-sided message which was the same as the one-sided message but included arguments about Japan's weaknesses. Research such as this tends to show that, if people are already broadly in agreement with a message, a one-sided argument is more persuasive. If the recipients of the message disagree, a two-sided message is more effective in persuading them towards the opposite view. Overall, though, group averages show no differences.

- In *Mein Kampf* ('My Struggle', 1925), Adolf Hitler combined the power of the one-sided message and **repetition** when he wrote of the importance of repeating slogans and never allowing contradictory messages to intervene. Indeed, more recent psychological research by Zajonc (1968) has shown how repetition can lead to liking. He calls this the 'mere exposure effect' and there are many examples of this in advertising. Repetition of brand names during commercials is shown to be effective in people's purchasing patterns when they choose familiar products over equally good but less familiar ones. During election campaigns, political candidates make sure they are in the public eye as much as possible. However, it is important to guard against over-exposure and causing people to become irritated. Repetition works best if people are not paying too much attention to the message. If they are likely to pay closer attention, repetition with variation works well and guards against boredom. The Gold Blend coffee adverts which weave a mini soap-opera around coffee-drinking are a good example of this.

Channel Variables

These concern which medium is used to convey a message, for example TV, video, newspapers, magazines, radio, or mail shots:

- **Audio** and **visual** messages depend more on making an immediate, if superficial, impact. In practice, this means that the characteristics of the communicator (credibility, attractiveness and so forth) come to the fore. They can distract the recipient away from the message making its content less important.
- If the message is **written** it allows for more careful thought and checking so the quality of the arguments is more important. When Kennedy and Nixon were battling for election to the US presidency in the 1960s, Kennedy appeared many times on TV looking tanned and relaxed. Nixon, on the other hand, looked pale and troubled. Although it was generally felt that, on paper, Nixon's arguments were sounder and more compelling, Kennedy still won by a narrow margin.

Audience Variables

These include individual differences such as intelligence, personality, self-esteem and gender, and studies of their effects give very mixed findings. Clearly they do not operate in isolation from each other, and they can affect all or some of the stages in the persuasion process differently. Here is a selection of the findings:

- Greater verbal intelligence seems to be linked to greater persuasion if the message is complex and sound, and less persuasion if the message is simple and flawed.
- Some studies have shown a negative relationship between persuasibility and self-esteem but others (for example Rhodes and Wood, 1992) think people with moderate self-esteem are more persuasible. They are not so distracted by the wish to make a good impression that they will not listen, neither are they so sure of themselves that they are immovable.
- Bless *et al.* (1990) discovered that people in a good mood were more likely than people in a bad mood, to be swayed by superficial persuasive messages. People in a bad mood, however, could still be persuaded but only by good quality arguments.
- Cacioppo and Petty (1982) think that people differ in their 'need for cognition' (understanding). They developed a scale to measure this and used it to distinguish high scorers who tend to work hard to comprehend messages from low scorers who do

not. To persuade the former group it proved important that persuasive messages were of high quality as they are more likely to spot the flaws in weak arguments.

Recent Models of Persuasion

Studies in the Yale tradition have done much to examine the effects of 'Who says what by what means to whom?' but they have tended to skirt the issue of why certain communications work better than others. Recent models have focused much more on the cognitive (thought) processes people employ when faced with a persuasive message.

We are bombarded by messages from many sources and cannot possibly process them all. Some psychologists describe people as 'cognitive misers', who like to take 'mental shortcuts' and are lazy about how much information they will process. At other times, they give information their full attention. Would-be persuaders know that both lazy and thoughtful processing can lead to persuasion under different circumstances. Two models of persuasion have emerged which use these ideas.

1. *The Elaboration Likelihood Model (ELM)*

In this model (Petty and Cacioppo, 1981) there are two routes to persuasion:

- The central route involves active (thoughtful) processing of a message and careful scrutiny of its content, merit and logic. We are more likely to process actively (elaborate) if a message has personal relevance and we feel involved with it. The success of this route tends to depend on the quality of the arguments presented.
- The peripheral route involves relatively shallow (lazy) processing. There is little attention to its content, merit or logic. We are less likely to elaborate a message which is not particularly personally relevant or involving. Its success in persuading us depends more on superficial cues, such as communicator variables, than on the content of the message itself.

2. The Heuristic Model of Persuasion

This model (Chaiken, 1987) broadly agrees with the distinction between central and peripheral processing made by the ELM but substitutes the terms 'systematic' and 'heuristic' processing. It goes on to add that, when we are disinclined to give a message our full attention for whatever reason, we apply 'heuristics' or 'rules of thumb'. These enable us to process a message with minimum effort. For example, a heuristic we often use is that people who have personal experience of something are generally right about it. Another heuristic is that people will express opinions more honestly and openly if they believe they are having a private conversation. Both of these heuristics are used in certain 'hidden camera' washing powder advertisements in which a celebrity approaches a woman buying the advertiser's powder. She clearly has plenty of experience of washing the family's clothing and expresses a favourable opinion to him about the product. Only then is it revealed to her that she is being filmed.

In both the above models, it is agreed that **central** (or systematic) **processing** leads to more lasting retention of the message than does **peripheral** (or heuristic) **processing**. It should, therefore, be easier to predict people's behaviour after they have carried out central processing of a message than after they have carried out peripheral processing. Nevertheless, many advertisers are successful in encouraging peripheral processing of messages that lasts long enough for us to buy their products.

Putting Theory into Practice

Many of the early recommendations from the Yale studies can be re-interpreted in the light of newer models of persuasion and used by advertisers and propagandists to increase the chances of persuasion. Careful manipulation of communicator, message, channel and audience variables in combination with an understanding of central and peripheral processing should enable them to develop effective persuasive communications which will then, they hope, translate into attitude and behaviour change. There are many other tactics which potential persuaders might use, all of them derived from psychological research. Figure 6.1 lists some of these, and the reader is asked to refer to this before reading on.

FIGURE 6.1
Some Techniques Used in Persuasive Communications

1. *Techniques based on social influence*

- Creating 'granfalloons' ('proud and meaningless associations of human beings'). This is based on Tajfel's (1982) idea of minimal groups where people can be given a feeling of group identity sometimes on the flimsiest of pretexts. Persuaders encourage this by giving their product a 'personality' so that buying it gives the consumer a sense of belonging to a special group
- Using non-verbal aspects of communication well, e.g. use open gestures and a direct, but not overbearing, gaze. This avoids intimidating the audience and makes the persuader seem honest
- Creating a norm of reciprocity. If someone gives you something, it is usual to give in return. A small free gift or sample given before making a serious attempt to persuade can induce this in people and encourage them to return the favour by buying from the giver
- Using a number of persuaders and/or use 'converts' as models. Seeing that a number of people are already persuaded can help to increase pressure to conform

2. *Techniques which encourage peripheral processing or use of heuristics*

- Choose wording of the message carefully (e.g. 'There is no cheaper insurance') or use 'purr words' such as 'best ever'. There may be plenty of others that are equally cheap and the advertiser's 'best ever' may still be inferior to a competitor's product! Words can deceive and create misperceptions
- Use 'decoys' i.e. compare the product to an inferior one. This produces a 'context effect' and makes the advertiser's product look better than it really is. (But it is not often used by well-known brands. Why give the competitor free publicity?)
- Appear to argue against self-interest or for no personal gain. If the communicator finds the message that compelling there must be something in it
- Package the product carefully to encourage heuristics such as 'Brown paper packages contain wholesome products.' 'Soberly dressed politicians are more trustworthy'
- Use vivid images, distract attention from weak messages with humour, music or plenty of action. This makes the message more memorable and attention-grabbing and discourages central processing

Figure 6.1 *continued over*

3. *Techniques which play on cognitions and emotions*

- Allowing the audience to draw its own conclusions. This 'self-persuasion' technique works well with interesting and fairly simple messages but care must be taken not to patronise the audience
- Creating a feeling of 'cognitive dissonance' in people then offer them a way to reduce it, e.g. uncomfortable feelings raised by charity appeals can be reduced by giving to the charity
- Creating 'factoids' (Mailer, 1973), i.e. facts that did not exist before the media created them. Once created, these are difficult to undo. Hitler and Goebbels created factoids about Germans as the 'master race' and the Jewish people as 'conspirators' against it
- Encouraging people to mentally role-play. 'Slice of life' adverts do this by showing families not too unlike the viewer's own. This makes it easy for the viewer to imagine themselves enjoying the benefits of a product
- Creating a sense of scarcity, e.g. 'Buy now while stocks last!' The promise of possessing something allegedly rare and desirable can discourage us from considering alternatives

4. *Well-known sales techniques*

- Foot in the door'. Make a small request first followed by a larger one. Some advertisers offer a short-term trial subscription to a magazine and then ask for a longer commitment
- 'Door in the face'. Ask for too much, wait for the refusal and then ask for something less. Unscrupulous salespeople may initially offer something at too high a price and then appear to 'do you a favour' by grudgingly dropping the amount
- 'Low-ball', i.e. obtain agreement and only then let the person know there are strings attached. Some garages offer free roadside assistance if you buy your car from them (but only if your car is regularly, and expensively, serviced by them)

Source: Pratkanis and Aronson (1991).

In the real world, persuaders know that they can never be 100 per cent successful, but they can make some impact by combining everything they know about persuasion. Three examples which illustrate this are given by Pratkanis and Aronson (1991). The first of these (the Greenpeace appeal) leans more towards advertising. The second example (how cults create converts) leans more towards propaganda. The third example directly concerns how propaganda has been used in warfare. All of them borrow from the same stock of persuasion techniques.

The Greenpeace Appeal

Greenpeace's appeal for donations involved the following techniques which encourage a mixture central and peripheral processing:

- They targeted those most likely to be able to contribute, for example home-owners.
- They used a mailshot knowing that written material could be carefully scrutinised.
- The envelopes they used stood out through being larger than usual and by having an eye-catching message on the outside.
- The envelopes were an official looking colour thus creating an impression of credibility.
- Inside there were free stickers thus inducing the norm of reciprocity. In addition, use of the stickers would mean adopting the Greenpeace group identity. The appealing animals on the stickers would also serve as a distracter from central processing.
- The enclosed letter was addressed 'Dear Friend' (a **granfalloon** technique – see Figure 6.1).
- A questionnaire about toxic waste was included. Completion of this would encourage the individual to think about the issues involved and thus engage in a kind of self-persuasion.
- Information in the letter raised fears about toxic waste and offered a 'do-able' solution; that is, contribute to a group who were actively and, allegedly, successfully engaged in reducing the risks of such waste (and who were prepared to take the real risks for you).
- A choice of contributions was offered ranging from $15 to $100. The contrast effect thus induced would, hopefully, result in the choice of more than the minimum amount.

How Cults Create Converts

When we hear of the power of cults to persuade, it is tempting to think there is some sort of 'brainwashing' involved (as used by the Communist Chinese on American POWs during the Korean War). Pratkanis and Aronson explain that brainwashing entails nothing more exotic or irresistible than the persuasion techniques already outlined and that many groups, not just the more unusual cults, can be seen to use them. They list seven ways in which cults can be persuasive once a suitably impressionable person has been found:

- A new social reality is presented. To do this, the cult 'filters' information to the potential convert about what is and is not acceptable. This message is driven home through frequent repetition and reward. The convert may be cut off from others (for example family) who may challenge the message.
- A 'granfalloon', or feeling of identity, is created perhaps through giving up possessions and adopting particular habits, foods and ways of dressing that make it difficult to integrate with others outside the group.
- Commitment is encouraged through creating dissonance then offering a way to reduce it. The 'foot in the door' technique works well here. Once an initial commitment has been made, it is harder to go back on it than to go along with it. The creation of opportunities to reduce guilt is also effective.
- The credibility and attractiveness of the leader is established perhaps by creating myths about their connection to God or Jesus.
- The potential convert can be sent to give the message to non-converts. This acts as a form of self-persuasion.
- The potential convert can be distracted from questioning the group's doctrine, for example through rituals and self-depriva-tion (e.g. of food or sleep). Anti-cult thoughts are dismissed as being 'from Satan'.
- A vision of the 'promised land' can be created towards which the potential convert will need to work. (This is similar to creating a 'factoid'.)

Propaganda and Warfare

During World War I the use of propaganda by the US and Britain proved to be one of the vital ingredients in ensuring the defeat of Germany. Adolf Hitler learned a great deal from studying the tactics that had been used and this undoubtedly helped him to establish and maintain a German state controlled by the Nazi party. To assist him in this, he created the Ministry of Popular Enlightenment and Propaganda and appointed Joseph Goebbels to oversee it. Hitler and Goebbels favoured what we now call the peripheral route to persuasion and often used appeals to the emotions. They were scathing about the intellects of most people, and limited most of their propaganda to a few key points and frequently repeated slogans. Hitler concerned himself very little with the ethics of his propaganda ministry's actions arguing that the ends (swift victory) justified the means. Some of the techniques employed were as follows:

- Once in power, the Nazi party gained control of the mass media to ensure that the information reaching the people was selectively filtered. Journalists were carefully chosen and systematically rewarded and punished for their efforts (for example, in some cases, by being allowed privileged access to certain stories). A bold Nazi image was created through the use of attention-getting posters and slogans. Pro-Nazi messages were mixed into popular entertainment programmes and linked to Aryan prowess at the 1936 Olympic Games.
- Goebbels suggested phrases and images to people to encourage '**factoids**'; for example he coined the term *Schleichende Krise* (creeping crisis) to help persuade the German people that England was in an increasingly weak state of economic and political unrest.
- Films of mass rallies helped to give the impression of consensus with Hitler and approval of him.
- Massive stadiums were built as meeting places. These allied the Nazis in people's minds to great and powerful cultures of the past and left them feeling dwarfed by the scale of Nazi power.
- Initially a band of loyal supporters (Hitler Youth) was created, easily identified by their brown shirts. The ridicule that this sometimes provoked would have created unpleasant feelings of dissonance which could then be dispelled by becoming even more dedicated to the cause.
- One of the most powerful techniques used was to combine the 'granfalloon' with existing fear and frustration. World War I had left Germany in serious and demoralising economic difficulties and many people felt insecure about the future. Hitler and Goebbels began to create the idea that the Jews were responsible for draining the nation's resources. This had the effect of turning Jews into an **out-group** and Aryans and Nazis into an **in-group** with a strong identity. It also created a scapegoat for the in-group's feelings and legitimised persecution of the Jews for the purposes of restoring Germany's status.
- During World War II, radio was used by all sides in attempts to weaken the enemy's resolve. The Nazis used the British traitor William Joyce who broadcast German propaganda to the British

under the name 'Lord Haw Haw'. Iva Ikuko Toguri D'Aquino broadcast to the Allies from Japan under the name of 'Tokyo Rose'. These broadcasts were in addition to frequent leaflet drops from the air.

- Before each new aggressive move in Europe, the German ministry of propaganda started a 'war of nerves' against their target by, for example, alleging that German minorities were being persecuted in the target country and that the German forces were invincible. This had the effect of weakening and dividing the target country and causing its allies to hesitate.
- The answer to the nation's problems was firmly located with one man – Adolf Hitler – who was portrayed both as a benevolent and modest father-figure and as a steadfast military man supported by the mass approval of the people.

Naturally, the Allies had their own propaganda agencies which worked hard to counter the enemy's messages and demoralise its military forces and civilians while, at the same time, keeping up morale and strengthening resolve at home. Propaganda is a prominent feature of any modern war and there are many examples of its use in Vietnam, Korea, the Falklands and, more recently, in the Gulf and former Yugoslavia. Many of the tragic consequences of war are clear for all to see but it is always technically very difficult to assess whether propaganda played in the loss or protection of people's lives. Furthermore, once a war is over, propaganda which could be wildly inaccurate is seldom corrected and it is not known how persistent its effects, if any, are. For the survivors, the messages they were exposed to may well be retained helping to keep low-level hostility and prejudice ready to re-surface during the next conflict.

Understanding and Resisting Persuasion

Pratkanis and Aronson express concern that people have seen so many examples of the use of persuasion to coerce and manipulate that they have grown weary even to the point of inactivity, for example no longer bothering to vote in elections or make donations to charity. They suggest that inaction is not the most constructive solution and that there must be a middle route between 'naïve acceptance on the one hand and total cynicism on the other' (1991, p. xii) about the content of messages received from others and their intentions in trying to persuade us. Their book, *Age of Propaganda*, aims to inform people about persuasion techniques so that they can:

- understand what is happening;
- tell a 'con job' (p. xiii) from an honest message;
- protect themselves if they so wish;
- ultimately come to use persuasion wisely.

Many attempts to persuade, as we have seen, exploit the idea that people are 'cognitive misers' who can be reached through the peripheral route to persuasion and are more open to mindless propaganda than to thoughtful persuasion. This is of particular concern since Gerbner *et al.* (1986) showed that the mass media give us a grossly misleading picture of the world. Heavy viewing of television in particular tends to correlate with holding certain views, for example seeing women as less capable than men and society as more violent than it really is. After research by Iyengar and Kinder (1987) had shown that the effect of heavy viewing on people's views is causal, Pratkanis and Aronson concluded that 'the content of the mass media sets the public's social and political agenda' (1991, p. 54). Thus the burden is on the recipients of the message to scrutinise it carefully and to realise that they do have a choice about whether to accept it, or indeed whether to think about the message at all. There are at least four things that can be done:

1. Understand persuasive tactics and how to resist them (see Figure 6.2 with reference to Figure 6.1).
2. Induce 'reactance'. This is brought about by letting people know that attempts are being made to persuade them. The resulting 'reactance' causes them actively to resist the message because they feel their personal freedom is being threatened.
3. Use 'inoculation'. McGuire (1964) exposed people to a weakened form of a persuasive message before giving them the full message. This prior warning 'inoculated' them in that it allowed them time to formulate counter-arguments and made them more resistant to persuasion. Inoculation works particularly well with issues that have personal relevance.
4. Establish regulatory bodies. The role of these is to monitor messages and ensure that they are fairer and more honest. This raises a particular dilemma in democracies which advocate free speech since regulation could be seen as a form of censorship or

FIGURE 6.2

Some Persuasion Techniques and How to Resist Them

Persuasion technique	*Ways of resisting persuasion*
1. Techniques based on social influence • Granfalloons	• Come to terms with the disappointment of not being a member of a 'special' group (e.g. ask 'Is it really worth it?'). Look for common ground between the desired goal and alternatives. Think of the out-group as individuals like yourself. Don't get all your self-esteem from this one source
• Non-verbal aspect of communication	• Observe these carefully. What does the communicator have to gain?
• Creating a norm of reciprocity	• You are not obliged to give in return
• Using a number of persuaders and/or converts	• Recognise that you can act independently and that the image of consensus is probably superficial
2. Techniques which encourage peripheral processing or use of heuristics • carefully-chosen wording • decoys • arguments against self-interest • packaging • distracters	• Try rephrasing the message • Focus on the actual merits of what is being advertised • Question the motives of the persuader • Beware of your own heuristics! • Ask why it is necessary for the persuader to distract you
3. Techniques which play on cognitions and emotions • self-persuasion • cognitive dissonance • factoids	• Play 'devil's advocate' and try to counter-argue • Consider alternative ways of reducing dissonance • Question the motives of the persuader and consider the consequences of being persuaded

• mental images	• Recognise that you are being sold a (probably unobtainable) dream
• sense of scarcity	• Be prepared to walk away if you cannot get what you want. Recognise that frustration is a natural response to being thwarted so give yourself time to 'cool off'
4. Well-known sales techniques (foot in the door, door in the face and low-ball)	• Realise that you can say 'no' at any time and consider how you got into the situation in the first place

Source: Pratkanis and Aronson (1991).

'gagging'. Yet, regulatory bodies do exist and persuaders respond by arranging their messages very carefully to stay within the limits of the law. That this is not always successful can be seen in the number of prosecutions brought against advertisers and in the number of official apologies made on TV and in other mass media.

Persuason and Ethics

The scale of influence exercised by persuaders is enormous, ranging from charity advertising to attempts by fanatics to recruit followers. In addition, many professions, such as law, politics, teaching and medicine, depend on successful persuasion. Persuasion can be used for both good and evil ends and this raises important ethical questions about what its role should be and what the values of the persuaders themselves are. Pratkanis and Aronson (1991) say that ethical issues can be approached in three ways:

• Consider whether the **ends** justify the **means**. If we needed to persuade in order to save lives then the answer is probably yes. If we were a car salesperson on commission trying to persuade customers to buy then the answer is less clear.
• Consider the means rather than the ends. It is generally agreed that we should avoid misleading, false, filtered information that

arouses unpleasant emotions, but there are always fuzzy areas here such as when we tell 'white lies'.
- Consider both the means and the ends. Try to balance the importance of persuading people with the means of persuasion.

This is obviously a very complex problem with no easy answers. Pratkanis and Aronson comment that very often, the means determine the ends. If we feel honestly dealt with we may accept a message but if we suspect foul play we will reject it. The experience of British and American propagandists acts as a warning here. During World War I, they created long-term problems by failing to consider both the means and the ends of their successful anti-German campaign, concentrating instead on short-term gain. Once it became known that their propaganda had, at times, been less than honest it was harder to persuade the sceptical World War II Allies about the reality of Nazi atrocities against the Jews.

Pratkanis and Aronson say that we should ask 'What forms of education and persuasion will serve society and ourselves best?' (ibid., p. 218). Sadly, open and honest debate about the techniques of persuasion and wise evaluation of them does not seem to be commonplace. In addition we seem to be reluctant to engage in honest and reasoned argument about important issues, preferring instead to lazily process other people's messages about them while growing ever more cynical about the motives of the persuader. The danger in this is that we could become so ill-informed about both techniques of persuasion and important issues that we are unable to act appropriately when it matters. If that were to happen, Hitler's view that the masses are ignorant could, eventually, become a reality.

Concluding Note on Psychology and Warfare

In his book *War on the Mind*, Peter Watson (1978) debates the important question of whether war is an inevitable part of human life and, reluctantly, concludes that it is. A selection of research areas on the psychology of war ('psywar') are listed in Figure 6.3. Other important writers, such as Sigmund Freud and Konrad Lorenz, have expressed similar views, but not all psychologists would agree. In particular, learning theorists stress environmental determinants of behaviour and argue that, theoretically, it should be possible to avoid conflict. The truth probably lies somewhere in between. Humans may have a biological predisposition to fight with other humans but they can also bring higher cognitive abilities to bear on the situation. For psychologists, studying the role of heredity, environment and cognition in human conflict is more than an interesting academic exercise. The fact that humans can now conduct wars using technology that could destroy the planet is too important to ignore and makes an understanding of the psychology of war ever more pressing.

The use of persuasion techniques in spreading wartime propaganda is only one way in which psychology can be applied to war. Watson documents many other applications some of which are listed in Figure 6.3. All of them raise important ethical questions. In discussing these, Watson says 'the military use of science is justifiable but only when it is used to conserve life or if it is in

---

FIGURE 6.3
A Selection of 'Psywar' Research Areas

- Why wars occur
- How wars can be prevented or halted
- Peace maintenance
- Recruitment to the military
- Military leadership and followership
- Military group dynamics
- Loyalty and treason
- Selection of military personnel to work behind enemy lines
- How soldiers can be trained to spot booby traps
- Identification of people who are good at code-breaking, sensing danger or keeping secrets
- Assessment of the effects of different attitudes to risk-taking in military personnel
- Design of weapons, war vehicles, radar screens, control panels etc.
- Improving perception under less than ideal conditions, e.g. in the dark
- Why atrocities occur and what can be done to prevent them
- How to stop people 'chickening out' of combat
- Training people to kill
- Preparing prisoners to withstand the effects of captivity
- Helping military personnel to cope with stress before, during and after combat
- How survivors survive

Source: Based on Watson (1978).

response, direct or anticipated, to some new threat. The deliberate development of weapons of unnecessary suffering, on the other hand, is out' (Watson, 1978, p. 18). However, few applications of 'psywar' research are ethically quite so clear cut as in the two examples given by Watson, so in this area, as in others, psychologists find themselves facing ethical dilemmas.

No psychological research is ever entirely objective. It always takes place against a background of social, cultural and political values. Psychologists are not immune from these, consequently it would be naïve to think that all psywar research is for the noble purpose of self-defence or to make conflict less likely. Psychologists know that the same findings can be turned to both defensive or offensive ends. As Watson, says 'Psychology can be a worrying science in the hands of the military' (ibid., p. 18). However, psywar research is not something that psychologists can ignore simply because it is distasteful or can be abused. It has the potential to affect the fates of vast numbers of people for better or worse which makes it, perhaps, one of the most socially-sensitive research areas of all.

Self-assessment Questions

1. Explain what is meant by advertising and propaganda.
2. Give one example each of source, message, channel and audience variables as identified in the Yale studies.
3. Outline the ELM and heuristic models of persuasion.
4. Explain some of the persuasion techniques that might be used in charity appeals or to convert people to cults.
5. Describe some of the propaganda techniques used by Adolf Hitler and Joseph Goebbels during World War II.
6. Explain four ways in which people might resist persuasion.
7. Comment on the ethics of psychological research into advertising, propaganda and warfare.

SECTION II   PSYCHOMETRIC TESTING

Introduction

The term 'psychometric test' refers to any technique which has been devised for quantifying (measuring) an aspect of psychological functioning. Such tests are derived from the 'psychometric model' of human behaviour. According to Kline (1992), this model:

> . . . claims that all behaviour is explicable in terms of factors of ability, personality, motivation and state or mood together with the situation in which individuals find themselves. (p. 101)

The most widely known tests are those that measure intellectual abilities or personality, although psychometric techniques can be applied more widely than this. People are most likely to come into contact with testing in the following settings:

- *Educational* – used to assess accomplishments, to select and sort children according to ability, to diagnose problems, to predict future performance and to check the effectiveness of teaching techniques;
- *Occupational* – for purposes of selection, careers guidance and assessment of training needs;
- *Clinical* – used for diagnosis and to assess treatment needs and progress.

Kline (1992) explains that psychological tests fall into five categories. (There is some overlap between the first two). Only some of these can be considered truly psychometric in that they are based on established population norms (average scores) against which individual scores can be compared. Projective techniques and motivational tests, for example, are generally known as **ipsative** tests. They are not based on pre-established norms, and comparisons between individuals on the basis of test results cannot be made:

1. *Ability tests.* Intelligence tests are included here and typically measure general reasoning ability along with verbal, numerical and spatial ability.
2. *Aptitude tests.* These usually measure a collection of traits that might come in useful in a specific situation, for example high scores on hand–eye co-ordination could form part of a test for selecting trainee pilots to fly high-performance aircraft.
3. *Personality tests.* These usually take the form of questionnaires but also include projective techniques.
4. *Motivational tests.* These can measure present state, mood or interests.

5. *Other tests.* Clinical and neuropsychological tests are included here.

In all of these cases, tests should be carried out only by properly trained professionals. The consequences for individuals of the way in which test results are used can be far-reaching. For this reason it is vital that the tester knows the limitations of a given test and how to interpret the results. Test results should not be used in isolation but as a supplement to other techniques as part of an overall assessment. They should be thought of only as an aid to reaching decisions. (See Birch and Hayward, 1994, for more detail on testing.)

Intelligence Testing

Assessment Methods

The form that intelligence tests take will be determined by the underlying theory of how intelligence is structured. Kline (1992) says that modern tests tap into two kinds ability. The first of these is 'fluid intelligence' comprising basic reasoning skills which are not much affected by environmental experience. The second is 'crystallised intelligence'. This is the social manifestation of fluid intelligence which differs between cultures and is, therefore, affected by experience. Both of these can be measured in intelligence tests. British and American tests often contain verbal, numerical and spatial items as well as testing general knowledge. They generally reveal one or more IQ (intelligence quotient) scores. Examples include:

- The Stanford Binet Intelligence Scales. These cover a wide age range and test verbal, numerical and spatial reasoning and short-term memory.
- The Wechsler Scales cover ages ranging from pre-school to adulthood. They give verbal (word and number items) and performance (visual and spatial reasoning) IQ scores as well as a general IQ.
- The British Ability Scales (BAS) can be used with children and adolescents and comprise 23 tests which give visual, verbal and general IQ scores.
- Raven's Progressive Matrices have no verbal items at all. Test items include shapes and patterns and can be used with virtually

any age, educational level or cultural background. This test is more 'culture fair' than others which have a strong verbal element.

- The Mill Hill Vocabulary Scale is the verbal companion to the Raven's Matrices. It comprises two sets of 44 words of increasing difficulty which the test-taker has to define. Again, the test can be used from childhood to adulthood.
- AH series tests can be given to groups of people simultaneously. They contain numerical and verbal items and are used for selection to apprenticeships, various occupations or higher education.

Clearly, most of these tests draw heavily on the culture in which they were designed and this lays them open to accusations of cultural bias, especially if they are used with people from different cultural backgrounds. (This is an issue we will discuss later in this section.) A solution offered by some psychologists is to use measures of brain activity that have been shown to correlate with intelligence test scores but, as Kline says, these are physiological, not psychometric, tests.

Personality Testing

Assessment Methods

In personality testing, as with intelligence testing, the underlying theory determines the assessment method. Theories differ according to whether they are nomothetic or idiographic.

- **Nomothetic** theories are based on the idea that there are universal principles that can be applied to everyone and used to compare them with each other. These approaches give rise to normative tests ('questionnaires' and 'inventories') which depend largely on self-report (for example the Eysenck Personality Inventory or EPI, the Minnesota Multiphasic Personality Inventory or MMPI, Cattell's 16 PF). Some of these tests measure characteristics that are assumed to be normally distributed such that most people will score within a given range around the mean. A score at one of the extremes would, statistically speaking, be very unusual.
- **Idiographic** theories start by identifying characteristics that all people may have to some extent but see the individual's

combination of these characteristics as unique. These approaches give rise to ipsative tests which encourage individuals to reveal their own personality structure through self-assessment (for example Kelly's Repertory Grid; the Q-sort). Psychodynamic assessment techniques can also be fitted in here, for example projective techniques such as the Thematic Apperception Test (TAT) or the Rorschach inkblot test. The material in these is relatively unstructured. The client 'projects' meaning onto it and can then work on interpreting responses with the help of the analyst.

As Kline (1992) reminds us, only normative tests are truly psychometric. Ipsative tests do not yield scores which can be compared to norms. Problems arise if different people are compared on their ipsative test scores or when comparisons are made between normative and ipsative measures of a similar characteristic. Meaningful comparisons are only possible when comparing scores from the same normative test.

Controversies Surrounding Psychometric Testing

Technical, practical and theoretical considerations place limits on how much we can trust test results to give a true measure of psychological functioning. In addition to this, ethical considerations arise when we consider the testing situation itself and the uses to which test results are put. Here we will consider some of the many issues that make the use of psychometric tests so contentious. The following points apply to all kinds of testing although some of the ethical issues are more pertinent than others to specific types of tests.

Technical and Practical Considerations

Psychologists strive to devise technically-precise tests which have a number of important qualities:

- *Reliability.* The test should give consistent results over time (test–retest reliability). The items in it should also be measuring the same thing. (This can be assessed through 'split-half' or 'part–whole' reliability testing.)
- *Validity.* The test should be relevant, that is it should test what it claims to test. It should look as if it is relevant (**face validity**), it

should contain items that are meaningful to the test-taker (**content validity**), results from it should correlate positively with other tests of the same thing (**concurrent validity**), it should forecast future performance in particular areas (**predictive validity**) and it should measure a concept that is meaningful (**construct validity**).

- *Standardisation.* This involves 'trying out' test items on a representative sample of the population for whom it is intended and making appropriate adjustments. This results in the establishment of 'norms' against which individuals can then be compared.
- *Discriminatory power.* A test should be sensitive enough to enable us to tell people apart.

Testers also have to take into account a number of practical matters:

- *Standardisation of testing conditions.* The conditions under which people take the test should be the same for everyone in terms of instructions, treatment by the tester and so forth, in order to guard against the possible effects of tester-bias. Even the best designed test can be abused in unskilled hands. This is why educational, occupational and clinical psychologists must be trained to use tests. People outside these professions can obtain BPS training.
- *Mood and motivational state of test-takers.* These can influence test performance. Some testing procedures take their influence into account. Others do not.
- *Socially desirability bias.* Test-takers may alter their answers, or even lie, if they want to project a certain image. Some tests try to guard against this by building in 'lie scales'.
- *Test-wisdom.* Through familiarity with tests or coaching, people can become test-wise and affect their results considerably, for example to raise their IQ score. This makes a nonsense of comparing the score against norms or other individuals' scores (unless of course they are all similarly test-wise!)

No psychometrician has yet come up with a perfect testing technique which overcomes all these problems. Experienced and properly trained testers are fully aware of the limitations they impose on the veracity of test results. Unfortunately, less well-informed people may over-value test results.

Theoretical Considerations

There are a number of general issues concerning testing which we should always be aware of when interpreting and applying results, for example:

- *Theoretical assumptions underlie all tests* and tend to be determined by the dominant cultural group (see 'cultural bias' in Chapter 4). The test items, norms and interpretations are thus based on the dominant group's values. This could introduce bias which might prove disadvantageous to people in other cultural groups; for example, denying them access to certain jobs or educational opportunities.
- *There is a risk of reification* (the process by which theoretical concepts assume reality in people's minds). Concepts such as intelligence and personality became real to us once their existence was suggested and extensively researched, but we should remember that they are not absolute truths but inventions which have proved convenient and useful.
- *Psychometricians assume that certain characteristics are stable* (for example intelligence and personality) and that their tests tap into this relatively stable 'core'. Variations in scores over time simply indicate that the individual is superficially adapting to change. However, it is debatable whether we do have stable characteristics which operate independently of our circumstances and which can, therefore, be reliably measured.
- *Psychometricians assume that test results are reliably linked to behaviour*. If they were not there would be little point in them. However, there is some evidence (for example Hartshorne and May, 1928) that this is not always the case. The strongest critics of testing say that test results vary so much over time that they are no more to be trusted in predicting behaviour than astrology or graphology.

Ethical Considerations

There are many examples of undue reliance on test scores which are then used to inform decisions which affect people's lives, perhaps through unfair discrimination in education or at work or through misdiagnosis of a clinical condition. The development of the 11+ test, used for educational selection in Britain, is one example.

Doubts about its theoretical and statistical basis ensured that it had all but disappeared by the 1970s, but it had already had an enormous impact on the educational careers of many schoolchildren. More recently, Palmer (1995) described a case, which eventually went to court, in which a suspect personality test was used to select 20 nurses for 10 posts. The 10 successful candidates were White and the 10 unsuccessful candidates were Black. In clinical settings, the possible over-diagnosis of schizophrenia in Black compared to White patients is well-documented (Fernando, 1991). Understanding technical, practical and theoretical shortcomings of tests is clearly a vital part of test-users' training but they must go further than this to take account of the wider, ethical implications of their work. Here we will consider some of the ethical issues faced by test-users and their clients.

1. Test Bias

Tests often show differences in scores between certain groups, for example Kaplan and Saccuzzo (1989) quote evidence that Black Americans typically score up to 15 IQ points below White Americans. This unpopular finding is not in dispute but the reason for it is. There are at least two possibilities:

- The test is biased – it is culturally loaded in favour of certain groups and therefore the content is not valid for other groups;
- The test is not biased and shows up real differences.

Regarding test bias, Kaplan and Saccuzzo say that content validity is no longer a central issue. For example, the widely used Stanford Binet test, which was standardised on white children and adults, has been widely validated on other groups. Furthermore, during the 1970s, psychologists working on the educational enrichment programme 'Headstart' found that differences in Black and White children's performance remained on both Black and White dialect versions of this test. Excluding items that were potentially biased also produced no change. To complicate the issue, other studies in the United States and Britain have shown that groups such as Jewish and Oriental people score higher than the white population that provided the test norms (Colman, 1991). Clearly, there are factors other than test bias at work.

Blaming the test avoids the more difficult politically and socially-sensitive possibility that there are real differences. Some psychologists have argued that these differences are largely due to innate, unchangeable racial differences in intelligence (for example Jensen, 1969). Others claim that this is racism under the cover of science and that it has been used in a political conspiracy to justify discriminatory practices. Indeed, in some American states, concerns about bias in testing have led to outlawing certain kinds of tests or severely restricting their use.

An alternative and much more plausible view is that test results reflect environmental factors such as social disadvantage. In this case social inequalities must be addressed which is an eminently more challenging and lengthy process. Colman (1991) concludes that differences in test scores are due to real differences, rather than to test bias, and that the evidence for this is strongly in favour of environmental influences. Nevertheless, psychologists are still not sure how these influences operate and to what extent they affect measures of intelligence.

2.   Labelling

Some critics complain that tests are reductionist (see Chapter 2). They over-simplify a complex person by applying a convenient label. The problem with this is that labels may become self-fulfilling, meaning that people begin to behave in ways which fit their labels. In clinical settings (for example Rosenhan, 1973) mental disorder labels carry stigma with them and seem to be particularly 'sticky' in that they are very difficult to shake off. In schools, labelling a pupil as a 'spurter' as a consequence of testing (for example Rosenthal and Jacobson, 1968) was thought to enhance the child's ability. In the workplace, labelling an employee as lacking potential could be extremely damaging to their self-esteem and job performance.

Studies such as these appeal to folk-wisdom. We are inclined to believe that labelling works. However, close examination of research findings reveals very little evidence that it does, at least in the direct way the studies have claimed. Defenders of testing also reply that a test score only gives a general indication of functioning and is part of a more general assessment. In professional hands tests have many uses when combined with other techniques, for example they can provide a vehicle for interaction and allow the tester time to make other less-formal assessments. Just in case there is a danger that labelling could work to the test-taker's disadvantage, testers prefer to describe results in general terms rather than to use a rigid label or test score.

3. The Test-taker's Rights and the Tester's Responsibilities

There are a number of issues to consider under this heading. All of these highlight the importance of proper training of the tester whose responsibility it is to safeguard test-takers by explaining to them the following rights before testing takes place:

- To refuse to be tested;
- To know test results (but see 'communicating results');
- To know who will have access to the results and why;
- To expect confidentiality of results;
- To expect that test results will be secure.

4. Divided Loyalties

Testers may sometimes find themselves with a conflict of interests between the test-taker and the institution that pays the psychologist to carry out the testing. For example, if a test could show which employees are most likely to crack under stress, would the employees or the institution benefit most from knowing the results? Information given to the employee could allow the purpose of the test to leak out to others who could then prepare themselves and render further testing useless. Information given to the institution could be used to justify staff changes or redundancies. The tester must decide where their loyalties lie and let all parties know this in advance so that ownership of data is clarified. (See also 'communicating results'.)

5. Communicating Results

Understanding all the limitations of testing and their likely abuses has an important bearing on how test results are communicated. Trained testers follow strict procedures when doing this taking into account, amongst many other things, the likely impact on the person or organisation receiving the information. Generally, results are communicated in broad terms rather than in the form of precise scores or specific labels. For example, an employer might be told a particular employee has a 'low probability' of cracking under pressure and that this prediction is accurate 68 times out of 100. It is important that test results on their own are not over-valued and misunderstood. It is for this reason that counselling to discuss the interpretation of results should be available.

6. Privacy

In personality testing in particular, it is sometimes necessary to disguise the purpose of a test to prevent the test-taker from manipulating the situation and distorting the result. However, in disguised tests, test-takers might believe that they could unwittingly give something away that they would rather have kept to themselves. Clearly, a delicate balance must be struck between the costs and benefits to test-takers of intrusions into their privacy. In defence of such tests, Kaplan and Saccuzzo (1989) say that they are not as revealing as people imagine and that privacy is only invaded if intrusion is unwelcome or detrimental. In addition, the trained tester is bound by procedures outlined in 3, 4 and 5 above. The only circumstances where confidentiality can be breached is when test results indicate a danger to the test-taker or others or when results can be subpoenaed by the courts. If people know all these things in advance and still consent to being tested it is highly unlikely that they are unwilling test-takers.

7. Use of Test Results

Test results are worth nothing unless they can be used, but how this is done is an important ethical issue. In connection with selection for work or education, Hunter and Schmidt (1976) say that what selectors do depends on whether they believe tests are biased. There are four possible courses of action:

- *Unqualified individualism.* Take the highest scorers on the grounds that they will do the best job. Use other factors, such as age, race or sex, if they help to improve prediction of performance.
- *Qualified individualism.* Take the highest scorers as above but ignore other factors on the grounds that this helps to counteract discrimination – the best will come through regardless.

- *Quotas.* This is a kind of proportional representation. Test-takers are divided into sub-groups and the highest scorers are selected from each group in the same proportions that occur in the target population.
- *Compromise.* This strikes a balance between individualism and quotas. Test results from disadvantaged groups are adjusted to take account of possible bias. All scores are then pooled and the highest scorers selected.

Kline warns that test results should not be used on their own in this way but should be put to 'humane use' (1992, p. 4). The mechanical and inhumane use of testing results from:

- over-valuing test scores;
- failing to use other relevant information to supplement them; or
- failing fully to discuss test scores.

The introduction of Standard Assessment Tests (SATs) in state schools in England and Wales is a case in point. The tests, in English, Maths and Science, were fully introduced in 1995 for 11-year-olds at Key Stage 2 of the National Curriculum. Many teachers agree that test results are a useful measure of achievement and that they can be used diagnostically to identify areas of weaknesses. It is the issue of using test results to produce schools league tables which is hotly disputed. At the time of writing (1996) opponents of the publication of tables argue that:

- the SATs are still in the experimental stage;
- undue weight will be placed on test performance leading to a narrowing of the curriculum;
- they fail to take into account the many factors that influence children's performance. In particular they ignore the 'value-added' factor, that is the amount children have actually gained taking into account their different starting points;
- it will be divisive. Failure to discuss the full meaning of results will result in parents moving children to the 'better' schools. Government funding will follow leading, eventually, to the closure of schools that are successful in ways not shown by their position on the league table.

In this case, the use of test results to produce league tables, rather than to inform parents and teachers about children's educational needs, has become an important and unresolved political issue which could have far-reaching effects on the education of many English and Welsh children.

Conclusion

In this section, we have concentrated on the many shortcomings of psychometric testing at the expense of their strengths. Kline (1992) says that, properly used, psychometric tests can save time and money that would otherwise be used in lengthy assessment procedures. They are easy to administer, sometimes to many people at once. Some of them can even be given and efficiently scored by computer, thus giving immediate results as a basis for further assessment. Well-constructed tests, he claims, are far more objective than some other forms of assessment. Teacher assessments, for example, may be influenced more by a child's effort rather than by actual ability. Tests can never be totally free of inaccuracies but they are, in theory at least, good for promoting equal opportunities.

A cynical way of viewing tests is that they are a major and profitable commercial interest and that this is one reason for their proliferation, particularly in the workplace. In the real world of applied psychology Imich (1991) writes that, when working with individual children, increasing numbers of educational psychologists believe that psychometric tests have no positive value. They prefer instead to concentrate on helping children to achieve skills which will give them access to the National Curriculum. In the field of clinical neuropsychology, Hall (1991) comments on a decrease in the use of personality tests in favour of sophisticated tests of cognitive functioning. If trends like these continue, the fear that psychometric techniques may, one day, become so sophisticated that they will be administered, scored and interpreted by computer will soon be a groundless one.

Self-assessment Questions

1. What is meant by the term 'psychometric test'?
2. Give examples of the use of psychometric tests in educational, occupational and clinical settings.
3. In what ways do theories of intelligence and personality affect the form of the tests which arise from them?

4. Outline technical, practical, and theoretical limitations of psychometric tests.
5. What ethical considerations are there in the field of psychometric testing and how have psychologists attempted to resolve them?
6. According to Kline (1992) what strengths do psychometric tests have?

FURTHER READING

R. M. Kaplan and D. P. Saccuzzo (1989) *Psychological Testing: Principles, Applications and Issues*, 2nd edn (California: Brooks Cole).
P. Kline (1992) *Psychometric Testing in Personnel Selection and Appraisal* (London: Croner).
A. Pratkanis and E. Aronson (1991) *Age of Propaganda: Everyday Uses and Abuses of Persuasion* (New York: Freeman).
P. Watson (1978) *War on the Mind* (New York: Basic Books).

HIM ? HE'S THE EDUCATIONAL
PSYCHOLOGIST.

Psychology in Action   7

When you have finished this chapter you should be able to:

1. describe some of the main fields of pure and applied research in psychology;
2. identify the relationship between research and the application of psychological concepts in therapy and in other areas of work; and
3. be more aware of the career openings for psychologists and the demands which they make in terms of qualifications and the work itself.

Introduction

Psychology is not only an academic subject but also a profession. It is under the control of a professional body, the British Psychological Society. This body offers graduate membership to those with a degree which has sufficient psychological content.

Graduate Basis for Registration (GBR)

The most straightforward way of gaining GBR is by taking a Society-accredited honours degree in psychology. However, if your degree course is not accredited or is in a subject other than psychology, you may gain GBR by one of the following routes:

- By sitting the Society's own qualifying examination.
- By obtaining a Society-accredited postgraduate qualification.
- By taking a conversion course which converts your degree to the equivalent of an honours degreee
  with psychology as the main subject. These are run on a full-time or part-time basis in many universities.

Note: Many degree courses are now run on a modular-basis and it may be necessary to take particular modules to qualify for GBR.

For example the Open University lists those courses which together provide sufficient psychological content for the degree to be Society-accredited.

The BPS regulates the way in which psychologists behave professionally and grants the status of Chartered Psychologist to those working in the field. Those on the register of Chartered Psychologists may use the title Chartered Psychologist (abbreviated to C. Psychol.)

If you thought you might like to work in psychology what might you find yourself doing? What are the next steps you would need to take? The purpose of this chapter is to give you a fuller picture of career opportunities using psychological qualifications.

Psychology and Psychiatry

Psychology is concerned with all aspects of the behaviour of people; it is the science of human behaviour and experience. Elsewhere in this book there is a full discussion of what science is and of the position of psychology in relation to science (Chapter 4).

Psychiatry, on the other hand, while it draws on a knowledge of psychology, is a branch of medicine and is concerned with the treatment of psychological problems and mental disorders. It uses drugs as well as psychotherapeutic techniques.

Educational basis

While GCSE, GCE A or AS level psychology have value as interesting subjects to study, they are only an introduction and the use of psychology as a career depends upon further study and training.

Applications of Psychology

Psychology is concerned with practical problems as well as attempting to explain behaviour. The BPS give some examples:

- What are the best shifts for air traffic controllers to work in order to minimise the risk of accidents?
- What effect does their parents' divorce have on children?
- How should parents best deal with their chidren's tantrums?
- How do you best train a blind person and a guide dog to work together?
- How do you learn to cope with stress or with particular fears and phobias?

- What kind of people are the most attractive to the opposite sex? (BPS, 1996, p. 3)

Careers in Psychology

If you thought you might like to work in psychology, what might you find yourself doing? What are the next steps you need to take? The purpose of this chapter is to give you a fuller picture of career opportunities, which require psychological qualifications. The areas of work which we shall discuss include the following:

- Pure psychological research;
- Applied research;
- Non-therapeutic work using psychological knowledge and skill;
- Therapeutic work of various kinds based upon psychology.

SECTION I PURE RESEARCH

Research carried out in university departments of psychology aims to extend basic knowledge in the particular areas of psychology in which members of staff are interested. Many of these psychologists are entered on the register as chartered psychologists by virtue of holding a postgraduate research degree in psychology. As with all scientific study, it starts with existing theories and knowledge. Based upon these theories a researcher will set up hypotheses which explore and question existing theories, and then test them using experimental or other methods. As a result of the work done, theories may be modified and subsequently tested further.

As an example of this process we consider **Sperling**'s (1960) research into how memory works. Sperling established the existence of what he called a Visual Information Store (VIS). This briefly prolonged a visual stimulus to enable it to be processed and passed to the short-term memory store. Treisman (1964a), using Sperling's work as a basis, attempted to establish the existence of an 'Echoic Store', the equivalent within the hearing modality of Sperling's Visual Information Store.

The fields of study covered in this kind of basic pure research are illustrated in Figure 7.1. We shall describe briefly the work carried out in each of these fields of study to give an idea of the scope of

FIGURE 7.1
Areas of Pure Research

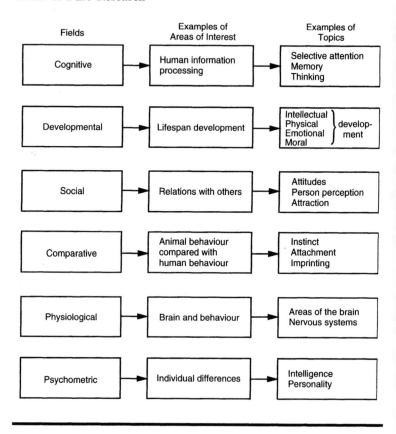

psychology, but even this is not exhaustive. The study of psychology includes anything that humans (or animals) do.

Cognitive Psychology

Cognitive psychology is a central discipline of psychology. It is concerned with the way in which human beings process information. Under the influence of the **behaviourists** (see Chapters 1 and 2) this area once tended to be neglected in favour of the study of stimulus (what went into the mind) and response (the behaviour which resulted). The way information was processed by the brain was thought to be inaccessible and so was ignored.

Typically, cognitive psychologists set up hypothetical models of what might be happening in the nervous system as information is processed and then test this model through empirical research. We might take as an example some of the work done on the topic of attention; that is how the mind selects *some* information to process out of the mass which is presented to it. Figure 7.2 shows the filter model of selective attention which **Broadbent** (1958) developed.

Broadbent (1958) suggested that the available capacity of the mind to deal with information was limited and that there needed to be a filter mechanism of some kind to select what most immediately needed to be dealt with. The model arose from observations made by Colin Cherry and others about the way in which individuals were able to focus upon one conversation in a crowded party, paying little attention to everything else that was going on.

What Broadbent was attempting to do in developing this model was to create a framework, based on observations already made, for an explanation of the stages of processing which are carried on in the brain – which after all is not accessible to direct observation. The framework can then be supported, refuted or modified as a result of data acquired through experiment.

FIGURE 7.2
Broadbent's Filter Model of Selective Attention

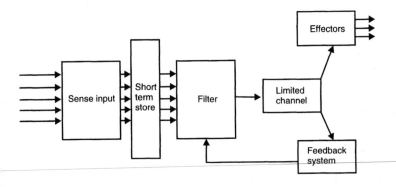

In Broadbent's case, this experimental evidence included 'split-span' experiments. In these, participants were presented through earphones with a series of digits to recall sent alternately to the left and right ears. He found that the participants would recall first all the digits presented to one ear, then all presented to the other: for example, 567821 might be presented:

left	*right*
5	6
7	8
2	1

Participants would recall 572 then 681. When they were asked to recall the pairs, 56:78:21, recall was only 20 per cent. He concluded that a filter system, such as he had hypothesised, had filtered out all the input to one ear before it allowed through to processing the input from the other ear. Other researchers, such as Treisman, concluded that Broadbent's model did not account adequately for all the observed data, and so modified the model to include an attenuating unit which weakens but does not eliminate entirely the message which is not being attended to immediately. In this way understanding of cognitive processes is advanced.

Cognitive Science

With the growth of the study of **artificial intelligence (AI)** and the increasing use of computers in the modelling of cognitive processes, there has been a growing demand for cognitive science to be recognised as a separate discipline. Brown (1990) has suggested that there are three alternative views regarding this development:

1. *The 'new-discipline' model of cognitive science.* This view suggests that mental states can be replicated and studied on computers. Cognitive science is therefore a new discipline with its own subject matter (intelligent systems, both natural and artificial) and its own vocabulary.
2. *The 'umbrella' view of cognitive science.* This second view emphasises the interdisciplinary nature of the new field of cognitive science. It is not a new and separate discipline but provides a whole range of new tools for the study of cognitive processes.

3. *Eco-cognitivism.* This view involves a rejection of the notion that it may be possible to study and replicate mental states independently of the ecology in which they occur; that is to say, causes and effects in the real world. There are two broad themes within this ecological view: (a) a denial that structured mental representation in isolation is as important as the cognitivists maintain; and (b) an insistence that any representation of mental process must have meaning 'in the world' rather than just 'in the head'.

Developmental Psychology

Developmental psychology is concerned with the way in which humans develop and change throughout their lifespan, though perhaps the focus has been particularly upon the development of children. A variety of methods have been used: observation, experiment and case study in particular. For example, **Perner** (1988) were interested in children's theory of mind and how they understand false beliefs. Their work could be described as a naturalistic experiment, the independent variable being the ages of the children and the dependent variable the children's predictions about what their friend would answer.

Participants in the study were 29 children between three and four years old. To begin with they were shown a Smartie box and asked what they thought was inside. They all answered 'Smarties'. The box was then opened and the children shown that it only contained a pencil. Then the children were asked a number of questions.

1. To make sure they remembered the situation they were asked what was still in the box. All knew that the box had a pencil in it.
2. Then they were asked what they thought was in the box when they first saw it. They again all answered correctly.
3. They were asked then to predict what would happen if a friend of theirs, waiting outside, was brought in and asked what was in the box.

The researchers found that of the 29 children, 16 who had answered the first two questions correctly, predicted that their friend would answer 'a pencil'. These were the younger children, nearer three than four, while the older ones were able correctly to report other people's false beliefs

An example of the use of observation in developmental psychology is found in the work of Sylva *et al.* (1980) investigating play in nursery classes in Oxfordshire. The researchers divided play into high, medium and low-yield activities – high-yield activities being such things as building, drawing and doing puzzles; medium-yield activities included pretend-play and play with sand or dough; and low-yield activities included unstructured social playing and rough and tumble. It was suggested that the high-yield activities were more cognitively useful than the medium and low-yield activities.

Case study has also been extensively used in developmental psychology, by such people as Piaget in his earlier investigation of intellectual development and by Melanie Klein in her studies of emotional development. Developmental psychology does not of course confine itself to childhood. Neugarten (1973, 1977) conducted studies into the way in which individuals approach the last years of their life, testing an earlier theory proposed by Cumming and Henry (1961) which became known as 'disengagement theory'. It suggested that, as individuals approach the last years of life, they progressively withdraw from social contacts and activities, become less concerned with the problems of the outside world, separating themselves from emotional attachments with other people. Neugarten suggested that, while this disengagement undoubtedly occurs, friendships and social relationships remain important and may compensate for losses during old age. This finding has been supported by Tesch (1983).

Social Psychology

Social psychologists are concerned to investigate the effects upon individuals' behaviour of belonging to a group or being involved with other people. Methods include both experimental observational and survey methods.

Nadler (1986), for example, was interested in the relationship between socio-cultural values and the likelihood of people asking for help. In this study, carried out in Israel, the participants were 110 school students, both male and female. Half of them lived in kibbutzim and attended a high school catering for the needs of kibbutz members. The kibbutzim emphasised collectivist values. Having a communal and egalitarian outlook was important and being cooperative was crucial. The other half came from two cities in

Northern Israel and went to their local high schools. The Israeli city context placed emphasis on individualism, personal achievement and competitiveness. All lived with their families and most were of a middle class background.

The participants were asked to solve 20 anagrams and it was suggested to them that their success in doing this was an indicator of future success in other domains of life. Several of the anagrams, they were told, had not been solved by people in the past. If they were unable to solve some of the anagrams they were told that they were free to seek help from the investigator.

The dependent variable was the proportion of occasions when a student sought help. For example, if an individual sought help with five anagrams out of ten unsolved ones, this would give a help-seeking score of 50 per cent.

Before taking the test they received instruction, half of each group in a group-oriented context, and half had individually-oriented instruction. In the group context the students were given to understand that their scores would be compared with the average scores of other classes, in the individually-oriented condition they were told their scores would be compared with those of other individuals.

Nadler's prediction was that help-seeking by these two groups would vary according to the nature of the instruction they had had. If the instruction was group-oriented the Kibbutz dwellers would be more likely to seek help, while if the instruction was individually-oriented the city dwellers would tend to seek help more often.

Results showed that in the kibbutz, the proportion seeking help was much higher where instruction had been group-oriented (35 and per cent against 15 and per cent). In the city context the difference was even more marked, with over 40 and per cent seeking help where instruction had been individually-oriented, as against about 10 and per cent where the instruction was group oriented.

Examples of studies using survey methods might include that of Joy *et al.* (1977) who studied the incidence of aggression in a small Canadian community before and after the introduction of television into the town. Observation, both participative and non-participative, was used by Corsaro (1985) to examine friendships made among nursery school children. He used one-way mirrors and videotapes as well as joining in with the children's activities. The results stressed the importance of the social context within which children operate and the way children's concepts about friendship emerge in response to the demands of everyday situations.

Comparative Psychology

Comparative psychologists study the behaviour of animals and make comparisons with human behaviour. Animals are less complex than humans: it is assumed, accordingly, that variables are easier to control. Also researchers are able to use animals in a way which would not be ethically possible with human participants. The question of the use of animals in research has been discussed more fully in Chapter 5.

Lea (1984) suggested that there are three main approaches to comparative psychology:

1.   Comparative Ethology

This is the oldest and best known of these approaches, exemplified in the work of Lorenz and Tinbergen, who suggested that behaviour might be studied in the same way as other aspects of life. Just as the biological forms of animals which belong to related groups of species will tend to be similar, so their behaviour is also likely to be similar. For example, Leyhausen (1973), investigating drives, noted that there is a build-up of drive energy which may be released by appropriate behaviour: hunger drive is released by eating, for instance. Leyhausen used cats' hunting behaviour by way of illustration. While a well-fed cat will not hunt much, in a glut of mice, when a cat has caught several without having to stalk them, it will start stalking more distant mice. It seems that the glut of mice has not 'released' built-up stalking behaviour. Ethologists concluded that there were 'action-specific energies'. Each fixed action pattern seems to have its own specifically related drive.

2.   Social Ethology

This represents the way in which biologists study societies. They start from the social environment of animals. In 1976, E. O. Wilson published *Sociobiology* and in 1977 Richard Dawkins published *The Selfish Gene*. They treated animal societies as biological entities. Of every piece of behaviour the question is asked whether the gene which produced that behaviour could survive in evolutionary terms. An important aspect of animals' environments, though, is other members of the species which form their social group.

3. Behavioural Ecology

Behavioural ecologists are also interested in behaviour, but from the point of view which considers how certain behaviours affect the distribution of a species. There has been interest, for example, in the way in which animals learn where to forage. Krebs, Kacelnik and Taylor (1978) arranged an experiment in which great tits could obtain food by hopping on to either of two perches, which provided them with different probabilities of obtaining food. At first the birds sampled both perches, but in the end hopped consistently onto the one which was more likely to yield food, a result which could have been predicted under Krebs *et al.*'s **optimal foraging** theory.

Physiological Psychology

The approach of physiological psychologists is to look for explanations of behaviour in the physiological structures of humans and animals. Animals are frequently used for the reasons described above, and so there are close links with comparative psychology. In particular, study is concentrated upon the brain and the nervous system as being most influential in determining behaviour, though the endocrine system is also important.

Methods of study include:

- Clinical examination of patients who have behavioural abnormality, usually as a result of disease or trauma; in the study of memory for instance, Shallice and Warrington (1977) showed that some patients with damage to the left parietal cortex had problems with short-term memory. Their digit spans were reduced to one or two items instead of the normal seven.

- Measurement of physiological phenomena such as heart rate, blood pressure, **galvanic skin response** (GSR) (a measure of emotional response, based upon the electrical conductivity of the skin), in relation to strong emotion; for example Sternbach (1962) showed children the film *Bambi* and measured the physiological changes that occurred in them as they watched the saddest, scariest, happiest and funniest parts of the film. An increase in GSR was noted in the saddest parts, while the happiest scenes were accompanied by gastric contraction.

- **Electroencephalography** (EEG) has been used to record the electrical patterns of the brain in sleep research.

- In animals, the use of **ablation** or **lesion** techniques – the removal or cutting of parts of the brain – interfering with normal brain structures and observing the resultant changes in behaviour has increased knowledge of brain function. Jouvet (1967), for example, was able to show, through making lesions in the brain stem, that an area known as the **locus coerulus** was responsible for rapid-eye-movement (REM) sleep. When the area was lesioned REM sleep was suppressed.

- The use of **microelectrodes** to record and sometimes to stimulate particular neurons within the brain has been demonstrated by, for example, Hubel and Wiesel (1962), who were able to record the activity of particular neurons in the visual cortex on the presentation of certain stimuli.

- **Chemical stimulation** is also used to alter the way in which transmitter substances affect neural activity in the brain. Grossman (1960), for example, found that an injection of acetylcholine into the hypothalamus resulted in drinking, while an injection of noradrenaline resulted in eating; thus he was able to show that motivation to eat and to drink was controlled by separate nerve pathways.

Psychometrics

Psychologists in the field of psychometrics attempt to measure attributes of human individual differences – intelligence, aptitudes, personality, attitudes – to mention only a few of the many measurements that are made. Whether this work comes strictly within the scope of pure psychology is perhaps debatable. As with many other fields there is a 'pure' element, the identification of a concept, say, creativity and the behaviours which make up the concept, and then tests are devised to measure those behaviours. Thus, Guilford (1950) worked on the structure of the intellect, identified 120 different abilities and devised tests for a large proportion of them. Very often statistical procedures such as factor analysis are used to find out the degree to which it is possible to identify factors which go to make up the concept under investigation. Guilford, in studying creativity, also proposed that it involved divergent thinking, some convergent thinking, and evaluation. A battery of tests was devised for these factors and the combined results of these tests purported to be tests of 'creativity'.

The value of psychometric tests in a practical context lies in their ability to reduce the need for guesswork in the selection of individuals for particular roles. However the use of psychometric tests for the selection of children for particular forms of education, for example, the 11-plus test for selection for grammar schools has been the subject of criticism. It was felt that the concept of intelligence which underlay the selection tests was not sufficiently well-understood and that it was not a unitary or a stable attribute, as had been assumed.

Psychopathology

Psychopathology is the study of mental disorder. Here again it is not easy to separate 'pure' research into the nature of abnormalities from 'applied' research into appropriate ways of treating those with abnormalities. Essentially those engaged in 'pure' research in this area might, for example, be investigating the function of dopamine as a neurotransmitter. Applied research might involve the development of drugs which could block the action of **dopamine** in the case of schizophrenia, or alternatively the development of drugs which increase its availability in the case of Parkinsonism.

Self-assessment Questions

1. What is the particular focus of developmental psychologists?
2. Why do cognitive psychologists use models?
3. What kind of issues do social psychologists address?
4. List some of the methods used by physiological psychologists
5. What are some of the reasons why comparative psychologists study animals?
6. What is the main thrust of those who engage in psychometric research?

SECTION II APPLIED RESEARCH

Non-therapeutic Applications

Applied research is carried out either in an academic environment – a university – or in a work context. Typically the problem posed will be a practical one, in contrast to pure research which tends not to be so much problem-based as theory-based. The work of the Applied Psychology Unit (APU) at Cambridge University is a good example. The APU was started by Craik and Bartlett, carried on by Broadbent and Baddeley, and produced not only practical solutions to problems but also theoretical contributions to areas of knowledge such as attention, vigilance and memory. At the same time, their advice has influenced such practical outcomes as the design of decimal coinage and postal codes. Broadbent has been concerned practically with such problems as how noise affects people's ability to make decisions and attend to the task in hand. Real problems, such as the ergonomic design of pilots' cockpit control panels or systems for radar operators are dealt with.

In an academic context such as that enjoyed by the APU, problems are solved mainly through simulating them in the laboratory, for example setting up a simulation of a radar operator's workplace and then testing for the effects of such things as stress on performance.

Alternatively, applied psychology may involve action research in the workplace. **Participant observation** might be used. Warr (1978) became a member of a trade union negotiating team to gain first-hand experience of the methods used by employers and unions. This is applied social psychology.

Again it is useful to look at some examples of applied research in the fields mentioned above.

Applied Research in Cognitive Psychology

Bach-y-Rita *et al.* (1969) worked on what became known as 'blind-sight'. This was the development of a tactile sensory replacement for normal sight. The user wears a vest with a grid on which are hundreds of tiny points that touch the skin. The vest is connected to a black and white camera; light and dark messages are gathered by the camera and translated into vibrations on the points on the vest. With this equipment blind people have been able to find things in a room quickly, read meters and even read an oscilloscope (a scientific instrument designed to display electrical activity which has a screen not unlike a television).

Applied Research in Developmental Psychology

The Cockcroft committee was set up to enquire into the question of why there seemed to be so many problems associated with the learning of mathematics in schools (Department of Education and Science, 1982). The committee received evidence of research on learning and teaching mathematics which was reviewed by Bell *et al.* (1983). They concluded that mathematics was hard to learn because it tended to deal with abstract relationships. This concentration on abstracts has been highlighted by the growth in the use of calculators to perform the basic symbol manipulations which had at one time been seen as the core of mathematics as learnt in school. If you could manipulate the right symbols in the right order you could get the answer right, whether or not you had any understanding of the underlying concepts. With the use of calculators the focus began to be placed on developing an understanding of the concepts, rather than just on symbol manipulation, and it has been this that has proved difficult for many children.

Piaget showed that abstract concepts were difficult to acquire. The formal operations stage of development was the point at which children began to be able to deal with abstracts. For most children this was at about age 11 and, for some, much later than this. In fact Shayer and Wylam (1978) claimed that only about 20 per cent of British children reach the formal operational stage by age 16. Assuming, therefore, that most of the children in secondary schools are still at the concrete operational stage, more attention should be paid to the level of thought required in working through textbooks in mathematics, which should themselves be directed more towards concrete operations. The solution is to use apparatus to build bridges between concrete and abstract thought and to encourage children to develop mathematical thought through language.

Applied Research in Social Psychology

Perhaps the most important application of social psychology lies in the field of **organisational psychology**. Blackler and Brown (1980) reported revolutionary changes in the field of job-design in the Volvo plant in Sweden. Because of high customer demand there was a need to increase production of trucks. The existing assembly lines were working at maximum capacity. A new and unconventional approach was adopted which involved a semi-autonomous team of workers assembling around a static chassis. Since the days of Henry Ford it had been thought that the static assembly of vehicles was much less efficient than moving assembly lines. With a motivated, skilled and co-operative workforce, however, it seemed that savings of something like 30 per cent could be achieved by this new method of static assembly. There was enthusiasm on the part of the workers for the new method and its potential began to be realised, so that even when demand slackened the company did not shut down the experimental unit, but continued to explore its feasibility. From a psychological standpoint it maximised the variety of work for an individual and provided learning opportunities, responsibility and involvement in the whole task. However, opinion among the managers at the factory hardened against innovation and eventually, when a new plant was built in 1979, it was along more conventional lines.

One reason why this experiment did not succeed was the conservatism of senior managers. It had become a feature of the experimental static plant that, once the quota for the day had been achieved, workers had been allowed some relaxation at their workstation. Management, however, reacted to this by increasing work quotas, and this had a demoralising effect. Loss of managerial control in the new method was considered to be an insuperable obstacle in the way of establishing what had at first been shown to be a more effective method of work

Applications of Comparative Psychology

It cannot be said that there is strictly applied research in the field of **comparative psychology**. A researcher does not deliberately set out to use psychological research to solve a particular problem, as in the example above of research into the learning of mathematics. It is, however, true that much has been learned about human behaviour from the studies of animals conducted by **ethologists**. For example, **displacement** activities have been much researched by ethologists where there is a drive-conflict situation. Animals will engage in totally unrelated activity in the stress of conflict between wanting to do and being afraid of doing something. A cock zebra finch in conflict between approaching a hen and flying away from her may wipe his beak violently on the perch. A human teenager waiting for a first date may indulge in one of a number of displacement activities – chewing nails, adjusting make-up, straightening a tie or smoothing a skirt. But this is not applied psychology. It is the application of pure psychology in explanation of behaviour.

Lea (1984) identified four ways of applying the results of studying animal behaviour:

1. Ethology provides insights which are of benefit in such situations as the interaction of humans with animals on farms, zoos and wildlife reserves, and the keeping of pets by individuals. In particular, the mating behaviour of endangered species can he singled out. It is necessary when natural habitats are destroyed to induce species to breed in captivity. Knowledge of normal mating procedures enables us to simulate the conditions which might enable them to reproduce.

2. In their study of animals, ethologists employ carefully planned observational techniques. These methods have been adapted and used for the study of humans. This **human ethology** has been particularly successful in the study of babies and young children. Among many examples described by Schaffer (1977) there is a detailed description of 'states' – classified by Prechtl and Beintema (1964) – of babies ranging from 'deep regular sleep' (state 1) to 'crying' (state 5). These states were seen as cyclical. Not only is the baby stirred into action by outside stimulation but internal forces regulate much of a baby's behaviour.

3. Sometimes the ideas and concepts of ethology may be incorporated into psychological theory. Hediger (1951) in his analysis of the behaviour of zoo animals developed the concept of 'individual distance', the space which individuals of the same species always seem to try to keep between each other. This has been adopted into the social psychology of humans as the concept of **personal space**.

4. Most questionably, results from ethological studies have been extrapolated into human study. Desmond Morris (1978) for instance has attempted this kind of extrapolation, concentrating particularly upon non-verbal communication.

Applied Psychometrics

Psychometric research has been largely applied in that tests of individuals' characteristics have been designed, not so much with the pure goal of better understanding the differences between people, as for the practical object of placing people in suitable employment, or – to stand that on its head – to find suitable employees to fill a vacancy. Trainability testing (Robertson and Downs, 1979) has also been developed. This is a form of testing where applicants are given a period of training in the skills they are required to learn and then systematically observed and rated as they attempt to carry out the task. It is job-specific and requires no prior knowledge or experience on the part of the candidate. Trainability tests have been shown to be valuable in relation to semi-skilled manual tasks, and in discovering management potential. Personality testing such as that using the Myers–Briggs Type Indicator is also quite widely used for job selection.

Therapeutic Applications

Different kinds of therapy spring from the main approaches to psychology: behaviourist, psychoanalytic, cognitive and humanistic.

Behaviour Therapies

One example of behaviour therapies in common use is the technique of **behaviour modification**. This has been used quite extensively in the treatment of abnormal behaviour, particularly in children. In essence, it amounts to the application of conditioning procedures, especially **operant conditioning**, to change the behaviour of those treated. It has been used, for example, to treat people with mental handicaps so that they exhibit behaviour which is more acceptable to the group with whom they are associated. The procedure is to isolate desired behaviour, which is then systematically reinforced, while reinforcement is withheld from undesirable behaviour. Research into the treatment by this means of agoraphobia (fear of leaving a safe and secure place) has resulted in increased effectiveness of treatment and reduction of therapist time.

Psychoanalytic Therapy

Psychoanalytic therapy arises from the practices of Freud and his followers, and is based upon the uncovering of problems concealed in the unconscious mind, perhaps from childhood, and with their revelation, coming to terms with problems currently exhibited. Interest is beginning to build up in Britain in this area of research with the establishment of a Psychoanalysis Unit in the University of London and of research into the process of psychotherapy in the Social and Applied Psychology Unit at Sheffield University. An example might be the use of play-therapy by Melanie Klein (see Chapter 2) and her associates (Klein, 1959). Klein provided carefully-chosen toys and play materials for children referred to her and allowed them freedom to play as they wished under her observation. She sat or knelt with individual children as they played and interpreted their behaviour in psychoanalytic terms; that is to say, she considered how the behaviour observed might have a symbolic relationship with some past experience which had become a part of the unconscious and was affecting the child's personality.

Cognitive Therapy

Cognitive therapy is being increasingly used by clinical psychologists in the treatment of depression and other disorders. Its initial effectiveness has been shown to compare favourably with the use of medication. Cognitive therapy is used on the assumption that a person suffering from depression tends to have a memory system biased towards negative material, and these negative memories contribute to the maintenance of the depressed mood. The aim of cognitive therapy is to replace these negative memories with more positive ones. Cognitive psychology has also been used in the treatment of occupational stress, a condition which is becoming increasingly common. Treatment with tranquillising drugs is common, but psychological therapies aim to help patients to see their world differently and to accept personal responsibility for their own lives.

Therapy Based Upon Humanistic Psychology

Client-centred therapy such as that offered by centres whose work is based on that of Carl Rogers is increasingly being used as an alternative to other treatments. The aim is to help clients to come to terms with themselves. By means of individual therapy, group or family therapy sessions, a more realistic evaluation of an individual's self-concept emerges which is closer to a conception of the person's ideal self. The process is one of non-intervention by the therapist whose role is to encourage clients to talk about themselves or to each other, and who is trained in counselling techniques designed to help people find their own solution to problems.

Self-assessment Questions

1. What contributions did the Applied Psychology Unit at Cambridge make to the solution of practical problems?

2. Describe one area of applied research in developmental or social psychology.
3. How has applied social psychology been used in an industrial context?
4. List four ways in which comparative psychology has been applied in practical situations.
5. Describe some therapeutic applications of psychology.

SECTION III CAREER OPENINGS FOR PSYCHOLOGISTS

The above sections will have given some indication of the kind of work done by psychologists in an academic context. The openings described below detail some of the ways in which professional psychologists work, together with an indication of career routes into those fields It is worth emphasising that psychology is a graduate profession and the openings described below assume the possession of a degree in psychology, or one that is recognised by the British Psychological Society.

Occupational Psychology

There are many who hold psychological qualifications employed in industry and the public services, in particular the Civil Service and HM Forces. The kind of work they do has already been alluded to. As employees are selected for employment the psychologist has a role in their selection and in their training. The development of aptitude tests for particular jobs is part of their function, as is the assessment of performance within their employment. Occupational psychologists work alongside other professionals, such as managers, trades-union representatives, training officers and other specialist staff.

Personnel Management

The management of personnel is an area heavily dependent on psychological skills. Postgraduate courses leading to membership of the Institute of Personnel Management will inevitably have a high psychological content. The National Institute for Industrial

Psychology runs training courses and validates tests of aptitude in this field of occupational psychology.

Occupational Health

Another area in which psychologists are becoming involved in the occupational field is occupational health. In particular there is growing concern about occupational stress and this has been a stimulus for development work in this area. Occupational health now embraces all aspects of employee health care.

The Use of Computers in Industry

Another area which has received attention from occupational psychologists is the interface between humans and computers. Factories, hospitals and small businesses are increasingly using micro-computers, word processors and so on, and the relationship between person and machine is becoming important for productivity, health, career development and work roles. There has been an overwhelming interest in applied research in this field. The issues include:

- Negative health consequences;
- Improvement of career prospects;
- Clarification of role relationships, which become increasingly confused with the growth of the use of micros. This has led to a new Inter-Research Council (the Economic and Social Reseach Council with the Medical Research Council) initiative in the field of human/computer interaction which will receive funding for both research and training and will have a major psychological component.

Minorities at Work

A further area of research among occupational psychologists has been concerned with the question of minorities at work – especially women and ethnic groups.

Women at work Research is being carried out into the way in which women are treated in industry, for example, their career paths, their health and the impact of their dual roles in families where both partners have careers. While this research has led to growing demands for change in the legislative field, little has as yet been done and so it is likely that research into women in the workplace will grow.

Ethnic minorities In the case of ethnic groups at work, the situation is not good. Little sytematic research has been done into what is an increasingly difficult problem in Britain. Areas to be tackled include **career development, stress, co-worker relationships** and **discrimination**.

There is also research into cognitive areas specific to occupational psychology. In particular, **performance appraisal** has become increasingly important and efforts are beginning to be made to apply psychological theory to appraisal at work.

The enormous change which is happening in Britain, industrially and socially, has also led to the need for research into the way in which people can plan and cope with organisational change in the work situation. Occupational psychologists are beginning to make a real contribution in this area.

Labels in Occupational Psychology

You may come across a number of different labels within this field. It is useful here to clarify some of them:

- **Ergonomics** is the study of the way in which humans fit with machines of many kinds – the best position for the steering wheel, seats and controls for a car, for example, are a matter of ergonomics. This is increasingly also being referred to as 'human factors'.
- **Industrial psychology** refers to the ways in which humans behave in an industrial situation. It might involve relations between managers and work people, for example.
- **Time management** relates to the efficient use of people's time.
- **Personnel mangement,** as we have seen, relates to how people are best fitted for a job.
- **Management consultancy** relates to how managers may best utilise the human resources which they have at their disposal.

The Route to Occupational Psychology

It is not now possible to train as an occupational psychologist 'on the job'. A chartered occupational psychologist must now have a

BPS-accredited first degree in psychology (that is, one which confers a Graduate Basis for Registration (GBR). Then the trainee would go on to an accredited one-year training course, followed by two years of practice under the supervision of a chartered psychologist. The only exceptions to this are for mature entrants. They may go straight into employment after graduation and join a training course at a later date. Those who complete the three-year training will be accepted for the Register of Charterd Psychologists (Division of Occupational Psychology). Mature entrants will be required to sit the Society's Postgraduate Certificate in Occupational Psychology. This examines academic knowledge in eight main areas, in five of which the trainee will need to gain supervised experience and demonstrate expertise. Figure 7.3 shows the routes available for occupational psychologists.

Clinical Psychology

Clinical psychology is concerned with the application of psychology to problems of mental disorder. Clinical psychologists work mainly with psychiatrists in a hospital context or in the community. There is need for a rapid expansion in the number of clinical psychologists, but funding for sufficient training courses for the ample supply of suitably qualified applicants is presently inadequate.. Most clinical psychologists are employed by Health Authorities, where their role is to work with psychiatrists in the treatment of patients suffering from psychological disorders. However, an increasing number are now working with children and adolescents rather than adults. They also work with the mentally handicapped, the elderly and those who have neuropsychological problems.

Some example of the kinds of work which clinical psychologists do include:

- Training people in self relaxation;
- Helping people with learning difficulties to care for themselves;
- Treating people with eating disorders, sexual problems, phobias, head injuries, strokes, HIV/AIDS and problems associated with ageing.

They may work from health centres, hospitals or in people's homes. Generally, they operate as part of a team including social workers,

FIGURE 7.3
Routes to a Career in Occupational Psychology

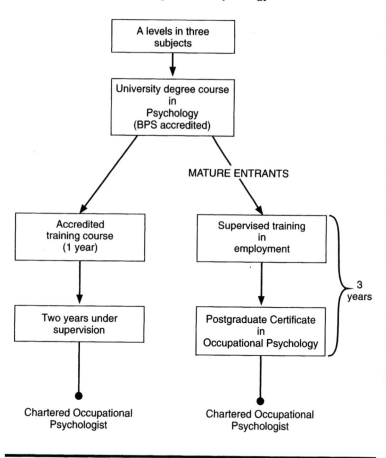

medical practitioners and other health professionals. While most work within the NHS there is growing work in private practice.

Clinical psycholoogists are also engaged in teaching and research into psychological treatment. Such research activity might inclde, for example :

- *Research into behavioural therapy.* For example, into the treatment of agoraphobia (a fear of open spaces) or the use of behaviour modification to change the behaviour of those with mental handicaps such as autism.

- *Research into psychological treatments for medical conditions.* There is strong evidence for the effectiveness of psychological therapy for the treatment of hypertension (high blood pressure), asthma, epilepsy and chronic pain. Cognitive retraining and rehabilitation of patients with neurological handicap (stroke victims, for example) have also received attention and this has in turn contributed to our understanding of human brain function. There has been an extension of treatment by clinical psychologists to groups of patients not treated by them hitherto, for example AIDS patients and cases of sexual abuse in children.
- *Research into the nature of psychological dysfunction.* This has been closely allied with that into the treatment of abnormality. For example there has been research into cognitive and attentional dysfunctions in cases of schizophrenia and emotional disorders. Social psychology has contributed to an understanding of the role of life-events and of social support in the etiology of emotional problems. Physiological psychology has contributed to an understanding of the behavioural effects of Alzheimer's disease.

A Career Path for Clinical Psychology

All the above indicate a rapid growth in the use of psychological expertise in clinical treatments, but this has not been matched by growth in facilities for training so that it is becoming difficult to enter this field. Many individuals gain experience in poorly paid work in hospitals to gain appropriate experience before applying for training.

Those aspiring to become clinical psychologists need a BPS-accredited first degree, usually with first or or upper-second class honours. After this there is a three-year training course accredited by the society. There are 20 applicants for each place on these courses, so that as well as a good degree applicants will need relevant experience either before or after graduation. It might be possible to work on a voluntary basis as an assistant psychologist or with one of the charities operating in this field. Figure 7.4 shows a career path to the register of Chartered Clinical Psychologists.

FIGURE 7.4
Career Path to Become a Chartered Clinical Psychologist

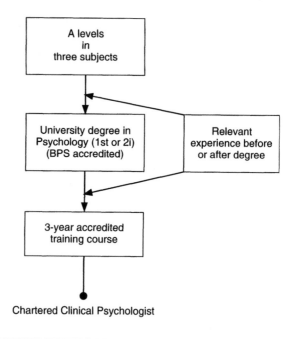

Chartered Clinical Psychologist

Counselling Psychologists

Counselling psychologists aim to improve people's well-being, alleviate distress and enable people to solve their own problems and take their own decisions. They work with individuals, families, couples or groups, either privately or in primary health care in the NHS (perhaps in GP's surgeries). Other contexts include counselling organisations, business and academic contexts. To become a Chartered Counselling Psychologist a BPS-accredited first degree in psychology is needed before taking the society's Diploma in Counselling Psychology. Some training courses accredited by the BPS confer exemption from all or part of the diploma. Figure 7.5 shows a route to registration as a Chartered Counselling Psychologist.

FIGURE 7.5
Career Path to Registration as a Chartered Counselling Psychologist

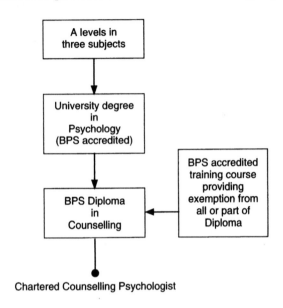

Chartered Counselling Psychologist

Many people work as counsellors without going through this route or becoming a Chartered Psychologist. An appendix to this chapter includes the address of The British Association for Counselling who are able to provide information about appropriate training courses.

Psychotherapy

Psychotherapy covers a wide range of treatments for mental or physical disorders. A wide range of methods are employed and psychotherapists work with individuals or with groups of patients, children as well as adults. These methods include:

- Long series of intimate discussions, often extending over two or three years.
- One or two intense interview sessions.

- Role-play or the encouragement of the expression of emotions.
- The use of hypnosis.

The BPS takes the view that psychotherapy or hypnosis is properly a postgraduate specialisation for medical practitioners, applied psychologists or social workers. Psychology graduates interested in training in psychotherapy should first acquire relevant basic training in another field of applied psychology and follow this with training in psychotherapy. Some of the training courses are inadequate though the United Kingdom Council for Psychotherapists (UKCP) have validated courses in Psychotherapy and set up a register of Psychotherapists. Similarly, the British Association for Counselling (BAC) have validated counselling courses and are finalising a register of counsellors. Both UKCP and BAC are collaborating with various universities to validate qualifications at master's level. Further information may be obtained from the organisations who addresses are listed at the end of this chapter. There is need for extreme care in the choice of private courses, and the BPS suggest that the following questions should be addressed by those wishing to take such courses:

- Is the course prospectus detailed enough to indicate the objects, methods and orientation of the course?
- Is the course long enough, and the amount of supervised experience sufficient ?
- What are the qualifications of the course organisers and supervisors?
- Is supervision of therapy provided for trainees, individually (or at least in pairs) on a regular basis?
- Does the course have a formal and externally validated method of assessing trainees?
- Has the course been approved by an accredited body other than the organisation running it ?

The NHS employs Child Psychotherapists. The Association of Child Psychotherapists whose address is listed in the appendix can advise on training.

Educational Psychology

The psychology of education has always been a central concern. There has been much theorising and empirical work carried out in this area. The Schools Psychological Service has had an impact within as well as beyond the classroom.

Educational psychologists work in schools, colleges, nurseries, special units or in the children's own homes in close collaboration with teachers and parents. The work consists of assessing children's progress, their emotional and academic needs and providing help and advice. It may be necessary for them to write reports about children in relation to their special educational needs, behavioural problems or court proceedings.

The Route to a Career as an Educational Psychologist

Someone aspiring to join the Schools Psychological Service will need, first, a good degree in psychology, and then a postgraduate teaching qualification (PGCE). Thereafter, some practical experience in teaching in schools will be followed by a specific qualification in Educational Psychology before a person may apply for appointment as a member of the Schools Psychological Service of a local education authority. It needs to be remembered that psychology is not a subject within the National Curriculum and consequently those aspiring to teach in secondary schools will need an appropriate subsidiary subject which is within the curriculum. Thereafter, some experience in teaching in schools will be followed by a specific qualification in educational psychology and a year of supervised practice before applying for appointment as a member of the Schools Psychological Service and to be registered as a Chartered Educational Psychologist.

In Scotland there is no requirement that educational psychologists should have teaching experience, but not having teaching experience will restrict the area in which a person may work. Authorities in England, Wales and Northern Ireland will require educational psychologists to have had teaching experience. Figure 7.6 shows a career path to become a Chartered Educational Psychologist.

While the majority of Chartered Educational Psychologists work in the public sector and are mainly employed by local education authorities, there are a growing number working independently as private consultants. Mature students are welcomed as aspiring educational psychologists. Qualified teachers who are not psychology graduates may train as educational psychologists but they must first study for a qualification conferring eligibility for the Graduate Basis for Registration (GBR) and then have postgraduate training

FIGURE 7.6
Career Path for Entry to Educational Psychology

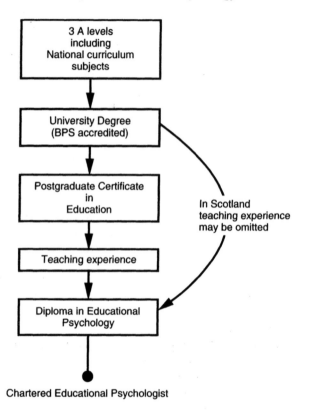

Chartered Educational Psychologist

as an educational psychologist. Further teaching experience is, of course, not necessary.

Despite the relevance of psychology to the training of teachers, there has been a reduction in recent years of psychological content in teacher-training courses and even a suggestion by government that psychology was not an appropriate discipline for aspiring members of the teaching profession. This has obviously caused problems for the recruitment and training of educational psychologists to work in the Schools Psychological Service. The educational psychologist's role has been to provide assessment and guidance for children referred to them by schools because their behaviour or progress has caused anxiety, and this role is, if anything, more necessary now than in the past.

Paradoxically, the changes brought about within education by the same government have led to a resurgence of interest in both the psychology of education and in educational psychology. Work in both academic and professional psychology in the field of education has been the catalyst for this developing interest in, and understanding of, the educational process.

Forensic Psychology

Forensic (or **criminological** and **legal psychology**) might involve therapeutic work with individuals or with groups of offenders. This kind of work aims at understanding and treating behaviour problems in those who have come into conflict with the law. Psychologists in this field may be involved with any of the following:

- The organisation and evaluation of custodial regimes.
- Clinical work with individuals after they leave the courts.
- The administration of the judicial system. They are increasingly involved in management issues, in dealing with stress and in dealing with such things as hostage situations.
- Work in prisons or in other secure establishments – detention centres or Regional Secure Units.
- Training and treatment of prisoners.
- Carrying out clinical interviews and administering behavioural and psychometric tests.
- research into the psychological processes that underlie certain offences, such as sexual offences or aggression.

They may also be members of the police force. They may be involved in producing profiles of criminals. In the community they are involved with the rehabilittion of offenders and in preventing the re-occurrence of offending behaviour

It is possible to identify four areas of work within this field:

1. *Clinical and rehabilitative work.* This involves attempting to establish the causes of anti-social or aggressive behaviour in order to improve it through treatment.

2. *Administration*. Secure institutions are likely to employ psychologists to be involved, initially, in the planning of the units and in operational policy within the unit – allocation of resources and design of the accommodation for instance. Psychologists are likely to sit on Home Office and Department of Health committees concerned with the future planning of special hospitals.

3. *Court work*. Criminological and legal psychologists may be involved in both criminal and civil court cases. In a civil case this might involve using psychometric or behavioural tests to help assess the impairment of an individual's functioning following an accident. In a criminal case a psychologist might be asked to see an individual charged with a petty offence such as shoplifting and perhaps establish what the intention of the offender was. This might influence judgement and sentence.

4. *Prison service work*. A psychologist might also work in the environment of a prison. Work might include helping prison officers understand the factors which produce a build-up of tension in the prison, leading to outbreaks of violence. Teaching aspects of criminology or advising on hostage-taking are also aspects of a psychologist's work with prison staff.

Route to Registration as a Chartered Forensic Psychologist

Chartered forensic psychologists working in special hospitals and regional secure units will usually have first qualified as clinical psychologists. Prison psychologists need to have a Society accredited first degree in psychology and then be selected for Civil Service Basic Grade Psychologist posts. There are no prison psychologists in Scotland and Northern Ireland. Their work is done by clinical psychologists. Experience will usually be gained as an assistant psychologist in the prison service, in the clinical setting or through the probation or social services. Figure 7.7 shows career paths for a Chartered Forensic Psychologist.

Health Psychologists

This is a new field of applied psychology. Health psychologists work in universities, hospitals and academic health research departments to promote better attitudes, behaviour and thinking in relation to

FIGURE 7.7
Career Paths to Become a Chartered Forensic Psychologist

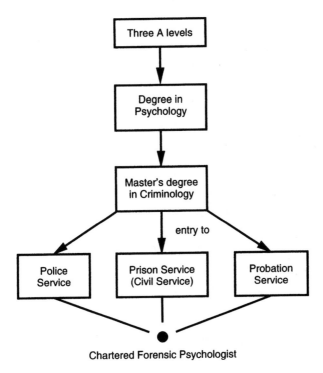

Chartered Forensic Psychologist

health issues. They may find themselves involved in any of the following:

- Advising about communication with patients.
- Evaluating the services provided for patients by hospitals and other health care organisations.
- Assessing the ways in which people's beliefs may affect treatment.

There is at present no established route for registration as a Chartered Psychologist in this field.

Sports Psychology

As with health psychology there is as yet no established route to qualification as a Chartered Sports Psychologist, but there are a number of psychologists on the register able to offer a service as sports psychologists. They are generally on the register on the basis of a postgraduate research degree. The British Association of Sports and Exercise Sciences keeps a list of approved sports psychologists. In the cases both of health and sports psychologists, admission to the register as Chartered Psychologists depends on the individuals meeting the criteria for registration as a Chartered Psychologist. There is at present no approved route nor any training courses accredited by the Society.

Teaching Psychology

Teachers of psychology work in schools, colleges and universities. They will usually have a degree in psychology but will not usually be Chartered Psychologists as they are primarily teachers rather than professional psychologists. There exists, however, a Diploma in Applied Psychology of Teaching, holders of which may apply to become Chartered Psychologists.

Self-assessment Questions

1. List those areas of work where psychologists are likely to be found.
2. What kinds of work would you expect an occupational psychologist to do?
3. What are some of the functions of clinical psychologists?

Appendix

Some useful addresses are listed below:

The British Psychological Society
St Andrews House
48, Princess Road East
Leicester LE1 7DR
(0116 247 0787)

Association of Child Psychotherapists
54, Gayton Road
London NW3 1TU
(0171 794 8881)

The British Association for Counselling
1, Regent Place
Rugby Warwickshire CV21 2PJ
(01788 50899)

The British Association of Sport and Exercise Sciences
114, Cardigan Road, Headingley
Leeds LS6 3BJ
(0113 230 7558)

United Kingdom Council for Psychotherapy
1st Floor, 167–9 Great Portland Street
London W1N 5JB
(0171 436 3002)

FURTHER READING

B. Ball (1989) *Manage Your Own Career* (Leicester: British Psychological Society Books).
British Psychological Society (1986) *How about Psychology: A Guide to Courses and Careers* (Leicester: British Psychological Society Books).
British Psychological Society (1996) *Careers in Psychology* (Leicester: British Psychological Society Books).

Bibliography

Ainsworth, M. D. S. and Bell, S. M. (1969) 'Some contemporary patterns of mother–infant interaction in the feeding situation', in A. Ambrose (ed.), *Stimulation in Early Infancy* (London: Academic Press).

Alexander, B. K., Coambs, R. B. and Hadaway, P. F. (1978) 'The effect of housing and gender on morphine self-administration in rats', *Psychopharmacology*, 58, 175–9.

Allport, G. W. (1961) *Pattern and Growth in Personality* (New York: Holt, Rinehart & Winston).

Allport, G. W. (1962) 'The general and unique in psychological science', *Journal of Personality*, 30, 405–21.

Allport, G. W. (1965) *Letters from Jenny* (New York: Harcourt, Brace & World).

Anastasi, A. (1958) in R. M. Lerner (1986) *Concepts and Theories in Human Development*, 2nd edn (New York: Random House).

Animals (Scientific Procedures) Act 1986, *Halsbury's Statutes*, 4th edn, *Current Statutes Service*, Issue 9, Vol. 2, 3–34 (London: Butterworth).

Argyle, M. (1987) *The Psychology of Happiness* (London: Methuen).

Aronson, E. (1992) *The Social Animal* (New York: Freeman).

Asch, S. (1956) 'Studies of independence and submission to group pressure: a minority of one against a unanimous majority', *Psychological Monographs*, 70 (9), (whole no. 416).

Asch, S. E. (1952) *Social Psychology* (New York: Prentice-Hall).

Asch, S. E. (1956) 'Studies of independence and submission to group pressure: a minority of one against a unanimous majority', *Psychological Monographs*, 70 (9) (Whole no. 416).

Atkinson, J. W. (1964) *An Introduction to Motivation* (Princeton, New Jersey: Van Nostrand Reinhold).

Atkinson, R. C. and Shiffrin R. M. (1971) 'The control of short-term memory', *Scientific American*, 224, 82–90.

Atkinson, R. L., Atkinson, R. C., Smith, E. E. and Hilgard, E. R. (1985) *Introduction to Psychology*, 9th edn (New York: Harcourt Brace Jovanovich).

Ayllon, T. and Azrin, N. H. (1968) *The Token Economy: A Motivational System for Therapy and Rehabilitation* (New York: Appleton Century Crofts).

Bach-y-Rita, P., Collins, C. C., Saunders, F. A., White B. and Scadden L. (1969) 'Visual substitution by tactile image projection', *Nature*, 221, 963–4.

Ball, B. (1989) *Manage Your Own Career* (Leicester: BPS Books).

Bard, P. (1934) 'The neurohumoral basis of emotional reactions', in C. A. Murchison (ed.), *Handbook of General Experimental Psychology* (Worcester, Mass.: Clark University Press).

Baron, R. A. and Byrne, D. (1991) *Social Psychology*, 6th edn (Boston: Allyn & Bacon).

Baron-Cohen, S., Leslie, A. M. and Frith, U. (1985) 'Does the autistic child have a "theory of mind"?' Cognition, vol. 21, 37–46.

Bateson, P. (1986) 'When to experiment on animals', *New Scientist*, 109 (1496), 30–2.

Bateson, P. (1991) 'Assessment of pain in animals', *Animal Behaviour*, 42, 827–39.

Bateson, P. (1992) 'Do animals feel pain?', *New Scientist*, 134 (1818), 30–3.

Baumrind, D. (1964) 'Some thoughts on the ethics of research after reading Milgram's "Behavioural study of obedience"', *American Psychologist*, 19, 4211–23.

BBC Horizon. 'Chimp Talk', broadcast on 21 June 1993.

Bell, A. W., Costello, J. and Kuchemann, D. E. (1983) *A Review of Research in Mathematical Education: research on learning and teaching* (London: National Federation for Education Research).

Belsky, J. and Rovine, M. (1987) 'Temperament and attachment security in the Strange Situation: a rapprochement' *Child Development*, 58, 787–95

Bergin, A. E. (1971) 'The evaluation of therapeutic outcomes', in A. E. Bergin and S. L. Garfield (eds), *Handbook of Psychotherapy and Behaviour Change: An Empirical Analysis* (New York: Wiley).

Berlyne, D. E. (1960) *Conflict, Arousal and Curiosity* (New York: McGraw-Hill).

Berry, J. W. (1983) 'The sociogenesis of social sciences: an analysis of the cultural relativity of social psychology', in B. Bain (ed.), *The Sociogenesis of Language and Human Conduct* (New York: Plenum Press).

Birch, A. (in press) *Developmental Psychology: from Infancy to Old Age*, 2nd edn (Basingstoke: Macmillan).

Birch, A. and Hayward, S. (1994) *Individual Differences* (London: Macmillan).

Birch, A. and Malim T. (1988) *Developmental Psychology: From Infancy to Adulthood* (London: Macmillan).

Blackler, F. and Brown, C. (1980) 'Job redesign and social change: case studies at Volvo', in K. D. Duncan, M. Grumeberg and D. Wallace (eds), *Changes in Working Life* (London: Wiley).

Blakemore, C. and Cooper, G. F. (1970) 'Development of the brain depends on the visual environment', *Nature*, 228, 477–8.

Bless, H., Bohner, G., Schwarz, N. and Strack, F. (1990) 'Mood and persuasion: a cognitive response analysis', *Personality and Social Psychology Bulletin*, 16, 331–45.

Bower, T. G. R. (1965) 'Stimulus variables determining space perception in infants', *Science*, 149, 88–9.

Bowlby, J. (1951) *Maternal Care and Mental Health* (Geneva: World Health Organisation).

Bradshaw, J. (1988) *Healing the Shame that Binds You* (Deerfield Beach, FL: Communications).

Brady, J. V. (1958) 'Ulcers in "executive monkeys"', *Scientific American*, 199, 95–100.

Brislin, R. (1993) Understanding Culture's Influence on Behaviour (Orlando, Fla.: Harcourt Brace Jovanovich).

British Psychological Society (1978) *Ethical Principles for Research on Human Subjects* (Leicester: The British Psychological Society).

British Psychological Society (1985) 'A code of conduct for psychologists', *Bulletin of the BPS*, vol. 38, 41–3.

British Psychological Society (1985) 'Guidelines for the use of animals in research', *Bulletin of the British Psychological Society*, 38, 289–91.

British Psychological Society (1986) *How about Psychology: A Guide to Courses and Careers* (Leicester: BPS Books).

British Psychological Society (1988) *Career Choices in Psychology* (Leicester: BPS Books).

British Psychological Society (1989a) *BPS Careers Pack* (Leicester: BPS Books).

British Psychological Society (1989b) *Putting Psychology to Work* (Leicester: BPS Books).

British Psychological Society (1990) *Ethical Principles for Conducting Research with Human Participants* (Leicester: The British Psychological Society).

British Psychological Society (1993) *Code of Conduct, Ethical Principles and Guidelines* (Leicester: BPS).

British Psychological Society (1996) *Careers in Psychology* (Leicester: BPS Books)

Broadbent, D. E. (1958) *Perception and Communication* (Oxford: Pergamon).

Broadbent, D. E. (1961) *Behaviour* (London: Eyre & Spottiswoode).

Brown, G. D. A. (1990) 'Cognitive science and its relation to psychology', *The Psychologist*, August, 339–43.

Bruner, J. S. (1976) 'Psychology and the image of man', *The Times Literary Supplement*, 17 Dec.

Bulhan, H. A. (1985) *Frantz Fanon and the Psychology of Oppression* (Boston: Boston University Press).

Cacioppo, J. T. and Petty, R. E. (1982) 'The need for cognition', *Journal of Personality and Social Psychology*, 42, 116–31.

Cannon, W. B. (1927) 'The James-Lange theory of emotions: a critical examination of an alternative theory', *American Journal of Psychology*, 39, 106–24.

Chaiken, S. (1987) 'The heuristic model of persuasion', in M. P. Zanna, J. M. Olson and C. P. Holson (eds), *Social Influence: The Ontario Symposium* (Vol 5) (Hillsdale, NJ: Erlbaum).

Chapman, A. J. and Gale A. (1982) *Psychology and People: A Tutorial Text* (London: BPS/Macmillan).

Clegg, F. (1982) *Simple Statistics - A Course Book for the Social Sciences* (Cambridge: Cambridge University Press).

Cohen, G. (1977) *The Psychology of Cognition* (London: Academic Press).

Coile, D. C. and Miller, N. E. (1984) 'How radical animal activists try to mislead humane people', *American Psychologist*, 39, 700–1.

Colman, A. M. (1991) 'Aspects of Intelligence', in I. Roth (ed.), *Introduction to Psychology*, Vol. 1 (Hove: Erlbaum).

Conover, M. R. (1982) 'Modernizing the scarecrow to protect crops from birds', *Frontiers of Plant Science*, 35, 7–8.

Coolican, H. (1990) *Research Methods and Statistics in Psychology* (London: Hodder & Stoughton).

Corsaro, W. A. (1985) *Friendship and Peer Culture in the Early Years* (Norwood, NJ: Ablex Publishing).

Cousins, N. (1989) *Head First: the Biology of Hope* (New York: E.P. Dutton)

Craik, F. and Lockhart, R. (1972) 'Levels of processing', *Journal of Learning and Verbal Behaviour*, 11, 671–84.

Crawford, M. and Unger, R. K. (1995) 'Gender issues in psychology', in A. M. Colman (ed.), Controversies in Psychology (Harlow: Longman).

Cumming, E. and W. Henry (1961) *Growing Old: A Process of Disengagement* (New York: Basic Books).

Cuthill, I. (1991) 'Field experiments in animal behaviour: methods and ethics', *Animal Behaviour*, 42, 1007–14.

Darwin, C. (1872) *The Expression of Emotions in Man and Animals* (London: John Murray: reprinted Chicago: University of Chicago Press).

Dawkins, R. (1976) *The Selfish Gene* (London: Oxford University Press).

Dawkins, R. (1993) 'Meet my cousin, the chimpanzee', *New Scientist*, 5 June, 36–42.

De Fries J. C. (1964) 'Effects of prenatal maternal stress on behaviour in mice: a genotype–environment interaction' (Abst.), *Genetics*, 50, 244.

Department of Education and Science (1982) *Aspects of Secondary Education in England: A Survey by HM Inspectors of Schools* (London: HMSO).

Deutsch, J. A. and Deutsch, D. (1963) 'Attention: some theoretical considerations', *Psychological Review*, 70, 80–90.

Dukes, W. F. (1965) 'N = 1', *Psychological Bulletin*, 64 (1), 74–9.

Ekman, P. (1985) *Telling Lies* (New York: Lyle Stuart).

Ekman, P., Levenson, R. W. and Frieson, W. V. (1983) 'Autonomic nervous system activity distinguishes among emotions', *Science*, 221, 1208–10.

Ellis, A. (1962) *Reason and Emotion in Psychotherapy* (New York: Lyle Stuart).

Erikson, E. H. (1963) *Childhood and Society* (New York: Norton).

Erikson, E. H. (1968) *Identity, Youth and Crisis* (New York: Norton).

Eron, L. D., Huesmann, L. R., Lefkowitz, M. M. and Walder, L. O. (1972) 'Does television violence cause aggression?', *American Psychologist*, 27, 253—72.

Experimental Psychology Society (1986) *The Use of Animals for Research by Psychologists* (Experimental Psychology Society).

Eysenck, H. (1973) *The Inequality of Men* (London: Temple Smith).

Eysenck, H. J. (1952) 'The effects of psychotherapy: an evaluation', *Journal of Consulting Psychology*, 16, 319–24.

Eysenck, H. J. (1966) 'Personality and experimental psychology', *Bulletin of the British Psychological Society*, 19 (62), 1–28.

Eysenck, H. J. and Eysenck, S. B. G. (1964) *Manual of the Eysenck Personality Inventory* (London: University of London Press).

Eysenck, H. J. and Wilson, G. D. (1973) *The Experimental Study of Freudian Theories* (London: Methuen).

Eysenck, M. (1994) *Perspectives in Psychology* (Hove: Lawrence Erlbaum Associates).

Fairbairn, S. and Fairbairn, G. (eds) (1987) *Psychology, Ethics and Change* (London: Routledge & Kegan Paul).

Falk, J. L. (1956) 'Issues distinguishing idiographic from nomothetic approaches to personality theory', *Psychological Review*, 63 (1), 53—72.

Fernando, S. (1991) *Mental Health, Race and Culture* (London: Macmillan).

Festinger, L. and Carlsmith, J. J. (1959) 'Cognitive consequences of forced compliance', *Journal of Abnormal and Social Psychology*, 58, 293-310.

Festinger, L., Riecken, H. W. and Schachter, S. (1956) *When Prophecy Fails* (Minnesota: University of Minnesota Press).

Fisher, S. and Greenberg, R. (1977) *The Scientific Credibility of Freud's Theories and Therapy* (Brighton: Harvester Press).

Frankl, V. E. (1992) *Man's Search for Meaning*, 4th edn (Boston, MA: Beacon Press).

Freud, A. (1936) *The Ego and the Mechanisms of Defence* (London: Chatto & Windus).

Furnham, A. and Pinder, A. (1990) 'Young people's attitudes and experimentation on animals', *The Psychologist: Bulletin of the British Psychological Society*, 3 (10), 444-8.

Gallup, G. G. and Suarez, S. D. (1985) 'Animal research versus the care and maintenance of pets: the names have been changed but the results remain the same', *American Psychologist*, 40, 968.

Gardner, A. R. and Gardne, B. (1969) 'Teaching sign language to a chimpanzee', *Science*, 165, 664-72.

Garnham, A. (1991) *The Mind in Action* (London: Routledge).

Gerbner, G., Gross, L., Morgan, M. and Signorielli, N. (1986) 'Living with television: The dynamics of the cultivation process', in J. Bryant and D. Zillman (eds), *Perspectives on Media Effects* (Hillsdale, NJ: Erlbaum).

Glassman, W. E. (1995) *Approaches to Psychology* (Buckingham: OU Press).

Goodall, J. (1978) 'Chimp killings; is it the man in them?', *Science News*, 113 (276) 327.

Graham, S. (1992) 'Most of the subjects were white and middle class: trends in published research on African Americans in selected APA journals, 1970-1989', *American Psychologist*, 47 (5), 629-39.

Gray, J. (1991) 'On the morality of speciesism', *The Psychologist: Bulletin of the British Psychological Society*, 4 (5), 196-8.

Gray, J. A. (1987) 'The ethics and politics of animal experimentation', in H. Beloff and A. M. Colman (eds), *Psychological Survey No.6* (Leicester: The British Psychological Society).

Green, S. (1980) 'Physiological studies I and II', in J. Radford and E. Govier (eds), *A Textbook of Psychology* (London: Sheldon Press).

Green, S. (1994) *Principles of Biopsychology* (Hove: Lawrence Erlbaum Associates).

Gregory, R. L. (1972) 'Visual Illusions', in B. M. Foss (ed.), *New Horizons in Psychology* (Harmondsworth: Penguin).

Gregory, R. L. and Wallace, J. G. (1963) 'Recovery from early blindness: a case study', *Experimental Psychological and Social Monograms*, 2.

Gross, R. (1995) *Themes, Issues and Debates in Psychology* (London: Hodder & Stoughton).

Gross, R. D. (1992) *Psychology: The Science of Mind and Behaviour* (London: Hodder & Stoughton).

Grossman, S. P. (1960) 'Eating or drinking elicited by direct adenergic or cholinergic stimulation of the hypothalamus', *Science*, 132, 301–2.

Guilford, J. P. (1950) 'Creativity', *American Psychologist*, 5, 444–54.

Hadow Report (1926) *The Education of the Adolescent* (London: HMSO).

Hall, J. (1991) 'Challenging psychometrics', *The Psychologist: Bulletin of the British Psychological Society*, 4 (5), 204.

Hare-Mustin, R. T. and Maracek, J. (1990) *Making a Difference. Psychology and the Construction of Gender* (New Haven CT: Yale University Press).

Hargreaves, D. H. (1967) *Social Relations in a Secondary School* (London: Routledge & Kegan Paul).

Harlow, H. (1959) 'Love in infant monkeys', *Scientific American*, 200 (6), 68–74).

Hartmann, E. L. (1973) *The Functions of Sleep* (New Haven, Conn.: Yale University Press).

Hartshorne, H. and May, M. A. (1928) *Studies in the Nature of Character; Studies in Deceit* (Vol. 1): *Studies in Self-control* (Vol. 2); *Studies in the Organisation of Character* (Vol. 3) (New York: Macmillan).

Hawks, D. (1981) 'The dilemma of clinical practice – Surviving as a clinical psychologist', in J. M. McPherson and M. Sutton (eds), *Reconstructing Psychological Practice* (London: Croom Helm).

Heather, N. (1976) *Radical Perspectives in Psychology* (London: Methuen).

Hebb, D. O. (1949) *The Organisation of Behavior* (New York: Wiley).

Hebb, D. O. (1974) 'What psychology is about', *The American Psychologist*, 29, 71–87.

Hediger, H. (1951) *Wild Animals in Captivity* (London: Butterworth).

Heidbreder, E. (1963) *Seven Psychologies* (Englewood Cliffs, NJ: Prentice-Hall).

Hess, E. H. (1959) 'Imprinting', *Science*, 130, 133–41.

Hess, E. H. (1972) 'Imprinting in a Natural Laboratory', *Scientific American*, 227, 24–31.

Hetherington, E. M. and Wray, N. P. (1964) 'Aggression, need for social approval and humour preferences', *Journal of Abnormal and Social Psychology*, 68, 685–9.

Hewstone, M., Stroebe, W., Codol, J. P. and Stephenson, G. M. (eds) (1988) *Introduction to Social Psychology* (Oxford: Blackwell).

Hill, C. J., Rubin, Z. and Peplau, L. A. (1976) 'Break-ups before marriage: the end of 103 affairs', *Journal of Social Issues*, 32(1), 147–88.

Hitler, A. (1962) *Mein Kampf* (Boston: Houghton Mifflin), originally published in 1925.

Hofstede, G. (1980) *Culture's Consequences: International Differences in Work-related Values* (Beverly Hills, Calif: Sage).

Holmes, J. (1994) *Abnormal Psychology* (New York: HarperCollins).

Holt, R. (1962) 'Individuality and generalisation in the psychology or personality', *Journal of Personality*, 30, 377–404.

Hovland, C. I. and Weiss, W. (1951) 'The influences of source credibility on communication effectiveness', *Public Opinion Quarterly*, 15, 635–50).

Hovland, C. I., Lumsdaine, A. A. and Sheffield, F. D. (1949) *Studies in Social Psychology in World War II* (Vol 3) *Experiments on Mass Communications* (Princeton, NJ: Princeton University Press).

Howitt, D. (1991) *Concerning Psychology: Psychology Applied to Social Issues* (Milton Keynes: Open University Press).

Howitt, D. and Owusu-Bempah, J. (1994) *The Racism of Psychology* (London: Harvester Wheatsheaf).

Hubel, D. H. and Wiesel, T. N. (1962) 'Receptive fields in the striate cortex of young visually inexperienced kittens', *Journal of Neurophysiology*, 26, 994.

Hull, C. L. (1943) *Principles of Behaviour* (New York: Appleton Century Crofts).

Humphreys, L. (1970) *Tea Room trade: Impersonal Sex in Public Places* (Chicago: Aldine-Atherton).

Hunter, J. E. and Schmidt, F. L. (1976) 'Critical analysis of statistical and ethical implications of various definitions of test bias', *Psychological Bulletin*, 85, 675–6.

Imich, A. (1991) 'Challenging psychometrics', *The Psychologist: Bulletin of the British Psychological Society*, 4 (5), 204.

Imich, A. (1991) 'Challenging psychometrics', *The Psychologist: Bulletin of the British Psychological Society*, 4 (5), 204.

Isaacs, W., Thomas, J. and Goldiamond, I. (1960) 'Applications of operant conditioning to reinstate verbal behaviour in psychotics', *Journal of Speech and Hearing Disorders*, 25, 8–12.

Iyengar, S. and Kinder, D. R. (1987) *News that Matters* (Chicago: University of Chicago Press).

James, W. (1 884) 'What is an emotion?', *Mind*, 9, 188–205.

James, W. (1890) *Principles of Psychology* (New York: Holt).

Jensen, A. R. (1969) 'How much can we boost IQ and scholastic achievement?' *Harvard Educational Review*, 39, 1–123.

Jouvet, M. (1967) 'Mechanisms of the states of sleep: a neuro-pharmacological approach', *Research Publications of the Association for Research into Nervous and Mental Disease*, 45, 86–126.

Joy, L. A., Kimball, M. and Zabrack, M. L. (1977) 'Television exposure and children's aggressive behavior', in T. M. Williams (Chair) 'The impact of television: a natural experiment involving three communities.' Symposium presented at the annual meeting of the Canadian Psychological Association, Vancouver.

Kaplan, R. M. and Saccuzzo, D. P. (1989) *Psychological Testing: Principles, Applications and Issues*, 2nd edn (California: Brooks Cole).

Klein, M. (1959) 'Our adult world and its roots in infancy', *Human Relations*, 12 (4), 291–303.

Kline, P. (1981) *Fact and Fantasy in Freudian Theory* (London: Methuen).

Kline, P. (1984) *Psychology and Freudian Theory: An Introduction* (London: Methuen).

Kline, P. (1992) *Psychometric Testing in Personnel Selection and Appraisal* (London: Croner).

Koestler, A. (1970) *The Ghost in the Machine* (London: Pan Books).

Kohlberg, L. (1975) 'The cognitive-developmental approach to moral education', *Phi Delta Kappa*, June, 670–7.

Koriat, A., Melkman, R., Averill, J. R. and Lazarus, R. S. (1972) 'Self-control of emotional reactions to a stressful film', *Journal of Personality*, 40, 601–19.

Krebs, J. R., Kacelnik, A. and Taylor, P. (1978) 'Optimal sampling by birds; an experiment with great tits (Parus major)', *Nature*, 275, 27–31.

Kuhn, T. S. (1962) *The Structure of Scientific Revolutions* (Chicago: University of Chicago Press).

Lamiell, J. T. (1981) 'Toward an idiothetic psychology of personality', *American Psychologist*, 36 (3), 276–89.

Lang, P. J. and Melamed, B. G. (1969) 'Case report: avoidance conditioning therapy of an infant with chronic ruminative vomiting', *Journal of Abnormal Psychology*, 74, 1–8.

Lange, C. J. (1967) 'The Emotions' (translation of Lange's 1885 monograph) in C. J. Lange and W. James (eds), *The Emotions* (New York: Haffner Publishing Co), facsimile of 1922 edition.

Lashley, K. S. (1929) *Brain Mechanisms and Intelligence* (Chicago, Illinois: University of Chicago Press).

Lazarus, R. S. (1971) *Personality*, 2nd edn (Englewood Cliffs, NJ: Prentice-Hall).

Lazarus, R. S. (1974) 'Cognitive and coping processes in emotion', in B. Weiner (ed.), *Cognitive Views of Human Motivation* (New York: Academic Press).

Lea, S. E. G. (1984) *Instinct, Environment and Behaviour* (London: Methuen).

Legge, D. (1975) *An Introduction to Psychological Science* (London: Methuen).

Lerner, R. M. (1986) *Concepts and Theories of Human Development*, 2nd edn (New York: Random House).

Leventhal, H. (1970) 'Findings and theory in the study of fear communication', in L. Berkowitz (ed.), *Advances in Experimental Social Psychology*, Vol 5 (New York: Academic Press).

Levy-Leboyer, C. (1988) 'Success and failure in applying psychology', *American Psychologist*, 43 (10), 779–85.

Leyhausen, P. (1973) 'On the function and relative hierarchy of moods', in K. Lorenz and P. Leyhausen (eds), *Motivation of Human and Animal Behavior* (New York: Van Nostrand).

Lilly, J. C. (1977) *The Deep Self* (New York: Simon & Schuster).

Lindsay, G. (1995) 'Values, ethics and psychology', *The Psychologist: Bulletin of the British Psychological Society*, 8 (11), 493–8.

Lindsay, G. and Colley, A. (1995) 'Ethical dilemmas of members of the British Psychological Society', *The Psychologist: Bulletin of the British Psychological Society*, 8 (10), 448–53.

Loftus, E. (1980) *Memory* (Reading: Addison-Wesley).

Loftus, E. and Hoffman, H. (1990) 'Misinformation and memory: the creation of new memories', *Journal of Experimental Psychology: General*, 118, 100–4.

Lorenz, K. (1937) in W. Sluckin (1972) *Imprinting and Early Learning*, 2nd edn (London: Methuen).

Lorenz, K. (1966) *On Aggression* (London: Methuen).

Lotus, E. F. (1979) *Eyewitness Testimony* (Cambridge, Mass.: Harvard University Press).

Lovaas, O. I. (1973) *Behavioral Treatment of Autistic Children* (Morristown, NJ: General Learning Press).

Luce, G. G. (1971) *Body Time: Physiological Rhythms and Social Stress* (New York: Pantheon).

Maier, S. F. and Laudenslager, M. (1985) 'Stress and health: exploring the links', *Psychology Today*, August, 44–9.

Mailer, N. (1973) *Marilyn* (New York: Galahad Books).

Malim, T. (1994) *Cognitive Processes* (London: Macmillan).

Malim, T. (1996) *Research Methods and Statistics* (London: Macmillan).

Malim, T. (in press) *Social Psychology*, 2nd edn (London: Macmillan).

Malim, T. and Birch, A. (1989) *Social Psychology* (London: Macmillan).

Malim, T., Birch, A. and Hayward, S. (1996) *Comparative Psychology. Human and Animal Behaviour: A Sociobiological Approach* (London: Macmillan).

Maslow, A. H. (1959) 'Cognition of being in the peak experences', *Journal of Genetic Psychology*, 94, 43—76.

Maslow, A. H. (1968) *Towards a Psychology of Being* (New York: Van Nostrand).

Maslow, A. H. (1971) *The Farther Reaches of Human Nature* (New York: Viking).

Masson, J. (1992) 'The tyranny of psychotherapy', in W. Dryden and C. Feltham (eds), *Psychotherapy and its Discontents* (Buckingham: Open University Press).

Masters, R. E. L. and Houston, J. (1966) *Varieties of Psychedelic Experience* (New York: Holt, Rinehart & Winston).

Masters, W. H. and Johnson, V. E. (1966) *Human Sexual Response* (Boston, Mass.: Little, Brown).

Matlin, M. (1993) *The Psychology of Women* (New York: Harcourt Brace Jovanovich).

McClelland, D. C., Atkinson, J. W., Clark, R. A. and Lowell, E. L. (1953) *The Achievement Motive* (New York: Appleton Century Crofts).

McGuire, W. J. (1964) 'Inducing resistance to persuasion.: some contemporary approaches', in L. Berkowitz (ed.), *Advances in Experimental Social Psychology*, Vol 1 (New York: Academic Press).

Medcof, J. and Roth, J. (eds) (1979) *Approaches to Psychology* (Milton Keynes, OU Press).

Mercer, D. (1986) *Biofeedback and Related Therapies in Clinical Practice* (Rockville, MD: Aspen Systems).

Milgram, S. (1974) *Obedience to Authority* (London: Tavistock).

Miller, N. E. (1985) 'The value of behavioural research on animals', *American Psychologist*, 40, 423–40.

Miller, S. (1975) *Experimental Design and Statistics* (London: Methuen).

Miron, N. (1968) 'Issues and implications of operant conditioning; the primary ethical consideration', *Hospital and Community Psychiatry*, 19, 226–8.

Moghaddam, F. M., Taylor, D. M. and Wright, S. C. (1993) *Social Psychology in Cross-Cultural Perspective* (New York: W. H. Freeman & Co).

Morris, D. (1978) *Manwatching* (St Albans, Herts: Triad/Panther).

Morris, J. B. and Beck, A. T. (1974) 'The efficacy of anti-depressant drugs: a review of research (1958–72)', *Archives of General Psychiatry*, 30, 667–74.

Morton, D. (1992) 'A fair press for animals', *New Scientist*, 11 April (1816) 28–30.

Mowrer, O. H. and Mowrer, W. A. (1938) 'Enuresis: a method for its study and treatment', *American Journal of Orthopsychiatry*, 8, 436–47.

Much, N. (1995) 'Cultural Psychology', in J. A. Smith, R. Harré and L. Van Langenhove (eds), *Rethinking Psychology* (London: Sage).

Nadler, A. (1986) 'Help seeking as a cultural phenomenon: differences between city and kibbutz dwellers', *Journal of Personality and Social Psychology*, 51, 976–82.

Neisser, U. (1964) 'Visual Search', *Scientific American*, 210, 94–101.

Neugarten, B. L. (1973) 'Personality change in late life: a developmental perspective', in C. Eisdorfer and M. P. Lawton (eds), *Psychology of Adult Development and Aging* (Washington, DC.: American Psychological Association).

Neugarten, B. L. (1977) 'Personality in aging', in J. E. Birren and K. W. Schaie (eds), *Handbook of the Psychology of Aging* (New York: Van Nostrand).

Newell, A. and Simon, H. A. (1972) *Human Problem Solving* (Englewood Cliffs, NJ: Prentice-Hall).

Newell, A., Shaw, J. C. and Simon, H. A. (1958) 'Elements of a theory of human problem solving', *Psychological Review*, 65, 151—76.

Norman, D. A. (1976) *Memory and Attention: An Introduction to Human Information Processing*, 2nd edn (New York: Wiley).

Norman, D. A. and Bobrow, D. G. (1976) 'On the analysis of performance operating characteristics', *Psychological Review*, 83, 508–10.

Olds, J. and Milner P. (1954) 'Positive reinforcement produced by electrical stimulation of septal area and other regions of rat brain', *Journal of Comparative Physiological Psychology*, 47, 419–27.

Onhe, M. T. and Evans F. J (1965) 'Social control in the psychological experiment: anti-social behaviour and hypnosis', *Journal of Personality and Social Psychology*, 51, 189–200.

Ora, J. P. (1965) *Characteristics of the Volunteer for Psychological Investigations*. Office of Naval Research contract 2149(03), Technical Report, 27.

Orne, M. T. (1962) 'On the social psychology of the psychological experiment: with particular reference to demand characteristics and their implications', *American Psychologist*, 17, 776–83.

Orne, M. T. and Evans, F. J. (1965) Social control in the psychology experiment: antisocial behaviour and hypnosis', *Journal of Personality and Social Psychology*, 1, 189–200.

Palmer, C. (1995) 'Psycho killers face employment trial', *The Observer*, 8 October, p. 15.

Pavlov I. (1927) (trans. G. V. Anrep) *Conditioned Reflexes* (London: Oxford University Press).

Peele, S. (1981) 'Reductionism in the psychology of the eighties: can biochemistry eliminate addiction, mental illness, and pain?', *American Psychologist*, 36 (8), 807–18.

Peirce, C. S. (1951) 'The fixation of belief', in M. H. Fisch (ed.), *Classic American Philosophers* (New York: Appleton-Century-Crofts), original work published 1877 in Popular Science Monthly.

Penfield, W. (1975) *The Mystery of the Mind* (Princeton, NJ: Princeton University Press).

Penfield, W. and Rasmussen, T. (1957) *The Cerebral Cortex of Man* (New York: Macmillan).

Perner, J. (1988) 'Higher order beliefs and intentions in children's understanding of social interaction', in J. W. Astington, P. L. Harris and D. R. Olson (eds), *Developing Theories of Mind* (New York: Camabridge University Press).

Pert, C. B. (1990) 'The wisdom of the receptors: neuropeptides, the emotions, and body-mind', in R. Ornstein and C. Swencionis (eds), *The Healing Brain: A Scientific Reader*, 147–58 (New York: Guildford Press).

Pervin, L. A. (1984) *Current Controversies and Issues in Personality*, 2nd edn (New York: Wiley).

Petty, R. E and Cacioppo, J. T. (1981) *Attitudes and Persuasion. Classic and Contemporary Approaches* (Dubuque, IA: Brown).

Pfaffenberger, C. (1963) *The New Knowledge of Dog Behaviour* (New York: Howell Book House).

Piaget, J. (1953) *The Origin of Intelligence in the Child* (London: Routledge & Kegan Paul).

Pike, K. L. (1967) *Language in Relation to a Unified Theory of the Structure of Human Behaviour* (The Hague: Mouton).

Popper, K. (1972) *Conjectures and Refutations: The Growth of Scientific Knowledge*, 4th edn (London: Routledge & Kegan Paul).

Pratkanis, A. and Aronson, E. (1991) *Age of Propaganda: Everyday Uses and Abuses of Persuasion* (New York: Freeman).

Prechtl, H. F. R. and Beintema, D. J. (1964) 'The neurological examination of the full term new born infant', *Clinics in Developmental Medicine*, 12 (London: Heinemann).

Putnam, H. (1973) 'Reductionism and the nature of psychology', *Cognition*, 2(1), 131–46.

Radford, J. and Kirby R. (1975) *The Person in Psychology* (London: Methuen).

Rhodes, N. and Wood, W. (1992) 'Self-esteem and intelligence affecting influenceability: the mediating role of message reception', *Psychological Bulletin*, 111, 156–71.

Riegal, K (1976) 'The dialectics of human development', *American Psychologist*, 31, 689–99.

Robertson, I. and Downs, S. (1979) 'Learning and the prediction of performance development of trainability testing in the United Kingdom', *Journal of Applied Psychology*, 64, 42–50.

Robins, L. N., Davis, D. H. and Goodwin, D. W. (1974) 'Drug use by the army enlisted men in Vietnam: a follow-up on their return home', *American Journal of Epidemiology*, 99, 235–49.

Robson, C. (1984) *Experiment Design and Statistics in Psychology*, 2nd edn (Harmondsworth: Penguin).

Rogers, C. R. (1951) *Client-centred Therapy* (Boston, Mass.: Houghton Mifflin).

Rogers, C. R. (1961) *On Becoming a Person* (Boston, Mass.: Houghton Mifflin), reprinted 1967.

Rolls, E. T. (1979) 'Effects of electrical stimulation of the brain on behavior', *Psychology Surveys*, 2, 191–269.

Rose, S. (1976) *The Conscious Brain* (Harmondsworth: Penguin).

Rosenhan, D. L. (1973) 'On being sane in insane places', *Science*, 179, 250–8.

Rosenthal, R. (1966) *Experimenter Effects in Behavioral Research* (New York: Appleton-Century-Crofts).

Rosenthal, R. (1969) 'Interpersonal expectations: effects of experimenter's hypothesis', in R. Rosenthal and R. L. Rosnow (eds), *Artefacts in Behavioural Research* (New York: Academic Press).

Rosenthal, R. (1969) 'Interpersonal Expectations: Effects of Experimenter's Hypothesis', in R. Rosenthal and R. L. Rosnow (eds), *Artefacts in Behavioral Research* (New York: Academic Press).

Rosenthal, R. and Jacobson, L. (1968) *Pygmalion in the Classroom* (New York: Holt, Rinehart & Winston).

Rubin, J. S., Provenzano, F. J. and Luria, Z. (1974) 'The eye of the beholder: parents' view on sex of newborns', *American Journal of Orthopsychiatry*, 5, 353—73.

Rushton, J. P. (1978) 'Urban density and altruism, helping strangers in a Canadian city, suburb and small town', *Psychological Reports*, 33, 987–90.

Rutter, M. and Rutter, M. (1993) *Developing Minds* (London: Penguin).

Rutter, M., Maughan, B., Mortimore, P. and Ouston, J. (1979) *Fifteen Thousand Hours* (London: Open Books).

Ryder, R. (1990) 'Open reply to Jeffrey Gray', *The Psychologist: Bulletin of the British Psychological Society*, 3, 403.

Ryder, R. (1991) 'Sentientism: a comment on Gray and Singer', *The Psychologist: Bulletin of the British Psychological Society*, 4 (5), 201.

Savage-Rumbaugh, S. (1990) 'Language as a cause-effect communication system', *Philosophical Psychology*, 3 (1), 55–76.

Scarr, S. (1988) 'Race and gender as psychological variables', *American Psychologist*, 43 (1), 56–9.

Scarr, S. (1992) 'Developmental theories for the 1990s: development and individual differences', *Child Development*, 63, 1–19.

Schachter, S. and Singer, J. E. (1962) 'Cognitive, social and physiological determinants of an emotional state', *Psychological Review*, 69, 379–99.

Schaffer, R. (1977) *Mothering* (London: Fontana).

Schulz, D. (1987) *A History of Modern Psychology*, 4th edn (New York: Academic Press).

Seligman, M. E. (1974) 'Depression and learned helplessness', in R. J. Freedom and M. M. Katz (eds), *The Psychology of Depression* (Washington DC: V. H. Winston).

Selye, H. (1956) *The Stress of Life* (New York: McGraw-Hill).

Selye, H. (1974) *Stress Without Distress* (Philadelphia: Lippincott).

Shallice, T. and Warrington, E. K. (1977) 'Auditory-verbal short-term memory impairment and conduction aphasia', *Brain and Language*, 4, 479–91.

Shayer, M. and Wylam H. (1978) 'The distribution of Piagetian stages of thinking in British middle and secondary school children II: 14–16-year-olds and sex differentials', *British Journal of Educational Psychology*, 48, 62–70.

Sherif, M., Harvey, O. J., White, B. J., Hood, W. E. and Sherif, C. W. (1961) *Intergroup Conflict and Co-operation: The Robber's Cave Experiment* (Norman OK: University of Oklahoma Book Exchange).

Sherrington, R., Bryjolfsson, J. and collaborators (1988) 'Localisation of a susceptibility locus for schizophrenia on chromosome 5', *Nature*, 336, 164–7.

Shostrum, E. L., Knapp, R. R. and Knapp, L. (1976) 'Validation of the personal orientation dimensions. An inventory for the dimensions of actualising', *Educational and Psychological Measurement*, 36(2), 491–4.

Sieber, J. E. and Stanley, B. (1988) 'Ethical and professional dimensions of socially sensitive research', *American Psychologist*, 43 (1), 149–55.

Simmons, J. V. Jr. (1981) *Project Sea Hunt: A Report on Prototype Development and Tests*. Technical report No. 746 (San Diego, CA: Naval Ocean System Center).

Singer, P and Cavalieri, P. (eds) (1993) *Equality Beyond Humanity* (London: Fourth Estate).

Singer, P. (1991) 'Speciesism, morality and biology', *The Psychologist: Bulletin of the British Psychological Society*, 4 (5), 199–201.

Singer, P. (1993) *The Great Ape Project* (London: Fourth Estate).

Skinner, B. F. (1938) *The Behavior of Organisms* (New York: Appleton-Century-Crofts).

Skinner, B. F. (1948) *Walden Two* (New York: Macmillan).

Skinner, B. F. (1953) *Science and Human Behavior* (New York: Macmillan).

Skinner, B. F. (1971) *Beyond Freedom and Dignity* (London: Jonathan Cape).

Smith, P. B. and Bond, M. H. (1993) *Social Psychology across Cultures: Analysis and Perspectives* (Hemel Hempstead, Herts: Harvester Wheatsheaf).

Solomon, R. L. and J. D. Corbit (1974) 'An opponent-process theory of motivation: Pt. 1. Temporal dynamics of affect', *Psychological Review*, 81, 119–45.

Sperling, G. (1960) 'The information available in brief visual presentation', *Psychological Monographs*, 74 (498).

Stephenson, W. (1953) *The Study of Behaviour* (Chicago: University of Chicago Press).

Sternbach, R. A. (1962) 'Assessing differential autonomic patterns in emotions', *Journal of Psychosomatic Research*, 6, 87–91.

Stoner, J. A. F. (1961) 'A comparison of individual and group decisions involving risk', unpublished master's thesis, Sloan School of Management, MIT, Cambridge, Mass.

Sylva, K. D., Roy, C. and Painter, M. (1980) *Childwatching at Playgroup and Nursery School* (London: Grant McIntyre).

Tajfel, H. (1982) *Social Identity and Intergroup Relations* (Cambridge: Cambridge University Press).

Tedeschi, J. T., Lindskold, S. and Rosenfeld, P. (1985) *Introduction to Social Psychology* (New York: West).

Tesch, S. A. (1983) 'Review of friendship development across the life-span', *Human Development*, 26, 266–76.

Teska, P. T. (1947) 'The mentality of hydrocephalics and a description of an interesting case', *Journal of Psychology*, 23, 197–203.

Thoday, J. M. (1965) in J. M. Meade and A. S. Parkes (eds), *Biological Aspects of Social Problems* (London: Oliver & Boyd).

Thomas, G. V. and Blackman, D. (1991) 'Are animal experiments on the way out?', *The Psychologist: Bulletin of the British Psychological Society*, 4 (5), 208–12.

Tinbergen, N. and Perdeck, E. C. (1950) 'On the stimulus situation releasing the begging response in the newly hatched herring gull chick', *Behaviour*, 3, 1–39.

Treisman, A. (1964a) 'Verbal cues, language and meaning in selective attention', *American Journal of Psychology*, 77, 206–19.

Treisman, A. (1964b) 'Monitoring and storing of irrelevant messages in selective attention', *Journal of Verbal Learning and Verbal Behaviour*, 3, 449–59.

Triandis, H. C. (1990) 'Theoretical perspectives that are applicable to the analysis of ethnocentrism', in R. W. Brislin (ed.), *Applied Cross-Cultural Psychology* (Newbury Park, Calif.: Sage).

UFAW, *Universities Federation for Animal Welfare Handbook* (1987) 6th edn (Harlow: Longman).

Valentine, E. R. (1982) *Conceptual Issues in Psychology* (London: George Allen & Unwin).

Valentine, E. R. (1992) *Conceptual Issues in Psychology* (London: Routledge).

Valins, S. (1966) 'Cognitive effects of false heart-rate feedback', *Journal of Personality and Social Psychology*, 4, 400–8.

Vernon, P. E. (1969) *Intelligence and Cultural Environment* (London: Methuen).

Vines, G. (1993) 'Planet of the free apes?', *New Scientist*, 5 June (1876), 39–42.

Vines, G. (1994) 'The emotional chicken', *New Scientist*, 22 Jan (1909), 28–31.

Wadeley, A. (1991) *Ethics in Psychological Research and Practice* (Leicester: British Psychological Society).

Walker, S. (1984) *Learning Theory and Behaviour Modification* (London: Methuen).

Wallach, M. A. and Wallach, L. (1983) *Psychology's Sanction for Selfishness* (San Francisco: Freeman).

Warr, P. B. (ed.) (1978) *Psychology at Work* (Harmondsworth: Penguin).

Watson J. B. (1919) *Psychology from the Standpoint of the Behaviourist* (Philadelphia: Lippincott).

Watson, J. B. (1913) 'Psychology as the behaviourist views it', *Psychological Review* 20, 158–77.

Watson, J. B. (1919) *Psychology from the Standpoint of a Behaviourist* (Philadelphia: Lippincott).

Watson, J. B. and R. Rayner (1920) 'Conditioned emotional reactions', *Journal of Experimental Psychology*, 3, 1–4.

Watson, J. B. and Rayner, R. (1920) 'Conditioned emotional reactions', *Journal of Experimental Psychology*, 3, 1–4.

Watson, P. (1978) *War on the Mind* (New York: Basic Books).

Weber, S. J. and Cook, T. D. (1972) 'Subject effects in laboratory research: an examination of subject roles, demand characteristics and valid inference', *Psychological Bulletin*, 77, 273–95.

Wertheimer, M. (1972) *Fundamental Issues in Psychology* (New York: Holt, Rinehart & Winston).

Westcott, M. R. (1982a) 'On being free and feeling free', paper presented to the 20th International Congress of Applied Psychology, Edinburgh.

Westland, G. (1978) *Current Crises in Psychology* (London: Heinmann).

Whyte, W. F. (1955) *Street Corner Society: The Social Structure of an Italian Slum* (Chicago: Chicago University Press).

Willard, M. J. (1985) 'The psychosocial impact of using Capuchin monkeys as aides for quadriplegics', *Einstein Quarterly Journal of Biology and Medicine*.

Wilson, E. O. (1975) *Sociobiology* (Cambridge, Mass.: Harvard University Press).

Windelband, W. (1904) *Geschichte und Naturwissenschaft*, 3rd edn (Strasburg: Heitz).

Witkin, H. A., Goodenough, D. R., Karp, S. A., Dyke, R. B. and Faterson, H. F. (1962) *Psychological Differentiation* (New York: Wiley).

Woolworth, R. S. and Sheehan, M. R. (1965) *Contemporary Schools of Psychology* (London: Methuen).

Worell, J. and Remer, P. (1992) *Feminist Perspectives in Therapy* (New York: Wiley).

Wundt, W. (1879) *An Introduction to Psychology* (trans. R. Pinter) (London: George Allen).

Young, R. F., Feldman, R. A., Kroenig, R., Fulton, W. and Morris, J. (1984) 'Electrical stimulation of the brain in the treatment of chronic pain in man', in L. Kruger and J. C. Liebeskind (eds), *Advances in Pain Research and Therapy*, Vol. 6, 289–303.

Zajonc, R. B. (1968) 'Attitudinal effects of mere exposure', *Journal of Personality and Social Psychology*, monograph supplement 9, 1–27.

Zimbardo, P. G. (1973) 'On the ethics of intervention in human psychological research: with special reference to the Stanford prison experiment', *Cognition*, 2(2), 243–56.

Zimbardo, P. G., Haney, C, and Banks, W. C. (1973) 'A Pirandellian prison', *New York Times Sunday Magazine*, 8 April, 38–60.

Zinberg, N. (1974) 'The search for rational approaches to heroin use', in P. G. Bourne (ed.), *Addiction* (New York: Academic Press).

Index